The Chase, the Capture:
Collecting at the Metropolitan

The Chase
the Capture: Collecting at the Metropolitan

THOMAS HOVING

Director, The Metropolitan Museum of Art

with essays by members of the staff:
Dietrich von Bothmer, Richard Ettinghausen,
Wen Fong, Henry Geldzahler, Morrison H.
Heckscher, Julie Jones, Christine Lilyquist,
Douglas Newton, Helmut Nickel, Olga Raggio,
Margaretta Salinger, and Susan Vogel

The Metropolitan Museum of Art

Designed by Peter Oldenburg with Arlene Goldberg
Cover design by Stuart Silver
Type set by Custom Composition Company, Inc., York, Pennsylvania
Printed by The Leether Press, Boston
Bound by Robert Burlen & Son, Inc., Hingham, Massachusetts

LIBRARY OF CONGRESS CATALOGING IN PUBLICATION DATA

New York (City). Metropolitan Museum of Art.
  The chase, the capture.

  1. Art—Collectors and collecting. 2. New York (City).
Metropolitan Museum of Art. I. Hoving, Thomas Pearsall
Field, 1931–   II. von Bothmer, Dietrich, 1918–
III. Title.

N610.A82   708'.147'1   75-34076
ISBN 0-87099-139-6 pbk.

Contents

The Chase, the Capture

THOMAS HOVING

Director

The chase and the capture of a great work of art is one of the most exciting endeavors in life—as dramatic, emotional, and fulfilling as a love affair. And love affairs, at least some of them, should be told about.

It is curious but true that the Metropolitan Museum has never attempted to tell the public about the endlessly fascinating aspects of its fundamental mission: collecting. This book attempts to explain the philosophy and techniques of collecting in an encyclopaedic museum. It is about curatorship and illustrates the complex processes by which a work of art comes into our possession. It reveals the story of the hunt, discovery, investigation, and capture of a work of art. It is also about connoisseurship. Thus, it is about quality, judgment, research, and analysis and about sensitivity, diplomacy, tension, courage, and occasional error. Finally, it has to do with the deep sense of gratification a curator feels when, after the chase and the period of study, the work of art is placed on exhibition to illuminate yet another chapter in the story of man's artistic achievement.

"The great days of collecting are over!" I've heard this lament from curators, private collectors, and dealers many times in the years I have been associated with professional collecting. I'm sure it goes back a long time, to a discouraged connoisseur in the days of Imperial Rome deploring the fact that original Greek bronzes are fast disappearing from the market, to a distinguished collector in the time of Louis XV complaining that others are destroying the field of drawings by their sudden (and perhaps untutored) desire to enter into competition. I've heard these words from dealers just before they have presented me with the most splendid works of art I have ever seen. I've begun to think that it is less a statement of fact than a subconscious tip that something great is just about to be offered. But today *is* different; it *is* over, people insist. Resources of traditional art have almost dried up. Too many people today know too much. Instant communication has destroyed that cocoon of secrecy in which every great collector likes to work. Prices are ridiculous. There are a host of new rules and laws that govern yesterday's laissez-faire collecting practices.

I feel that we are entering a new period of collecting. But I differ from others about its nature. For I feel that a distinguished moment of collecting is just *beginning*. It will be achieved through new attitudes about possession, by attempting the exchanges of cultural properties, by testing out mutual ownership of resources, and by experimenting with new techniques in searching for works of art. Traditional sources of traditional art are certainly dwindling, but other resources are becoming richer: those of the museums and national collections themselves. And it is from them that a new method of collecting will emerge through mutual-loan programs.

The strongest evidence that the great period of collecting is over is the recent promulgation of a UNESCO draft treaty to restrict the international movement of works of art. One aspect of this is that for certain categories of art—those that have been stolen or are of great archaeological importance to a state party—the legal title of the purchaser or subsequent owner will be challengeable unless the object is accompanied by a valid export license.

Implementing legislation is presently being drafted by the State Department, and at some point it will be submitted to the Congress for approval. The principles of the UNESCO treaty, which many museums in America have already honored, though they are not yet legally obliged to do so, has engendered predictions from some professionals that "no institution will ever again be able to collect anything in an archaeological field."

But is the situation so gloomy? I think not. Procedures already in practice at the Metropolitan and other institutions attempt to provide proper controls and at the same time permit and, indeed, encourage collecting. Whenever a work is offered to this Museum that does not have a clear provenance or plausible history, a letter is sent to the appropriate agency in the possible country of origin. This letter (Appendix 1, page 99) presents the known facts about the object and requests that we be supplied with any further information that may be available to the agency. Sometimes the letter is sent to more than one country. With certain Greek and Roman bronzes, for example, there is the possibility of their having been found in any one of a number of different areas of the ancient world. We wait at least 45 days for a reply to our letter. If none is received, we assume all is well and proceed with the purchase. This procedure, instituted in March 1971, has been effective. From over a dozen formal inquiries, we have received, in the case of two, evidence that the work of art was illegally taken from the country of origin. In one case, this confirmed our suspicions, in the other it surprised us. In most instances, the officials abroad to whom we have written have had no additional information and have raised no objections to our going forward.

Another manner of approaching the controls on the exportation of works of art is of potentially greater significance where the movement of cultural patrimonies is concerned. In January 1968 the Metropolitan and Mexico's Instituto Nacional de Antropología e Historia signed an agreement (Appendix 2, page 100) under whose terms we lend works of art to one another for public exhibition as well as exchange artistic, scientific, and educational knowledge in the fields of art and art history.

Working with the Ministry of Education and other Mexican officials in the summer of 1968, we were able to persuade a New York dealer to send back to Mexico a monumental stucco façade of a Mayan temple that had been torn from a structure somewhere in the Palenque jungle. Although legally imported into the United States, it turned out to have been illegally removed from Mexico. Since the piece had been at the Metropolitan on examination for a number of months before the information about its export came to us from the Mexican authorities, we were in a unique position to mediate with the dealer. The façade is now installed in the Instituto Nacional de Antropología e Historia.

In 1970, when the agreement was in effect, Mexico sent to our centennial exhibition, *Before Cortés,* some masterpieces of Precolumbian art of a quality never before seen in this country. In turn, we have on loan to the Instituto a number of Egyptian works of art and Cypriot antiquities,

FIGURE 1. Certificate of gratitude from the Museo Nacional de las Culturas, Mexico, the sponsoring organization of the Instituto Nacional de Antropología e Historia

particularly desired in Mexico. We expect that other splendid works of art will come from Mexico on long-term loan in 1977 to coincide with the opening of our Michael C. Rockefeller Wing, which is to house the collections of the Museum of Primitive Art, Nelson Rockefeller's collection of primitive art, and the Museum's own holdings in that field.

A problem not unlike that of the Palenque façade occurred in 1970 when the government of Guatemala raised a question about a stele owned by a private collector in New York. The stele, which had been published as from a known archaeological site in Guatemala, was scheduled to appear

FIGURE 2. The projected Michael C. Rockefeller Wing of Primitive Art in a scale model by Kevin Roche, John Dinkeloo and Associates, architects

in our exhibition. With our mediation, the collector transferred title to the stele to the Guatemalan government in return for an agreement that the object would stay on loan at the Metropolitan. It was also agreed that in the event the stele were recalled by Guatemala, the government would make available for loan to the Metropolitan an object or objects of approximately equal importance.

Recognizing the need at the Metropolitan for objects of the finest quality, and realizing that except for pieces still in private collections, few great works will ever again come on the market, we have proposed cultural exchange programs to various governments. These programs will enable us to have great foreign works of art on long-term loan in our galleries in exchange for loans of certain of our works.

Agreements covering works of art now exist, or are being drafted, between the Metropolitan and the museums of France, the ministry of culture of the U.S.S.R., a major museum in Germany, and the governments of Egypt and Iran. The required changes in attitude call for statesmanship, sensitivity, and patience on both sides, as well as an understanding that ownership is not necessarily any longer fundamental to collecting.

Thus, far from being over, collecting is only a different process than it was before, and whatever the international complexities are, collecting continues to involve connoisseurship.

Now, what is a connoisseur? A connoisseur is someone who clearly recognizes quality in all its subtle gradations. How does one become a connoisseur? This is less easy to answer. A "good eye" comes out of a mix of inborn talent and long experience. If there is one constant ingredient in an "eye," I suppose it is saturation. To have seen every single existing Limoges enamel of the thirteenth century and, in addition, every single surviving enamel of the same period from every other important center—amounting to hundreds of thousands of works of art—is at least to be a de facto "eye." Likewise to have studied every painting, sketch, or drawing by Peter Paul Rubens and most of the works of his contemporaries. Such an eye will presumably be able to look at a Limoges enamel or a Rubens portrait and know at once how it compares to the known indices of quality. Such saturation enables a person to react instantly: Buy it! or Don't bother, it's not good enough. But all that work, examination, knowledge, and experience do not necessarily make one a connoisseur. All too often we have an expert in Limoges enamels or Rubens, an expert on the thirteenth or the seventeenth century, and an expert who still does not have that instinct for quality that the French call *grand gout*. All the Ph.Ds in art history or archaeology available do not guarantee connoisseurship. I am constantly baffled by the presence of an expert who knows all the facts and documents but still does not have an eye, and thus does not really know how to collect. These experts sometimes tend to regard the connoisseur as being somehow shallow. But they don't recognize the mysterious, inexplicable side of connoisseurship.

Within the eighteen curatorial departments of the Metropolitan Museum, staffed by a goodly number of true connoisseurs, there are encompassed five thousand years of art history, exemplified in approximately three million separate and distinct works of art. (We must approximate that number. If one were to count every single object, down to individual ancient buttons, pieces of pottery, and single swatches of textile, the figure "nearly three million" would not be far off.)

For these museum connoisseurs the collecting process begins with the deepest possible knowledge of what is already in the Museum. Each curator must know each piece in his or her collection intimately, not only by direct personal examination but also through countless discussions with colleagues from all over the world. Special files are maintained in each department concerning each work of art, its basic description, its scientific data, its condition, provenance, bibliography, and all observations, plausible or fanciful, ever made about it by a visiting expert or letter writer. Each curator is well aware of the strengths and weaknesses of the department's collection. And from time to time the curator is asked to make a presentation of his assessment to the Acquisitions Committee of the Board of Trustees (Appendix 3, page 104). Often a curator will have established special categories of the collections under his or her keepership; for example, works of art of the highest quality, those whose condition is problematical, the outright fakes, the doubtful pieces, works of art under a fluctuating attribution, and study pieces that are of considerable educational value but are not of a quality to exhibit in the galleries.

The departmental storeroom is often the mark of a good or indifferent curator. One of the most intriguing storeroom arrangements I have seen was one in which the objects were all on view, grouped according to material. All were constantly being rearranged according to levels of quality. In this storeroom a restorer always was at work as if to force the continual physical examination of the holdings. The curator made it a point to visit the storeroom each day and touch and examine several objects. Important, for *touching* may be the ingredient equal to saturation in connoisseurship.

Contact with outside expertise is of vital importance. Sometimes it can be overlooked, owing perhaps to the embarrassment that a curator sometimes experiences when a learned visitor looks at a new acquisition and exclaims "My God, *you* didn't buy *that!*" But it is necessary. At an early stage in my curatorial career I was fortunate to have a great learning experience with one of the preeminent young connoisseurs of medieval art. Professor Erich Steingraber of the Bayerisches Nationalmuseum in

Munich had come to the Metropolitan on a fellowship to study the collections of the Medieval Department and The Cloisters. I was assigned the routine tasks of dealing with his needs in the storeroom and in the locked cases of the permanent exhibitions. In the ensuing eight months we must have looked at and touched every work of art in the extensive collections of both institutions. The masses of notes I took at the time still hold up well. We re-established the unquestionable verity of the great objects, compiled long lists of comparable material in collections all over the world, including private collections and dealers' collections—most of which I had never heard about, made observations about the condition of each work of art, discovered new, good things about a number of works that had been banished, and in turn banished a small number to the forgery bin. Steingraber's excitement when he touched works of art that he had known before only from photographs or catalogue descriptions was contagious. How thrilling it was to learn for the first time basic pieces of knowledge that an expert derives only from experience and that a neophyte could never gather from a seminar or the study of books. Saturation plus that inexplicable quality of "eye" enabled Steingraber to say "Something's wrong!" the instant I extracted from a cabinet a thirteenth-century silver reliquary in the shape of a finger and decorated with a ring set with a large emerald.

Something wrong? But, it's a famous piece from a renowned private collection with an extensive bibliography and an accompanying list of scholarly observations, all praising it! What's wrong? Well, first, the weight of the piece. Suspiciously heavy. Second, there are eight finger reliquaries in the world and this doesn't *look,* in general, like any other. Third, there are, on one of the delicate legs supporting the finger, three minute goldsmith's marks. But their design is of the seventeenth century for *gold,* not silver. Fourth, these marks are normally used for export—impossible in the thirteenth century. *And* they were not added later. Fifth, the reliquary is made with the ring and silver finger in one piece. All others have a ring or rings added later by a devoted worshiper who took a ring off his own finger and added it to the reliquary. Sixth, the niello inlay in the inscription of the saint's name is common tar, not niello. (We picked a minute piece out with a needle and tasted it.) Seventh, the feel, color, what-have-you of the silver—looking like crushed and melted cobwebs—is the color of silver produced in a forgery workshop of the 1920s in Paris, successors to the well-known Marcy workshop of the late nineteenth century. Further examination of documents revealed that the collector who had given us the reliquary was (1) fascinated with reliquaries, particularly finger reliquaries, and (2) was an avid collector of emeralds. Ah, well, at least the emerald was good.

The curator must also be aware of the basic philosophy and policy of collecting at the particular institution. At the Metropolitan we strive for quality, the best example possible in every area, a work that is the summation of its epoch or its artist, a work that has exerted strong influences throughout time, but above all is something that seems to grow continually and has a visual impact of mysterious, pure beauty. This, of course, is an ideal. One must recognize exceptions. Essentially the determination of quality involves two questions: How does the work relate to all of the works existing? How does the work relate to all that are available?

Very rarely one manages to discover a work of art that embodies all or nearly all of the ideal characteristics. The Merode altarpiece by Robert Campin, the calyx krater by Euphronios and Euxitheos, and the *Juan de Pareja* by Diego Velázquez are prime examples of the ideal. For the latter we know when the portrait was painted, precisely under what circumstances, when it was exhibited for the first time, what the reaction of the cognoscenti was then—"It is not mere art, it is truth, itself." We know that the painting stands high among all the known works of Velázquez, that it had a strong influence not only in its own day but long thereafter from the number of copies made of it; we know its history through the years except for a relatively short time; we know that the condition of the picture is perfect today; and we know that it is a sensitive, compelling, human portrait, ranking among the best portraits painted by anyone. Obviously, the *Juan de Pareja* is at the topmost end of the scale. For every one of such masterpieces there are the lesser works of art, unheralded, unsigned footnotes with no clear history, no historical impact but of keen importance to the collections nevertheless because they flesh out and explain in some fashion the rest of the material. And finally, there are many works of art of such nature that are extremely important, extremely beautiful, and yet, owing to the unfortunate vicissitudes of history, are totally silent. But they, too, are important in filling out the collections.

At the Metropolitan the working principle today is mainly the refinement of the collections. We consider that the encyclopaedia has been pretty nearly completed, in particular with the gift from Nelson Rockefeller of the collection of the Museum of Primitive Art. There are some gaps left to fill, weaknesses left to strengthen, but they are dwindling. We tend to seek only the rarest of the rare, those works of art of which we have none at all.

The current building program defines the farthest limit of the Museum's expansion, and a formal commitment to this effect was made by the Trustees in September 1970. It was agreed at the time that to expand farther would create a structure too big for a visitor to comprehend and enjoy. We are deliberately slowing down in the numbers of objects we collect and are concentrating upon true needs and true masterpieces. In order to reach for some of these rare great works of art, we are weeding out and disposing of numbers of works that once seemed essential to our collections but now are either redundant, superfluous, or not of the requisite quality. We have done this ever since the 1880s and, by and large, the process has worked well. Anyone familiar with the Museum remembers the hue and cry three years ago over the deaccessioning practices that were in effect at the time to enable us to purchase masterworks such as the *Juan de Pareja,* the Euphronios krater, the splendid paintings of the Sung and Yuan dynasties in the collection of C.C. Wang, and a host of other works of art. In retrospect much of the heat and controversy seem not to have been warranted. With the exception of one painting among the thousands of objects that were disposed of—the *Tropics* by the Douanier Rousseau—none have been missed, and the works of art that have come into the collections in their stead have been very much appreciated. Under the guidelines worked out between the Museum and the Attorney General of New York in 1973, the process of prudent disposal will continue.

There are three basic routes by which a work of art enters the Metropolitan: bequest, gift, and purchase. The majority of the collections have come by means of gift or bequest—about 85 percent of our holdings. It may surprise some to learn that our purchase funds are not the highest for an American museum, but indeed are at the low end among the five institutions that lead the nation. This fact has not as yet caused us problems, thanks to our ability to attract major donations of works of art and to raise, when needed, amounts of money to secure a great prize. But this could change.

A curator must be aware of all possible internal funding resources and, in addition, of whatever might be obtainable from donors. Typically, a donor is a member of the department's Visiting Committee or a collector who has been advised from time to time by the curator.

Works of art can come to the attention of the curator by chance. More usually he learns of them through his own work. The curator continually probes the marketplace, studies the auction catalogues, hunts for tips from a variety of sources that will enable him to know what is coming up at auction before the catalogue is published, and listens to all rumors indicating that a private collector is thinking of disposing of a certain object. The curator normally works from his list of prime desiderata and routinely establishes where every work of art on the list is at the moment. He tracks the movement of as many objects as possible and asks whether or not the object is available. He also lets important dealers know exactly what type of art he is seeking.

When the curator discovers a work of art, or the work of art discovers the curator, the complicated process of study begins. Each professional has his or her special technique for investigation. Essentially it boils down to a sort of checklist that varies only with the specific nature of the work—whether it is a sculpture or a painting, for example. A typical examination list will include:

1. Immediate impression

2. Description

3. Condition, wear, age

4. Use

5. Style

6. Subject matter

7. Iconography

8. History

9. Bibliography

10. Outside expert advice

11. Scientific analysis

12. Doubts list

13. Conclusion: Does the work stack up to the original impression?

It is extraordinarily helpful at the outset to write down one's immediate, spontaneous reaction to the work. A single word, a phrase, a sentence. Then the curator sets the feeling aside and comes back to it after the full analysis has been made. Most of the time the first impression, the subconscious one based upon years of experience, is what holds up after the long study process. Often a doubting word or a curious, apparently meaningless, phrase will later spotlight a flaw, dimly perceived at instant glance, but definitely there.

1.

The *immediate impression* might read: "Warm, good, strong feeling, looks red and solid, no doubts except perhaps not too high." This is what I jotted down a number of years ago upon first seeing a splendid gold, silver gilt, enameled folding reliquary shrine dating to around 1385 and once owned, it was said, by Queen Elizabeth of Hungary. My feeling was, obviously, one of contentment. I could see almost nothing awry. The work was strong at the instant and got stronger as the minutes passed. This is one of the best signs of all. "Red and solid" referred to the appearance of the gilding, which had that weighty, appropriately orange-yellow feeling it should have had. "Perhaps not too high" flagged what was later discovered, which was that the roof of the little shrine and some of the delicate finials were not original and made a lower profile than one would have expected in the High Gothic period. After the full investigation the shrine turned out to be indeed good and was acquired by The Cloisters.

2.

Description. The professional tries to make an exhaustive physical description of the work, forcing himself to recount its description to the point of boring detail. In doing this he may write down things that seem to ring a strange bell. When I first saw the splendid *Juan de Pareja,* and had gotten over the initial shock of its penetrating presence and magnetic power, I began to describe it to myself pedantically: "A painting, in oil, of a young man, whose image is set in the center of a vertical rectangular canvas." "Wait!" I wrote that down. It was a little unexpected to find a baroque portrait of the mid-seventeenth century set smack in the middle of the painting field. It would not have been uncommon in the neoclassic period of the early nineteenth century. Later, after we had purchased the masterpiece, it came as a surprise, but no great surprise, to discover that several inches on the top and side of the canvas had been carefully folded under to fit the face in the center of the canvas. When was this done? By the 1820s. Why? Because after that time all copies of the renowned painting were squared off, and did not have the infinite space on the top and side.

As the curator makes this plodding description he, in effect, touches and feels and weighs the work of art. He tries to put his eyes over every square millimeter, as if his eyes were fingers. He attempts to describe the work at various distances, very close, using the magnifying glass, then far off. One's impression needs different points of examination.

3.

Condition, wear, age. During the physical description the curator focuses in on the condition, noting the scratches, the wear, being careful to date the marks of age. He charts the wear, attempting preliminarily to date what would be the damage of, say, around 1300, then of the fifteenth century, and then of the recent past. He notes all visible repairs. Are they old or modern? Are the modern repairs made to look old? Often a forger deliberately adds an "ancient" repair. If it was repaired in antiquity it must be ancient—yes? No! Not always.

When the curator examines the wear and age of an object he tries to note the basic elements of corrosion even before he obtains a full scientific analysis —which is often precluded by the paucity of time and the circumstances under which the investigation is carried through. Every metal but gold corrodes, and even gold corrodes if it has the slightest mix of another metal. Customarily, therefore, the curator looks to see whether or not the bronze, silver, copper, steel, or iron exhibits the proper corrosion "sandwich." Every connoisseur has in his mind what constitutes the basic stratifications of corrosion of a variety of metals. Ancient bronze must inevitably set up in regular layers of cupric chloride—brown patina—underneath a cupric oxide surface—a green, crystalline, sometimes flaking level of corrosion. Old silver normally turns a dark blue-purple with a grainy consistency. If these characteristics are not present, a warning bell rings. But, careful! Sometimes an authentic ancient bronze will have been overly cleaned for one reason or other and then repatinated with false materials for sale. And if one rejects the piece because it has a modern surface, one can in a rare case condemn a truly ancient work of art. All is relative—and tricky.

4.

Use. This is an important point about any object, even a painting. Until fairly modern times almost all works of art—even sculptures and paintings—had a specific purpose and use. Minute examination with the glass will indicate if the wear, the aging marks, indicate that use.

The investigation of the wear-use factor is of vital concern not only for the question of authenticity but also for determining the history of an object. For example, a beautiful ivory plaque of the early thirteenth century depicting the Tree of Jesse, made in Bamberg and acquired in 1973 in association with the Louvre, has on its verso the distinct markings of a comb. And the probability is that earlier, perhaps in Carolingian times, even possibly in Early Christian times when combs were used in church liturgy, the comb was first made. In the thirteenth century ivory was exceedingly rare. Carvers used everything available, even ancient combs, recarving them. In the Carolingian period ivory was also rare, and artists of the time recut late Roman consular diptychs—ivory tablets with recesses for the wax on which proclamations were inscribed. Many great Carolingian ivory book covers have on the back, and sometimes even on the front, faint traces of the original and wholly utilitarian usage of a wax-filled tablet.

A medieval pax, intended to be kissed by the faithful, should show the wear of that use. If the pax is an adept forgery, the wear is apparent, but one can tell if the wear brought about by the passage of countless thousands of lips is real or artificially induced. However, in analyzing use, one must be cautious. There are rare, very rare works of art that were made as utilitarian objects and then, owing to burial custom, were used once or never. Certain Egyptian objects obviously fall into this category. For these—and all—objects it is wise to ask. Did it have any use at all? Perhaps if the question had been forcefully posed when the two large Etruscan warriors were discovered by the Museum before 1915 they would have been recognized as forgeries from the start. For indeed they have no plausible use. In the sixth century B.C. sculptures were not made merely to look at and appreciate, the way we look at a Rodin or a dancer by Degas. The Etruscan warriors would not have been solitary cult images, but would in all probability have been used as large decorations attached to the roofs of temples or other structures. But these two could not have been used for that purpose, for they are made in such a fashion that they stand up only with the aid of a modern metal support. In sum, they had no plausible use, and their principal interest lies in the fact that they are twentieth-century forgeries copied or adapted from Greek bronze statuettes or small East Greek vases in the shape of helmeted heads.

5.

Style. The professional asks whether or not the work has a distinct style, one that is consistent with the period in which it is said to have been made. Is the style consistent throughout or are there indications of several styles? If so, why? Could it be that we are dealing with a work of art of a transitional period, in which the artist was influenced by, and reflected, more than one confluent element? Is it a young work, an experimental one? Without a clearly definable style, the work is suspect. If it possesses a number of competing styles, it is either of a culture which, having no truly creative force of its own, drew upon other styles and other cultures or it is of no consequence. Or it is a forgery. The investigation of style leads inevitably to the date of the work, since all true styles can be placed in time. By the study of the style and individual styles, going deliberately from the general to the smallest specific, we can determine not only the authenticity of a work of art, but often its artistic quality. For the *Juan de Pareja,* for example, we go from the post-Renaissance period to the seventeenth century, to Spain, to Valencia, to Toledo, to the young Veláz-quez, to the part of his early work that must rest between the Bodegones and the emergence of his more mature works in 1648. Obviously, the more we know, the more historical data is preserved, the easier the process of analysis. The scholarship of art is, at least in one essential manifestation, the establishment of benchmarks or indices of known stylistic characteristics. And it is hard to force a work of art out of these indices.

A number of years ago in New York there was a special showing of a quite marvelous marble sculpture of the young Saint John the Baptist. Cocktails in a townhouse, guest list of the renowned in the art field, lecture by a distinguished expert in art history. At the end of his suave and persuasive talk the expert announced that the piece was an unknown masterpiece by Michelangelo Buonarroti. A keen scholar, standing near me, chuckled and whispered, "Too bad they've changed it." "What do you mean?" I asked. "Well, twenty-five years ago, in Florence, when I first was shown the piece, it was a splendid sculpture of some unknown but not incompetent Florentine of the mid-sixteenth century. Too bad they've changed it to Michelangelo."

Assessing the style of a work of art and pinning that style to a period, a locality, an artist, is pure diagnostic work. It sometimes takes a long time, particularly in those areas where a great body of comparable material does not exist. It also takes a considerable amount of faith and perseverance, plus an utter disregard of the circumstances under which a work of art is discovered. One of the greatest connoisseurs I have ever met, a dealer, renowned in the field for his remarkable discoveries, laughs openly at those who ask in astonishment, "Where did you find that?" "I found it on Third Avenue," or "in a fifth-rate auction house," he will say. Often, sadly, the velvet-festooned setting of a distinguished gallery is all that authenticates the work of art it offers for sale.

6.

Subject matter. Simultaneously with the examination of style one looks into the subject matter of the work in all its ramifications. At this point it is beneficial to begin to make comparisons, by list, of all other works of art in the general period, indicating what it is closest to and what it is farthest away from. I find it better to make basic stylistic comparisons slightly before comparisons of subject matter. Looking specifically at the latter tends sometimes to throw one off the objective assessment of style.

7.

Iconography. This is a specific art historical term denoting the precise manner in which a particular subject matter is treated. For example, in the scene of the Adoration of the Magi one iconographic tradition might show the Madonna seen from the side approached by two Magi; another might show the frontal Madonna approached by all three Magi. The subject is the same, the iconography varies. In general, iconography serves only to place a treatment of the subject matter into a general archetypal series. Iconography, except under highly specialized circumstances, cannot date a work of art or place it geographically. It is, however, an important field of study, particularly as regards the question of authenticity.

8.

History. At this point in the investigation one compiles the history of the object. Is it documented right back to the moment of its origin? Are there gaps in its history? Why? Where has it been exhibited? In whose collection has it been over the years? When the compilation is as complete as possible, the curator attempts to make a separate study of the reliability and authenticity of the documents themselves. The faking of documents is a common procedure. Also, the curator makes a routine check to learn whether the piece has been offered before to the Museum and, if so, under what circumstances.

9.

Bibliography. One makes a list of every book and article in which the work is referred to and a list of published opinions about it.

10.

Outside expert advice. Where feasible, the curator consults every connoisseur and professor in the field and obtains their views on all aspects of the work, in particular its quality. Contrary to what is generally believed, curators, directors, and private collectors are often delighted to volunteer information about a work of art, even if it is on the open market.

11.

Scientific analysis. A full scientific examination cannot take place in a dealer's shop, the home of a private collector, or the auction showroom. The conservation laboratory is the only place for that. However, if one is prepared, a remarkable amount of probing can be done "in the field." The working tools include a flashlight, a glass with two or three lenses, another glass that works as a high-powered monocle when set against a glass case containing a work of art, a pocket knife, a pick, tiny scissors, a small bottle of xylene and several swabs—used to quickly wipe off a tiny area of discolored varnish to see if the paint surface is undisturbed—and, possibly, a portable ultraviolet lamp. A Minox camera can also be useful, particularly when a collector refuses to give you a set of photographs to study, either because he wants to preserve as much secrecy as possible or is simply idiosyncratic.

Deft and rapid "scientific" analysis in the field can make a tremendous difference. One of the prize acquisitions of the Department of Western European Arts, a large and imposing lunette depicting the Archangel Michael by Andrea della Robbia, came to us because John G. Phillips, then in charge of the department, and one of its most able "eyes," made an unorthodox probe of the object's surface in the crowded auction room. The piece was considered to be rather uninteresting, despite its size, because the surface was lusterless, funny-looking. Most said that it was, at best, the work of a della Robbia follower, at worst a much later sculpture, possibly of the nineteenth century. But Phillips was able to slice off a bit of the surface with a knife, and see that the original glaze had been heavily coated with paint and varnish. We were able to purchase the piece for a modest price. When cleaned, it once again became a splendid creation of the master himself.

I remember going to an auction showroom with Margaret Freeman, then curator of The Cloisters, to examine a large armorial tapestry of the late fifteenth century. The tapestry was hanging. Peg Freeman insisted that it be taken down. We were scrutinizing its surface closely, counting up the number of repairs, when she detected that the upper three or four feet seemed thicker than the rest. Quickly, a knife was in her hand, the stitching of the back lining was cut, and she discovered that the thick area was part of the original tapestry, for some unknown reason folded back and concealed. The original selvage was preserved on the hidden portion. In this case, too, we were able to purchase the work for far less than its intrinsic value simply because everyone else who looked at the tapestry, hanging on the wall, assumed that it had been cut down from its original state.

For proper scientific analysis, one needs time. The object must be brought into the Museum. When a vendor pushes for a quick decision, beware. When the circumstances do not permit proper, slow examination, beware.

A number of years ago I traveled in Europe with the late James J. Rorimer, then the director of the Metropolitan and one of the most brilliant collectors in its history. A dealer let us know that a superb stone Madonna and Child of the rare period around 1400 was being offered under special circumstances by one of the great monasteries of Europe. It seemed that the government would allow its legal exportation in exchange for some kind of land transfer arrangement. The chance of a lifetime! We hastened to see the piece. In a hallowed crypt of the historic monastery it stood on an obviously ancient pedestal below a series of beautiful stained-glass windows of the fourteenth century and near one of the most resplendent gold and enamel shrines made in the entire Middle Ages. The sculpture took our breath away. The style was soft and elegant—the *weiche* or "beautiful" style of the art historian. The standing Madonna looked down gently at the Child held delicately in her arms. On each side of the serene and majestic figure coursed a perfectly formed series of sinuous "trumpet" folds, the mark of the style. Jim Rorimer had brought a flashlight and a small ultraviolet lamp, planning to determine immediately if the piece was truly old. If the stone fluoresced brownish yellow and buttery it would be ancient. If it came up purple or violet it would be either recut or modern. The dealer reluctantly allowed the examination to take place. The monks, he told us, wanted to make the sale discreetly. Everything about the sculpture was in order, he declared. After all, it had been here in the crypt for centuries. The only repair was at the neck. Sometime, long ago, the head of the Virgin had been knocked off and repaired. Our ultraviolet light showed the break clearly and indicated in the all-too-hurried probe that the stone seemed to fluoresce properly.

The price of $350,000 was established and we were shown the exportation permit signed by the government. When we were alone, Rorimer and I discovered that we were both suspicious. We determined to stall a bit on the basis that it would take several days to gather the funds. Meantime I would go to Paris with the set of photographs the dealer had furnished us and do some research. Rorimer would return to New York at once with the second set of photographs.

The fact that I was not able to find the splendid sculpture in any publication on the general period of 1400, or in any publication on the monastery itself, did not particularly bother me. Great pieces of art, after all, can be overlooked. Monastic orders sometimes discourage publication and reproduction in the hope that they can sell a work quietly. However, startling information soon reached me from New York. Rorimer had turned over the photos to William Forsyth, an expert on sculpture in the Medieval Department. Over the years Forsyth had collected thousands of photographs of Madonnas of all types and styles, dates, and regions. The instant he saw the photographs, Bill Forsyth knew that he had seen the piece before. But something—he couldn't decide what it was—seemed wrong with it. After a search in his photo collection he produced a sculpture that looked like our piece in certain details—the shape of the head, the almost exact nature of the Christ Child. This sculpture had once been in the collection of Junius Morgan, and in the distant past it had been offered to the Museum and not accepted because of its mediocre quality. For decades it had been in the inventory of a New York gallery. *But,* the picture that Forsyth produced from his file differed radically from the elegant piece Rorimer and I had viewed in the monastery. Forsyth's sculpture was dry, somewhat harsh. The Madonna did not look down at the Child. The cascades of folds at the sides of her robe were linear abstract elements, terminating in severe zig-zags, not in flowing trumpet shapes. This was a typical nondescript Madonna of about 1500, and was said to have come from a church in a small town east of Paris, slightly south of Rheims.

Forsyth had some further information for us. A year or two before our visit to the monastery a man matching Rorimer's description of the dealer had purchased the Junius Morgan statue for less than a thousand dollars from the gallery where it had been for thirty years.

In Paris, I called on a colleague in the Direction des Monuments Historiques. Here, after a brief search, we found an old photograph of the Madonna in situ and a recent notation by a departmental inspector reporting that the sculpture was still in the village church for which it had been made 400 years before. My colleague suggested that the piece once in the Morgan collection was probably an old copy that was subsequently recut to become a Madonna of 1400. It was all very interesting.

I rented a car, drove to the village, undid the wire lock on the door of the deserted church, and there the sculpture was, rigid face, zig-zag folds, and all. But upon closer examination I could see that the sculpture was not old at all. It was a cast, made of cement. When I reported this news to my colleague in the Monuments Historiques, he shrugged with Gallic resignation and made a note of the true facts.

The moment had arrived for my meeting with the dealer. At the end of a charming dinner, with the mellowing effect of some good wine, I produced an official-looking manila folder. My guest briefly seemed to think it contained currency. One by one I laid on the cleared table my photographs of the Madonna in its form of 1500 and its "reconstruction" of 1400. The dealer blandly conceded that my pictures recorded a remarkable coincidence. Over brandies he remarked that he presumed we were not going to purchase the piece.

The scientific analysis of works when they are on the premises of the Metropolitan is a much more thorough process. When we study a painting, it is normal to begin with X-ray, which points out not only damages in the canvas and how the artist may have changed the painting as he worked on it, but also reveals the structure of the brushwork and thus indicates where parts of the picture have been restored. X-ray can also tell us if the brushstrokes are different from those in other works by the same artist. Infrared light can look below the surface of the varnish and indicate damages and areas of repainting. Sometimes it is necessary to take microscopic cross sections through the multiple paint layers of the surface in order to determine whether these have been applied in the traditional manner. Or to take tiny samples of paint for chemical analysis so as to determine whether certain pigments are present, zinc white, for example, a type of paint invented around the middle of the eighteenth century and made commercially available only at the beginning of the nineteenth.

For objects of metal, we use such investigative methods as X-ray radiography, microscopic analysis of the sections and layers of corrosion, and neutron activation analysis. For pottery or terracotta sculpture, and for the ceramic core that may remain inside a cast metal object, thermoluminescence is helpful. In this technique a sample of the ceramic body is heated to emit a light that is proportional to the amount of nuclear radiation absorbed over the years by its mineral constituents. From the result, the scientist estimates the date when the object was originally fired.

For organic materials another possibility exists, carbon-14 testing, which will indicate the general age of the material. One of the difficulties, however, is that one needs a fairly significant amount of material with which to make the test.

One of the most fascinating tests, developed at the Corning Glass Center, involves examining a tiny chip of a glass object under microscope. Since, for a number of reasons, glass corrodes in a set layer of precise annual measurement, depending on whether it has been underground or in the sea, for example, one can count the rings of corrosion much as one would count the growth rings of a tree. Blind tests of this nature have been made in cases where the exact date of the glass is known by inscription, and the results have dated the object sometimes to the precise year.

Physical scientists are coming up with ever more sophisticated examination possibilities, especially in the field of computer techniques, but it would be a mistake to think that we have now been handed a magic box in which a work of art is placed, a button is pushed, and dials indicate to the now largely superfluous curator the date, locality, condition, quality, and esthetic essence of a work of art. The eye of the connoisseur is still primary. More often than not the detailed scientific analysis simply corroborates what the eye has already discovered.

12,13.

After all his study the professional returns to point number one: *immediate impression*. Does everything bear it out? If so, all is well. Then, the final step, the question to be asked coldly—Does the piece really have quality on its own? Is that quality pure and objective? Is it there distinct from one's human desire to add the work to the collection? If the original impression is far off from the conclusion, one goes to the doubts list and tries to pin down each item that has accumulated there. In the case of a forgery or suspected forgery the curator attempts to find solid proof of the fact. For, although it can be a mistake to collect a fake—a mistake that every great and adventurous connoisseur has made—it is a sin to brand as a forgery an authentic work of art.

There are several kinds of fakes. One, the simplest, is the straight copy. Next, the fanciful or romantic near copy. Third, the pastiche, in which the forger copies a number of original models and merges them. Fourth, the altered piece. Fifth, the truly creative, "original" fake. This is the hardest to produce, and it may prove the most difficult to detect. One thinks of Van Meegeren, the Dutch faker of the war years. His achievement was to formulate the "early" period of Jan Vermeer, of which no examples exist. But even the works of Van Meegeren collapsed in time. No matter how perfectly the forger recreates the style of an ancient period, his own style is there too. It is a rule of thumb that no forgery deceives for more than a generation. With the passing years, the elements of the style of the time when it was created stand out more clearly than those of the period in which it was supposed to have been made.

When the professional's doubts build up about a work of art, the piece begins to weaken. When the simple fault begins to emerge, the piece crumbles rapidly. Sometimes a brilliant forgery falls because of an extraordinarily stupid oversight. Once we were offered an Islamic painting of the sixteenth century. It seemed to be unique in that it was not a miniature but an easel painting. It was a splendid painting, I admit. But our X-ray photograph revealed that the forger had left a paperclip in the wood and parchment panel.

Now, the examination I have discussed here at some length need not in every case be as detailed as I have made it. An experienced curator can sometimes do most of this study in minutes. A good eye can spot a great piece or a nothing from a hundred feet away. A great connoisseur can walk into a gallery crowded with works of art and within half an hour choose unerringly the top five.

When the curator becomes convinced that a piece must be purchased, the next step is a formal one. At the Metropolitan we have an acquisition form that reflects the investigatory steps I have described and calls for the basic information needed by our General Catalogue and Registration. When properly written up, the form also provides what amounts to a standard exhibition catalogue entry. In this way at least some of the routine scholarly work surrounding the object is started right away.

A few comments about the form. The statement at VII, crucially important, is often the one that leads either to the pursuit and acquisition of the object or to its rejection. Areas IX and X cover the issue of legal exportation abroad. It may be noted that we seek not only hard facts but even hearsay or rumor. It is the full pattern of the evidence, including what might appear sometimes to be irrelevant, that can pin a work of art to its correct historical place.

RECOMMENDED PURCHASE BLANK

TO THE DIRECTOR AND THE ACQUISITIONS COMMITTEE: cc: Vice-Director for Curatorial and Educational Affairs (2 copies of this blank and 2 copies of Curator's Report) Registrar (this blank only) Secretary (this blank only)

I recommend the purchase of the object(s) fully described in the attached report and briefly captioned below.

Classification_____

Artist, title, date:

Vendor: Recommended loan class:

Price:

Additional expenses: Transportation $_____ Insurance $_____
                     Sender to pay   Sender to pay
                     M.M.A. to pay   M.M.A. to pay

                     Installation $_____ Restoration $_____

                     Other $_____

Recommendation approved: Submitted by:

_____   _____

Director   Curator of_____

                                    Date_____

FOR USE OF SECRETARY'S OFFICE ONLY

ACTION BY ACQUISITIONS COMMITTEE   To be charged against income from the

       (authorized)   _____Fund, 19

Purchase (not authorized) _____   Authorized at: $_____

Reported to Board_____

Reported to   Secured for: $_____

Acquisitions Committee_____   Purchase authorization no._____

                                                Accession no._____

RECOMMENDED PURCHASE—CURATOR'S REPORT

Classification

Attach at least one photograph of the object(s) to the Director's and Vice-Director, copies.

I. Name the title, artist, nationality or school, period, material, dimensions in inches and centimeters.

II. Full description of the object. Provide a complete visual account, including the description of all parts. Transcribe any inscriptions, describe marks and mention any added attachments or missing parts, etc.

III. Describe the condition of the piece, indicating any repairs and attempting a prognosis for future condition. Name the results obtained from scientific investigations, whether of microscopy, chemical tests, X-ray, infra-red, ultra-violet, spectrographic analysis, thermoluminescence, etc.

IV. State the function of the piece, and whether anything about the object indicates its function as part of a greater whole or as an independent work.

V. Describe the iconography of the object. Does it follow traditional iconography, or is there something unusual in its iconography?

VI. Stylistic considerations

    A. State briefly your initial reaction to the object.

    B. Describe the style and relate the style of the piece to the appropriate artist, school, period, etc.

    C. Discuss and illustrate the two or three pieces that make the best stylistic comparisons with this piece. Indicate what distinctive qualities this piece has in relation to them in terms of style, technique, condition, documentation, etc.

    D. Provide a list of all relevant works of art, whether copies, variants or other closely similar compositions, pointing out the relationship to each work named.

VII. State how the work of art complements the existing Museum collections or how it fills a gap.

VIII. Explain your plans for exhibiting and publishing the piece.

IX. Give the history of the piece, all known provenance with traditional documentation, when available. Include any hearsay evidence or traditional provenance, with source.

X. Give any significant archaeological information.

XI. List all published references, pointing out those of greatest importance. Also include any expert advice sought or volunteered from outside the Museum.

XII. Give a resume of your reasons for deciding to recommend the piece, being candid as to its strengths and weaknesses, its rarity of quality, technique, type, etc. Mention any problem outstanding that could affect the decision to buy.

XIII. Tell how long you have known of the piece and give a history of negotiations.

XIV. If possible, give recent market prices for comparable works of art.

XV. Financial considerations

    A. If the object is to be purchased, state the price _____ .

    B. State the name of the fund if you recommend that a specific fund be used.

    C. If the object is to be acquired by exchange, specify M.M.A. object(s) involved, including accession number(s), valuation and status of de-accessioning.

    D. Specify any anticipated additional expenses:

            Transportation $_____ Insurance $_____
               Sender to pay_____ Sender to pay_____
              M.M.A. to pay_____ M.M.A. to pay_____

            Installation $_____ Restoration $_____

            Other $_____

    E. State any conditions attached to the purchase. State chances for bargaining.

Part XII is the nub of the curatorial effort. The statements here distinguish the professional collector, who must be able to justify fully every reason for recommending a work of art, from the amateur, who is often impelled by love alone. We seek candor; we urge that the curator discuss the shortcomings of the work that must exist even in the rarest of masterpieces.

Parts XIII, XIV, and XV deal with the delicate nature of the negotiations for the acquisition and the appropriateness of the stated price. This information is essential to the Director in formulating his recommendations to the Acquisitions Committee of the Board of Trustees. It is this committee that makes final judgments, including determination of the amounts of money available in the current fiscal year or, possibly, several years ahead. The notes on negotiations and chances for bargaining enable the Director to measure how far the Museum can go. Normally, a plan of action is established concerning bargaining. The curatorial staff will go to a certain point, then, at the right moment, the department head will enter to apply more pressure. Normally, the Director does not enter the affair until after the work has been presented by the curator to the Acquisitions Committee and has been approved. The Director then determines what possibilities exist to bring the price down even further. It is wise to know the character of the individual you are dealing with, whether owner or agent. Precise timing is important. One squeezes, but not so much that the piece will go elsewhere. It is tense work, needing a cool, dispassionate attitude. Better to err on the side of loss than to break the discipline of the bargaining plan. There are, of course, exceptions to this, as there are in every aspect of the collecting mission. Some works of art are so important that one dispenses with the bargaining entirely.

Knowledge of comparable prices is almost as important as knowledge of all similar works of art. Most curators keep an updated data bank in their heads concerning prices of works by the same artist or of works of similar artists, schools, and the like. In collecting, this is a part of the "good, better, best" analysis of each work. Knowing prices takes training and talent. James Rorimer was astoundingly skilled in this area. When asked by the Museum's trustees what Rembrandt's *Aristotle with a Bust of Homer* would fetch at auction, two months before the sale, he said, "Two million, three hundred thousand dollars." That was precisely what it turned out to be. I remember bringing in fifteen or twenty varied works of early Christian and Byzantine art, some bronze, some silver, some gold, from a dealer Rorimer knew well. I deposited the objects on the desk before him. He had never seen them before. He examined them at some distance for little more than a minute and casually said, "Twenty-seven thousand, five hundred. Work hard and cleverly and you'll fetch them for twenty-three." I was amazed. The dealer was asking twenty-eight thousand. Eventually we obtained the pieces for twenty-three thousand.

For the layman, two of the deeper mysteries in the collecting process are how a price is established and how one knows that the price is right. People can understand the price of a car, a home, a fine piece of jewelry, or even the price of gold, which fluctuates according to a complex but recognizable set of economic factors. But a Rembrandt, a Jan Brueghel, a Precolumbian sculpture, a Jackson Pollock? More than once, I have seen professional appraisers cite widely varying figures for the same work. A certain Modigliani, for example, was appraised at $50,000, $35,000, and $27,000 by three experienced professionals. A fourth put it at "over a hundred thousand," but he, it turned out, had once owned the painting, had had the great luck to sell it way over its real value, and was now, of course, supporting the price. So, whom to believe? Frustrating though the answer may be to the layman, you can't believe anyone. You *feel*. You are comfortable, or not, more or less, in a rather large area of price possibilities. Certain simple indices help. At what price did the work sell before? What is the most recent price at auction for the closest thing possible? Simple enough, when it works. The problem is, what looks close, may not be. Condition, size, and quality—always that indefinable but ever-present *quality*—determines all about a work of art, even its value. If one takes the time to examine all the subtle differences in two very similar pieces, even by the same artist, the differences in quality and value become apparent.

One piece of Louis XV furniture brings $80,000, another, not wholly dissimilar, fetches $750,000. The first is of good, not splendid, quality. It is in acceptable condition but is undocumented, or unsigned. The second is by a known *ébéniste* working in the finest materials, producing a work of sublime quality. Let us say, in addition, that it bears on the underside of one of its drawers the number 6903. The quality and that number, logically enough, make the difference between a work of art costing $80,000 and one costing nearly ten times that amount. That number refers to the royal inventory, noting the existence of a superb piece of furniture made by one of the most accomplished cabinetmakers of the eighteenth century for the king himself. Now, if you were to ask why Louis XV's personal piece of furniture should not be worth $650,000 or $850,000, instead of $750,000, I could only reply that we are in the gray area of how different individuals assess quality, not to mention how the bidding of two or three avid collectors affects price. Put these collectors temporarily out of the picture and the "perfect," justifiable price might be $450,000. And if one cares to go back to the time when sublime furniture of Louis XV was, quite wrongly, considered to be decadent or even immoral, $7,625 was the "correct" price.

The Acquisitions Committee of the Board of Trustees regularly meets four times a year, more frequently when the need arises. There are usually about a dozen members, chosen for their special knowledge or their great interest in works of art. Many of them are connoisseurs in their own right, having private collections of great distinction.

Shortly before the meeting of the Acquisitions Committee, we go through a preliminary meeting with the heads of the curatorial departments. This process, which has been in effect for several years, enables the department heads, the Director, the Secretary and Counsel, and the Vice-Director for Finance to have a complete review of all the works of art the curators would like to present for formal consideration. Each curator makes a presentation of an object and must be prepared to defend it. There are usually tough questions from the other curators. If these are not answered satisfactorily, the object is either withdrawn or a more complete report is prepared within a few days. The Secretary and Counsel will, where necessary, ask for further information on the provenance and the circumstances of its export from abroad. The financial officer will advise as to whether restricted purchase funds are available. Normally there is an informal vote by the department heads in which they list their preferences among the works proposed. Almost invariably there is accord on the first four or five objects. Indeed, in the past seven years, encompassing twenty-six such meetings, the accord has been nearly universal. Sometimes, when one department presents a particularly important work, other departments will withdraw "their" objects so as not to compete for the same amount of unrestricted purchase funds. In the complex curatorial and fiscal structure of the Metropolitan, there is no process that works more efficiently than this one. Small wonder, for the collecting mission is the heart of the curatorial endeavor.

After this preliminary meeting, I review the works tentatively chosen by the curators with the President of the Museum and the Vice-Director for Curatorial and Educational Affairs. Depending upon the available money or, infrequently, the volume of the objects, I may cut some of them off the list to be presented to the Acquisitions Committee. When this happens, it doesn't necessarily mean they are banished forever. Sometimes they will reappear at a subsequent meeting.

It is in the meeting just described that the professionals have an opportunity to practice their presentations to the Trustees. One of my roles is to offer advice on the way an object is presented and defended. Sometimes I edit the oral proposal.

Curators take great pains with their presentations. Often they follow the Recommended Purchase Blank, enlarging upon it where necessary for dramatic effect. The hoped-for result is that a scholarly "brief" is presented with all the wit and excitement possible. I remember brilliant scholarly presentations and purely emotional ones that were equally effective.

One of my favorites in the latter category was delivered by Robert Beverly Hale in 1952, when he presented the splendid *Autumn Rhythm* by Jackson Pollock. The Trustees looked upon the near-spontaneous drips and meanderings of Pollock's action painting as practically dangerous. It was almost certain they were going to reject the enormous abstract-expressionist canvas, despite the fact that money was available for it in a special fund for living American painters. Faced with the possible loss of this grand picture, Bob Hale, partly for the effect and partly because of his deep conviction, broke into tears. Few Trustees can stand the sight of a weeping curator. The painting was approved. Years after this *coup d'émotion,* I was seeking advice from Hale with respect to a particularly important acquisition. He told me to think about crying. "But, remember," he said, "you can only do it once." I'm still waiting for the perfect opportunity.

After the curators have presented their briefs and shown their objects to the Acquisitions Committee, and after these Trustees have reviewed the state of the purchase monies, the curatorial staff is excused and the executive session begins.

Before each vote, I am asked to give my recommendation. Not every object presented has had my blessing, but almost always the curator who can make a strong case has been allowed to present the work. I have been overruled by the Acquisitions Committee from time to time and have in a sense overruled myself on occasion when a curator set forth an irresistible argument. Occasionally, one of the objects I support vigorously is voted down by the Trustees. The director of another museum once told me that, for him, this would be grounds for his resignation. I have no such feeling, and have found, in retrospect, that the few turn-downs have been quite right. The check and balance of the Trustees is vitally necessary to an institution such as the Metropolitan.

Under normal circumstances, every work of art to be acquired by the Museum, whether from a private collector or a dealer or at auction, goes through the process just described. In the case of an auction, the final offer is fixed by the Acquisitions Committee.

In past years the Director was granted a sizable sum of money—as much as $250,000—to enable him to purchase objects he might encounter in his travels around the world. I prefer not to have such a discretionary account for two reasons. First, the business of directing the Metropolitan has changed, and I am more of an overall manager and chief executive than a super curator. Second, I no longer have time for that all-important saturation, and for keeping up with all the details concerning possible acquisitions I rely on the curatorial staff, which should do this job and does it well.

Perhaps the question now arises, between the quarterly meetings of the Acquisitions Committee, what happens when works of art of modest significance and no great cost suddenly become available—or what happens when something grand suddenly surfaces in the auction room? Part of the problem is solved by the yearly allocation to each curatorial department of a small sum for what is called curatorial purchases. In addition, certain departments—Prints and Photographs, Drawings, Islamic Art—are granted $25,000 or $35,000 a year with which to buy abroad, in order to obtain things at lower prices than would occur if a middleman were involved. A sum of $50,000 is made available for use at my direction to acquire medium-range works, of up to $5,000 each, or to supplement curatorial purchase funds up to the limit. Finally, the Acquisitions Committee can always be polled by memorandum for those works of art that appear between regular meetings and are of sufficient importance to acquire quickly.

Despite all these sensible plans, exceptional events occur that require us to act quickly and in secrecy.

One morning in September 1970 Theodore Rousseau, then Curator-in-Chief, rushed into my office with word that one of Diego Velázquez's greatest portraits, the *Juan de Pareja,* belonging to Lord Radnor, was soon going to be auctioned by Christie's in London. He convinced me then and there that we must make the greatest effort to secure this universally acknowledged masterpiece, which was a sensation from the moment it was first exhibited, on March 19, 1650, in the Pantheon in Rome.

According to old accounts, Velázquez painted Juan, his assistant and traveling companion, shortly before beginning his portrait of Pope Innocent X. Velázquez had been sightseeing in Italy for months, never touching brush to canvas. In order to limber up his fingers, it was said, he painted this intensely human and sensitive portrait. One story had it that Juan himself took the picture to several artists' studios just after it was finished, knocked upon the door, and simply stood there holding the portrait. One painter declared that he could not tell which was the man, so deeply and vibrantly had the essence of life been transmitted into the paint.

The Radnor family had owned this supreme Velázquez for a hundred and fifty years. Dealers, private collectors, and museums had been after it for years. A member of the family once told me of an afternoon in the 1930s when, at teatime, Lord Radnor's butler brought him word that a dealer was seeking to purchase the picture. On the butler's tray lay a check for a very large sum. Lord Radnor tore the check to bits and instructed the butler to send the dealer packing. My informant said the butler presently reappeared with the same message and a new check, signed but otherwise blank. That check was also destroyed.

Ted Rousseau did not immediately know why the *Juan de Pareja* was going to auction. He himself had approached Lord Radnor not long before about the possibility of the Metropolitan's buying it and had been pleasantly rebuffed. We soon learned the reason for Radnor's change of mind. A thief had entered the Radnor country seat intending to steal the *Juan de Pareja.* Not being a connoisseur, he had cut the wrong painting from its frame—a portrait by Franz Hals of about the same size. In the aftermath, Radnor had decided it was time to dispose of his too-valuable property.

The auction was to take place in November, little more than a month hence. (Curiously, the *Juan de Pareja* had been sold once before at

FIGURE 3. Diego Rodriguez de Silva y Velázquez (1599–1660, Spanish). *Juan de Pareja*. Oil on canvas. Purchase, Fletcher and Rogers Funds and Bequest of Miss Adelaide Milton de Groot (1876–1967), by exchange, supplemented by gifts from friends of the Museum, 1971.86

Christie's in 1801, when the bargain price was 39 guineas.) I quickly assembled a team to examine the painting: Ted Rousseau, Everett Fahy, then our curator of European Paintings, and Hubert von Sonnenburg, our conservator of paintings. Next, we needed a bidder. For this service I sought Louis Goldenberg, president of the eminent house of Wildenstein and Company. Wildenstein was the perfect choice, a firm among the best in the auction room and one whose professionalism, discretion, and wisdom had always been held in high regard by the Museum. Also, I thought it likely that Wildenstein would either be going after the painting themselves or would soon be asked to bid for it on behalf of some other institution or collector. There was still another factor that sent me to Goldenberg. It was thought in certain quarters of the art world that Wildenstein and the Metropolitan were at odds. This was an entirely specious supposition, but, in the events to come, it was one that would help insure secrecy about our interest.

Goldenberg confirmed at once that his firm was hoping to purchase the portrait for itself. Wildenstein, he said, was contemplating a price around $4,000,000. I told him that Douglas Dillon, the Museum's President, and I had already discussed the matter preliminarily and that the Museum was seriously considering going higher than his figure. It was agreed that if the Metropolitan met or surpassed the Wildenstein price, Wildenstein would act as our agent for no commission, but that if the Museum dropped out, Wildenstein could, if it wished to, make a final effort to claim the picture.

With Goldenberg's help, we started at once upon an analysis of all the potential bidders in Europe and the United States. Our aim was to discover the identity of the underbidder and the exact figure the underbidder would select. Impossible? Not at all. Despite the high confidentiality of the situation, a surprising amount of precise information can be pieced together if one keeps a daily account of all rumors, hints, and casual conversations. While our record grew, we waited for what we assumed would happen: that the opposition would tip its hand by trying to find out if *we* were going to be involved. We devised, at the same time, a program to befuddle the competition. My personal image at that time was of a brash, publicity-seeking character with little experience in the big-time auction arena. We decided to capitalize on the image. The general plan was for me to appear keenly enthusiastic about the painting, then discouraged about my chances, then perhaps a bit frantic and finally utterly bored.

The first step was to take the team to Christie's and examine the painting as carefully as possible. We would then took at as many other great paintings by Velázquez as possible in order to make the all-important comparison of quality.

Visitors from all parts of the world were arriving at the venerable auction house, eager to view the masterpiece and prepare their own programs to capture it. The first time we studied it, we simply looked at it for the two hours we had been assigned. My God, what a painting! It was indeed life and truth, not just art, as had first been said nearly 350 years before. The young Black seemed on the point of speaking to us. It was, I thought at the time, the most supremely natural work of art I had ever seen.

The condition appeared to be superb, but it was difficult to be certain. The varnish was so yellowed with age that the true color of the background—a mouse gray, we thought—and the slate green of the cloak were not wholly perceivable. And, perhaps most important of all, it looked as if the painting had never been relined. A blessing, if true, for often relining involves the application of an additional piece of canvas to the back of a picture with the result that the peaks and mountains of the paint are flattened ever so slightly. The average eye seldom notices this. Consequently, many old-master paintings are so treated. But to place side by side a relined picture of the seventeenth century and one never touched is a revelation. In the baroque period the painter worked in scumbles, lightly applied impastos, deliberately and carefully building complex landscapes, relief maps of glistening reflecting surfaces of great subtlety. With Velázquez, this is of the utmost importance. Sadly, many of his greatest pictures have been so poorly treated over the centuries by dedicated conservators that they have lost much of their original vitality. But the *Juan de Pareja* had been stuck off in some room of a country seat in that splendidly offhand manner practiced only by the nobility and seemed to us at first sight never to have been touched. We picked out one detail to study. Even though we were not able to examine it with our pocket glasses we could see that the paint surfaces—those microscopic mountains—were sharp, so sharp as to be almost brittle. Could it be true? We left, booking a longer appointment two days hence, and went to Apsley House, the seat of the Duke of Wellington, to view the great early Velázquez, *The Water Carrier*. Then to the Wallace Collection where the Director, Sir Francis Watson, a friend and colleague, let us inspect the collection's three magnificent Velázquez paintings without their protective glass. One of these, the portrait of the beautiful *Lady with a Fan,* was of particular importance to us. We were stunned to see how much the picture deteriorated when the glass was removed. For the viewer, the glass acts like varnish. Without its glass, that portrait became as flat as a piece of newsprint. It had been relined and flattened.

After we tuned our eyes further on the Velázquez paintings in the National Gallery, we returned to Christie's for our second session. During that visit the young representative assigned to guard the painting left us alone with it for a few minutes, giving us the chance for a very close inspection of its surface. The picture looked as if it had just left the master's brush! We were careful to appear somewhat disappointed when the young guardian returned.

Next day we flew to Madrid to study Velázquezes in the Prado. All of the paintings, we discovered, had suffered somewhat over the years from having been cleaned. According to the Director, Xavier de Salas, a Velázquez expert, Lord Radnor's Velázquez was perhaps in the best condition of all the artist's intimate portraits. Later, after the auction, I learned that the Prado had bid a million dollars for the *Juan de Pareja*—a staggering sum for Spain.

After the Prado we went to Rome to study the single greatest portrait by this most accomplished of portrait painters, that of Pope Innocent X. It is in a private palace, still owned by indirect descendants of the subject. The painting hangs by itself in a sort of side chapel off one of the great halls that make up the Doria-Pamphili picture gallery. It is lighted superbly by an overhead window. A series of mirrored doors is arranged so that the visitor sees a reflected image of the painting before he sees the portrait itself. The effect is startling. Again, what seems to be projected is "truth, not art." It has been observed that this powerful, brooding, vital image of Innocent X is the most universal and most sensitive portrait that history has accorded us. Despite the superlative nature of that statement, I agree with it. Velázquez achieved a unique cohesion of all his incomparable gifts in his *Innocent* X. Italy itself was a grand part of the portrait's magic, as it was, too, of the *Juan de Pareja.* The court painter had traveled throughout the land for months before reaching Rome. He had feasted his eyes upon all the majesties of this land of superb art. His frame of mind was peaceful, happy, unharried by the constant demands of the Spanish court. He came to Rome saturated with the rich works of the Venetian colorists and the mighty works of Correggio in Parma. It was as if all elements converged to give him a confidence that in Spain he did not always possess. Something happened, for sure, in Italy. The works completed there, the *Juan de Pareja,* the *Innocent X,* and those completed shortly after his return to Spain, *Las Meninas,* and *Las Hilanderas,* are acknowledged as the pinnacles of his creativity.

Our study tour completed, we returned to London to examine the *Juan de Pareja* for the last time before making the decision to go for it. We had almost four hours with it. Part of this time we were alone with it, which enabled us to examine the back carefully. We held the portrait up to the light and saw pinpricks of the sun's rays through it. Now we had final proof of what our other examinations had suggested: the painting had never been relined.

As we left the auction house we made another of our plays to alert the representatives of Christie's to the fact that the Metropolitan was not interested. As we waited for the elevator, knowing that a genial attendant was listening, I said to von Sonnenburg, the conservator, "You never know about a work of art, do you? Some things called great *do* grow every time you see them. Others weaken and begin to fade. I would have thought the *Juan de Pareja* would have grown tremendously. But it's really fading away." Hubert agreed and added a few remarks about its "curious" condition. As we left the place we were asked if we wished to reserve seats for the auction. We declined.

Upon our return to New York we reported to an informal meeting of the Acquisitions Committee our unanimous feeling that the *Juan de Pareja* was one of the most beautiful and accomplished portraits by the master, and that it appeared to be in near-mint condition.

I checked with Louis Goldenberg to find out what he had discovered about the price. The picture, he said, would most certainly fetch two million guineas plus a bid or two. Thus, with the increments of the bidding being 100,000 guineas each, the *Juan de Pareja* could bring anywhere from $5,000,000 to $5,500,000! An enormous price, certainly, even if not the highest ever paid for a single work of art.

The members of the Acquisitions Committee were all of the view that we should try for it. There might never be another opportunity. Although certain great treasures were still around, few in number, to be sure, and others would present themselves in the future, within the works of Veláz-quez, the *Juan de Pareja* was the last particle of sand in the hourglass. One of the members of the committee, Charles Wrightsman, related that he had spoken confidentially about the picture to his friend Lord Clark of Saltwood, who said that the Velázquez was one of the greatest achievements of the master and, if bought by a collector overseas, would probably be the last great treasure ever to leave Great Britain. Five years later, Lord Clark's opinion about exportation has become a historical fact. I doubt if it will ever change.

Within the Museum we discussed the manners of fund-raising available to us. Among these, a private fund drive from very special friends (a procedure used in the past), the use of a part of the principal of our Fletcher Fund, and the selling of a variety of works of art represented in the collections by superior examples.

I then suggested that we try to purchase the portrait jointly with two or three American institutions, arguing that the work was clearly of national importance and could easily travel, thanks to its superb condi-tion. The Acquisitions Committee liked the idea. We selected, as possible partners, the National Gallery in Washington and the Cleveland Museum. I consulted Sherman Lee, the Director of the Cleveland, and Douglas Dillon discussed the possibility with the Chairman of the Board of the National Gallery, Paul Mellon.

After some consideration Lee told me that he and his trustees felt that although the concept had merits—particularly for the future—it would not be feasible with the *Juan de Pareja*. Time was one factor. (I grant that my novel plan was proposed rather suddenly.) Lee also felt that no ar-rangement could be worked out that would be consistent with the security and the delicate condition of the picture. That surprised me, for I would have surmised that the experts from Cleveland had studied the painting as intensely as we had. Then, getting to the meat of the matter, Lee told me that since the collection of Spanish paintings at Cleveland was so superior, the trustees were going to authorize their own bid for the work. I suggested that it would be sensible for us to compare our highest bids in order not to run the painting up senselessly, as had occurred earlier with our *Aristotle.* Lee agreed that a comparison would be helpful. Somehow, no doubt owing to the rush of events, we did not exchange the information. It didn't matter, for Cleveland eventually bid up to $3,500,000 and quit.

Douglas Dillon brought us word from Paul Mellon that the National Gallery was not interested in a joint purchase and furthermore had no current interest in the painting.

We then attempted to form another combine, including the Museum of Fine Arts in Boston and the Art Institute of Chicago. For various reasons, primarily financial, this effort also failed.

At a special meeting of the Acquisitions Committee, eleven days before the auction, the seven Trustees present agreed that the *Juan de Pareja* must come to the Museum. One of them stated that nothing could be more correct than for the committee to vote in favor of the acquisition. Quality is supreme, he said, and this is supreme quality.

There was a brief discussion of the unfavorable publicity we might get if we bought the painting. The gist of it was that we should not be concerned with possible flak. Despite the criticism after our purchase of the *Aristotle,* said one Trustee, that purchase was absolutely correct. Another Trustee said, "It's always better to buy a few things of great quality than to fritter the funds away on numbers."

I gave a report of the latest word on possible price, after which I was asked who the underbidder would be. The National Gallery in Washington, I said. The attitude of no interest there was a pose, I said, just as ours at Christie's had been. Officials of the Gallery had spent considerable time examining the picture, and the Director, Carter Brown, had even inquired of Wildenstein what they thought the bid increments would be. Furthermore, an official in the public relations department of the National Gallery had recently telephoned a colleague in our Museum, and had attempted to find out, "if anything interesting was going on at the Met."

Now, Dillon presented the financial situation and recommended that the bulk of the bid money come from the unrestricted Isaac D. Fletcher Fund with the understanding that $2,000,000 would be paid back to Fletcher from the Jacob S. Rogers Fund. The loss of income from both the funds, extended over a fifteen-year period, he explained, would amount to only $368,000 annually. Dillon advocated later discussions concerning the disposal of certain works of art to reduce the drain upon the Museum's unrestricted acquisitions funds, and he gently reminded everyone present that Trustee aid would also be critically important.

The vote in favor of acquiring the painting was unanimous. The feeling was one of confidence and enthusiasm. In slightly under five minutes, from the seven members of the committee present, President Dillon was able to raise $550,000. Later on that figure would rise to $750,000, thanks to additional donations from two of those present.

Charles Wrightsman did not want to see us trapped into landing on an even 2,000,000 guinea bid and urged that Wildenstein be given the flexibility to break away from that position. He requested that his very generous pledge be used specifically for this purpose.

President Dillon formed a resolution to instruct Louis Goldenberg to attempt to purchase the *Juan de Pareja* for the Metropolitan, at no commission and no cost to the Museum other than normal expenses, which Wildenstein had suggested by a sum not to exceed 2,000,000 guineas plus one bid. The resolution was unanimously adopted.

I began to feel that the competition might well make one bid over the even 2,000,000 guineas. But we had to be a bit more creative than this, and, in a discussion with Douglas Dillon, I recommended that our final position be 2,000,000 plus one additional bid *back to us* and that the bidding team assigned by Wildenstein try to enter rather late and at an even bid. This gave even greater flexibility, of course, but would mean an additional outlay of $250,000. The President gave his approval, and our instructions with respect to the "break" bid were communicated to Wildenstein two days before the auction. This in essence won the painting for us.

Auctions that deal with treasures of such glory as the *Juan de Pareja* take only two or three minutes. In the early going there were five or even six bidders. At about $4,000,000 the competition dwindled to three or four. Louis Goldenberg entered at 1,600,000 guineas. This was the precise even bid he had been maneuvering to obtain. His entry caused shock waves in the jammed room. Think of it! An incredibly strong bid so late and so firm. All but one other bidder retired. The one who remained was Geoffrey Agnew, of Agnew and Sons, a renowned London dealer in old-master paintings. Agnew had entered earlier, pushing his way deliberately into an odd bid, it seemed to Goldenberg. The prospect excited him tremendously. At Goldenberg's 1,800,000 bid, there was a long pause from Agnew. Then, he indicated 1,900,000. For a second, Goldenberg wondered whether he should halve his bid from 100,000 to 50,000. He tossed the idea aside, figuring, correctly, that his strongest card would be swiftness and vigor. With hardly a pause he bid 2,000,000. Now there was a very long pause from Agnew before he went to 2,100,000. Goldenberg's counter bid of 2,200,000 was entered a fraction of a second later. Another long pause. Silence. The painting was hammered down to Wildenstein and Company at the Metropolitan's final possible bid of 2,200,000 guineas or $5,544,000. The crowd burst into applause.

When the painting arrived in New York, following the issuance of the exportation permit by the British Board of Trade, Hubert von Sonnenburg made the discovery (which we had discussed in London as a distant possibility) that 1⅜ inches of the canvas at the top and 2¼ inches at the right side had been folded under with perfect care. Some unknown owner of the painting, possibly a member of the Radnor family, had combined an instinct for saving things with the impulse to alter Velázquez's composition.

Suddenly, the lively and sympathetic young Juan de Pareja was liberated from his constricting proportions of the early nineteenth century. With these 104 additional square inches of canvas restored to view, Juan was at once in infinitely more real and convincing space. As soon as von Sonnenburg removed the yellowed ancient varnish, the original colors throughout the entire painting were astonishingly fresh, dynamic. The veil of centuries disappeared, and the portrait once again became the astounding image of 1650.

When the painting was put on exhibition in the Metropolitan, we were pleasantly surprised at the absence of controversy. An editorial in the *New York Times* observed: "It is virtually impossible to think of the new Velázquez without thinking about its price tag. This is a shame because the association deforms a great work of art. All secondary questions aside, the Metropolitan's acquisition of this superb painting enhances the quality of its great collection and permanently enriches the life of the city."

Another extraordinary meeting of the Acquisitions Committee was called in 1972 to consider our action regarding the now much-publicized calyx krater by the painter Euphronios. The story of this remarkable object had begun several months before the meeting, when the curator of the Greek and Roman Department, Dietrich von Bothmer received a letter from an American dealer in antiquities, Robert Hecht, saying, in part:

> I once made a hint asking if you and your trusted associates would make a super gigantic effort. Now please imagine this [vase] broken, but *complete* and

in *perfect state*—by complete I mean 99 44/100% and by "perfect state" I mean brilliant, not weathered. It would hardly be incorrect to say that such a thing could be considered the best of its kind—I don't say necessarily it is, but except for two Munich Kleophrades Painters and a Munich Euthymides it is hard to find competitors.

FIGURE 4. Calyx krater: Sleep and Death lifting the body of Sarpedon. Attic. About 515 B.C. Signed by Euxitheos as potter and Euphronios as potter. Bequest of Joseph H. Durkee, Gift of Darius Ogden Mills, and Gift of Mr. and Mrs. C. Ruxton Love, by exchange, 1972.11.10

Von Bothmer immediately showed the letter to me and Ted Rousseau. We soon wrote that the Museum would be most interested in seeing the object, and Hecht came to New York with photographs of the vase unrestored, showing all of the cracks. Even in the bland and "technical" photographs, the vase looked like a brilliant work of art. Dietrich von Bothmer explained to President Dillon, Rousseau, and me that the vase was painted by Euphronios, one of the greatest painters, if not the greatest, of the late sixth century, B.C. Euxitheos, a prime potter, had also signed the vase, making it that much more significant. The moving scene from the *Iliad* of the dead Lycian prince, Sarpedon, being transported back to his homeland by the figures of Sleep and Death was certainly one of the most beautiful in the works of the sublime artist that have survived. Moreover, the condition of the vase was excellent. Although broken into about 40 or 45 pieces, nothing was missing.

Compared with the 27 other extant vases or fragmentary vases either signed by Euphronios or attributed to him, this fine, large krater was most surely one of the top three and possibly even better than that.

We arranged to go immediately to Zurich to examine the vase. A speedy decision was essential, since Hecht had told us that he had dispatched the exact same letter he had written us to two museums in Europe, a private collector in Switzerland, and the Cleveland Museum.

On the morning of June 27 von Bothmer and I arrived at the house and laboratory of Fritz Bürki, a restorer of antiquities, who had worked on the piece. Hecht was already there. Ted Rousseau arrived shortly after we did.

These are my notes on the meeting:

> I caught a very quick glance of the krater indoors, but too quick for any impression at all. Good for that. The weather is perfect spring light and clear so I inform Hecht that I would prefer to have the full impact of the vase out-of-doors in the sun. So a table is arranged on the terrace and the enormous vase is lifted, not without some straining, out the door and up on the table. It is immense. Later I'm told that it holds, or held, twelve gallons of wine mixed with water. My impression is that it's far bigger than the Euphronios krater in the Louvre depicting Hercules and Antaeus. But that's surely a mistake since they are identical in size.
>
> Seeing it now in the perfect, full illumination of a beautiful morning I'm struck by its great presence. I suppose it's a bit unorthodox to call a vase an edifice, or edificelike, but this is truly a piece of architecture. The proportions

are sure and very strong. The angles and the curves are so right and solid as to be architectonic. Now I know fully what Dietrich meant by the principal scene being similar to a wall painting. When you look at it at some distance the scene of Sarpedon being lifted away by Sleep and Death fits perfectly within the curving area of the great stomach of the vase so that no part of the complex scene drifts away out of focus because of the curvature. In this sense it is far, far more successful than the Louvre Hercules and Antaeus where the figures are so large that parts of them disappear round the bend. This disappearance is even true of the great volute krater in Arezzo.

Now close to examine the drawing itself. What impresses me at once is the utter sureness of the drawing without a scintilla of hardness or *effort*. Sureness, certitude, confidence, without travail! All is completely in order and under control, but no part—even the tiniest detail—is too disciplined. The figures are drawn with an absolute sureness that staggers the imagination. All lines stand out sharply in considerable relief (how *did* Euphronios *do* it? With a sort of hollow needle?). The long line that in a simple stroke continues the wing of Sleep, through his arm in one, pure, unbroken, unhesitating line, is one of the most splendid passages of drawing that I've ever seen.

What makes all this even more extraordinary is that the artist could just barely see what he was drawing—or couldn't see it at all. In a sense, it was like drawing with invisible ink. The reason is that the glazes and the drawing, also glazes, were applied either by brush (or by the needlelike, brushlike implement) on the brownish gray color of the damp clay in a bistre kind of color. Thus, before firing, it would be almost impossible to see the lines. How could he do it? How could this artist have gotten every tangent, every overlap, every junction, every loop and whirl of these hundreds and hundreds of different lines just so right? Did he practice the scene, in all its bewildering complexity, time after time? Unthinkable, then dryness would enter. And there's no dryness of style here at all! But perhaps like a brilliant pianist, he could achieve warm perfection without the stultification of practice.

The condition is great. Thank God. Bürki simply glued the pieces together with no restoration at all! Nothing's missing except for infinitesimal slivers along some of the breaks. And here's a most interesting detail: at certain, three or four, joinings of pieces, there are clusters of very tiny pieces all carefully glued together. Hecht has a logical answer for this, which is that the vase has been stored for several decades in a box only partly put together and when Bürki got it he was able to find and preserve the smallest fragments that had broken by being jostled around.

I must commend Bürki on his efforts. The piece is radiant, beautifully preserved, and superbly put together.

There's an ancient repair consisting of three pairs of drilled holes made for bronze staples, now missing, which indicates that the vase was repaired in antiquity. Dietrich tells me that it's very rare to find the repair brackets carefully placed to avoid crossing any of the lines of the drawing. On countless lesser vases, the repairman just put the staples any place, smack in the drawing or wherever he pleased.

The figures on the back, men arming themselves, seem less accomplished than those of the Sarpedon group. My first idea, that this is another hand, is wrong. Invariably the reverse scene on a calyx krater is by the master painter, and is not less accomplished, merely swifter. Why? Because the artist is working on an unfired clay object which must remain soft enough to allow the glaze to sink in, somewhat like fresco, I suppose, and he must paint with dispatch, lest drying cracks set in. Even the floral decoration, the impressive, large leaves and clusters, become slightly more summary as the painter turns the vase, holding it on his knees as he paints.

We have studied the vase for several hours and I have no doubt that the Museum must make a major effort to acquire it. Simply said, it would become the most important object in our very good vase collection and in addition one of the most significant works in all the collections. Dietrich says it even more forcibly: "It would be the culmination of my career."

On our way to lunch, "What's its history?" I ask Hecht. Excellent. Apparently it has been in a private collection for two generations, at least since the time of the First World War. Hecht explains that it is not his vase, he is an agent for the dealer Dikran Sarrafian, who lives in Beirut. I tell Hecht that I cannot move until I have in writing evidence of ownership from him. This he agrees to furnish. All is legal. The piece has been owned by the Sarrafian family for over fifty years. It was brought to Hecht in Zurich on consignment, from Lebanon. If the Museum is to seriously consider its purchase it will be taken to the United States with a full customs declaration that includes its offering price.

After the pleasure, now the difficult work begins, at lunch. Essentially, there is only one real problem: the price, which is incredible, to say the least—$1.5 million. In attempting to reduce it, I tell Hecht that the vase is superb. There is no sense to denigrating the piece. It is superb, and a man like Hecht will become annoyed and simply sell it to someone else, quite possibly for less. Because of the Museum's reputation we are often the first to be offered a work of art, and for this privilege we sometimes have to pay a higher price. But I tell Hecht that the figure of $1.5 million is out of the question for us. He counters by spelling out the importance of the vase. His points are not inaccurate. He says that it is certainly worth the $1.5 million, possibly more, and that the owner refuses to go much below, under any circumstances, especially with the uncertainties of the value of the dollar. I try to probe all payment possibilities, mentioning time payments, purchase in part by cash and in part by exchange, even a large lump of cash, such as $650,000, paid upon purchase. But Hecht is adamant, and keeps falling back upon an argument which is impossible to counter; namely, he doesn't own the piece; he is working for a commission. If he owned the piece he would accommodate the Museum, but he cannot. What he can do and all he can do is to suggest a 10 percent reduction if we pay $850,000 in mid-July and the rest in September. That would make the price $1,350,000. I tell him that I wouldn't recommend such an arrangement to my Trustees.

Then Hecht says that if he owned the vase he would suggest that the Museum hand over to him two collections of Greek and Roman coins that the Metropolitan had already deaccessioned and is negotiating for sale through two coin dealers in Switzerland. He would give us the vase for the coins plus $100,000 in cash. For him this arrangement would be brilliant; he is a coin collector and dealer of international recognition. For us? It might be perfect, for the top assessment by two of the most eminent coin dealers in the world for our coins is at this time $950,000. But Hecht's offer clearly means that their appraisal was too conservative. I excuse myself and talk to Ted Rousseau about this unexpected turn of events. We agree that the $950,000 evaluation offer must be much too low. I immediately telephone New York to find out whether or not the contract has been signed by the Swiss or by us. It has not. I give instructions not to sign any contract until I can visit another house in London and attempt to achieve a higher guarantee and a more favorable percentage above and beyond the guarantee.

Shortly thereafter, we found ourselves in the situation of being in the middle between a partnership of two Swiss auction houses, on the one hand, and Sotheby's, on the other, eager to handle our coins. In the end, instead of a $950,000 guarantee plus a percentage, we received from Sotheby's a guarantee and cash advance of $1,520,000 against the future proceeds of the sale and a percentage above and beyond that. Thus, an inconclusive negotiation for a Greek vase led us to a far more profitable arrangement for the sale of our coins.

I did not resume contact with Robert Hecht for a number of weeks, even though I knew he was actively seeking a purchaser. Strong rumor had it that one private collector was willing to pay up to $800,000 for the vase. Another, less certain, hinted that a European museum was willing to go to $600,000 for the treasure.

Shortly after we had received the $1,520,000 check as an advance on the coins, I called Hecht before he could hear the news and offered $850,000 for the vase. We finally settled for a flat million. Hecht said that although that price was the absolute bottom requested by Sarrafian, he would persuade him to agree.

On August 31 Hecht brought the vase to New York. On September 12, at a special meeting in my office, the vase, with the cracks this time lightly restored at our request by Bürki, was presented to the Acquisitions Committee. I had prepared a written statement in advance, as had von Bothmer. In our oral presentations we quoted from these statements:

> To be offered an object of superior quality is not uncommon at The Metropolitan. The Velázquez, *Aristotle* by Rembrandt, Robert Campin's Merode Altarpiece, the Bury St. Edmunds cross are each pungent examples. But to be offered the kind of quality that raises the stature of not merely one department of the Museum, but literally the entire Museum is exceedingly rare. This afternoon I have the extraordinary opportunity to present to you the rarest of the rare. The object is this monumental calyx krater depicting the death of Sarpedon of Lycia, a tale from Homer's *Iliad*. This surpassing work of art, embodying all that makes Greek art truly universal, was made by the potter Euxitheos and signed by the painter Euphronios, a man generally regarded as one of the greatest of all vase painters. It was made around 510 B.C. This object is, in my opinion, the finest pot by the finest painter of pots. Twenty-seven other whole or fragmentary vases signed by this man or reasonably attributed to him are known to exist.
>
> Since my association with this institution started in 1959, I have not encountered a finer work of art.
>
> As I will explain after Dietrich's historical expertise, we have funds available for its purchase. The price? Well, first Dietrich.

This was Dietrich's written statement:

> Greek art has been collected in America by private individuals and by museums for over a hundred years and is fairly represented across the country. It is not, however, nearly so abundant on this continent as it is in Europe. The great collections in London, Paris, Munich, Berlin, and Leningrad were begun fifty or a hundred years earlier, and in spite of great efforts and vast expenditures, American collections still lag behind.

An extraordinary opportunity to correct our position has recently come our way through the offer of purchase which is before you. Though the sheer beauty and monumentality of the object is such as to impress even the most casual observer, its special place in Greek art (as well as its very special price) demand something of an explanation.

Greek art is generally divided into three phases, the archaic, the classic, and the Hellenistic. Within the last fifty years, the archaic has become recognized as the most important of these phases, and the last quarter of the sixth century has evoked the greatest interest. For it is during those mere twenty years that Greek art advanced more energetically and more quickly than at any time before or after. In Greek art the emphasis is at all times on the human form, and it is in the late archaic period that human anatomy is for the first time not only fully understood, but competently translated into artistic terms. This holds true for both sculpture in the round and in reliefs, as well as for two-dimensional representations. For the latter we have come to rely almost exclusively on the paintings on vases. In this field we are fortunate that great artists are known and recognized, and when we speak of style, it is not in abstract generalizations, but is identified with the works of individual artists, hence something intimate and personal. By a curious coincidence most of the vase-painters of the last quarter of the sixth century are known to us by their real names, indeed the majority of all known signatures on vases occur in this very period. The artists that are credited with the most important innovations form what is called the Pioneer Group. In this group of about a dozen artists Euphronios, Phintias, and Euthymides are the leaders; of this trio, Euphronios is considered the best.

The vase now offered to the Museum is signed by Euphronios as painter, but even without the signature there would have been no hesitation in attributing the paintings to him. Any vase by Euphronios is almost automatically called a masterpiece: the newcomer surpasses all the others, and this claim can be substantiated. Paintings on vases cannot and should not be detached from the ceramic form on which they appear, and a good painter is governed and guided in the choice of his subjects, in his composition, and in the drawing of his figures by the proportions of the vase, its size, and its curvature. This vase is a calyx-krater, a relatively new shape, introduced into the repertory of Attic pottery not more than fifteen years before. As a piece of potting it is, even without the paintings, quite impressive, and we are not surprised that the potter, in this case Euxitheos, signed it. On a calyx-krater the painted scenes are habitually shown on the almost straight walls that are bordered above by a rim and a lip, and below by the convex cul that issues from a massive foot. The two lateral lifting handles are attached to the cul and curve upward, thus projecting into the picture zone. The handles have to be taken into account when the vase is painted, and they divide the zone into an obverse and a reverse. This distinction is by no means artificial or accidental, but quite deliberate. At this period, and especially in works by this painter, the division is further underlined by a change in the patterns: the more formal double chain of palmettes and lotuses gives way on the reverse to a less restrained row of six big palmettes lying on their sides. The rim, which is not interrupted, is decorated with 38 upright palmettes, of which every other one has two tendrils above. Since the upper circumference is bigger than the lower one, the picture fields are thus trapezoidal in projection, and this the painter has taken into account. He has wisely refrained from having all his figures bolt-upright, for, in that case, their heads would be farther apart than their feet. He has also observed that the human eye cannot take in an entire scene if it were painted right to the edges, that are blurred by the curvature. He has therefore made his panels narrower and placed elaborate palmette configurations in the space above the handles. The oraments thus serve as lateral frames without doing violence to the ceramic form that would not tolerate anything harsh. The painter has given much thought to the composition of the scene. Next to the palmette frames he has put two secondary figures that flank the principal scene and serve as transitions from the rather light palmettes to the center. The figures have been given conventional Trojan names, Laodamas and Hippolytos. As both wear Corinthian helmets pushed up on the head, they are smaller in scale than the upright figure of Hermes who appears in the center of the background, his head slightly to the left of the central meridian. Between the onlookers and Hermes are shown Hypnos (Sleep) and Thanatos (Death), both bending over to lift the body of the Lycian prince Sarpedon. Sleep and Death, though twin brothers, are no mirror images of one another, but differ in volume and contour, as well as in many particulars of wings, armor, hair, and expression. They are larger in scale than Hermes, that is to say they are thought to be nearer the spectator, in the second plane. The front plane is occupied almost for its entire length by the body of Sarpedon. Since he was stripped of his cuirass and helmet by Patroklos, his nudity is, of course, in keeping with Homeric tradition. At the same time, however, and this must be stressed, it is the drawing of the nude that has made Euphronios so famous. Here the limp body of Sarpedon is turned toward the spectator through the lifting action of Sleep and Death and contrasts with the other fully dressed figures. The contours of his body are drawn in unerring long relief-lines, and it must be remembered that in painting a vase, corrections or erasures are virtually impossible. If in the previous generation the principles of the red-figured technique were established, the Pioneer Group introduces refinements that become an integral part of it. Most important of the innovations is the use of diluted glaze and glaze washes, which serve both for entire areas and for linear details. Thus we have a light brown that covers the chitons of Sleep and Hermes as well as the wing-bows of Sleep and Death, the platelets of the armor of Death, and the wing-bows on the hat and boots of Hermes. A similar wash is also employed for the forehead hair of Hermes and the hair of Death and Sarpedon, rendered even more striking, since the individual locks are painted over the wash in a somewhat darker brown. A light wash is also used for parts of the abdominal musculature of Sarpedon, and lines drawn in diluted glaze appear throughout for sinews, tendons, and muscles. Other touches of color are the various instances of added red, most prominent in the three wounds on the body of Sarpedon. The blood does not drip down vertically, but gushes forth. The diagonal direction of the blood is a subtle indication of the movement from left to right. The same movement is given by Hermes and by the position of Sarpedon's head on the right. In most of Greek art any action is shown as moving from left to right, and this is the direction in which pictures should be read. Yet the movement is not violent and does not take away from the more static and severely symmetrical contour of the vase.

The arming scene on the reverse, though deliberately less ambitious, is executed with the same attention to compositional problems. Of the five figures, three face right and two face left. The latter are similar but not identical, and repetition is also avoided by varying the angle at which the three spears are being held. The two warriors facing left are ready and impatient; the warrior between them is almost ready. The one on the left lacks only his shield and helmet, while the second from the left is just beginning to arm. Four of the warriors are youths; the last is bearded. All of them are given names taken from the register of Greek or Trojan heroes, whose exploits are not further known from literature. An allusion to a contemporary figure is perhaps presented by the shield device of the third warrior: it is a crab playing the flutes with its claws. The same device occurs on two contemporary vases and cannot be just a playful way of showing a crab. There was, later in the fifth century, a tragedian who bore the name Karkinos, which in Greek means crab, and this Karkinos had a grandson, also a tragedian, with the same name. Could it be that the grandfather of the first Karkinos, or crab, was a famous flute-player who is here commemorated by this punning device?

That much for the artistic analysis of the paintings. Something, however, remains to be said about Sarpedon. He was the son of Zeus, a prince of Lycia, and hence a natural ally of the Trojans. When in the battle for the ships the Trojans seemed to be winning, Patroklos prevailed on his friend Achilles to allow him to join the battle. In the ensuing fight, Patroklos killed Sarpedon, who in the words of Homer, went down like the oak, or the poplar or the tall pine that high in the mountains is cut down by the axe of the woodsman. A fierce fight developed over his body, but Patroklos succeeded in removing his armor. Only then did Zeus, Sarpedon's father, command Apollo to remove the body from the battlefield and to wash it in a river. After this, Sarpedon was to be carried by the twin brothers Sleep and Death to his home in Lycia to receive there the customary burial.

Sarpedon does not often appear in Greek art. On Corinthian vases we see him once as a mere companion of Hector, and later his body is shown in a battle scene that features Patroklos. On the Siphnian treasury at Delphi, securely dated between 530 and 525 B.C. the fight over Sarpedon's body appears. Ten years later, on an unpublished cup signed by Euphronios, he is carried away by Sleep and Death who are shown as ordinary warriors, without wings. The actual lifting of the body occurs for the first time on this krater, and the moment depicted is repeated on three Attic vases that are somewhat later. A fourth representation, on a calyx-krater in Agrigento, shows a shrouded body removed from the battlefield by two warriors, who may, on the analogy of the inscribed unpublished Euphronios cup be Sleep and Death, even though they lack the wings. On two South Italian vases, of which one is in New York, Sarpedon is carried aloft on his return to Lycia. Both pictures are doubtless painted under the influence of Attic tragedies, especially the one by Aeschylos. The pictures by Euphronios, in contrast, are inspired by Homer, save that Apollo has been replaced by Hermes, whose special function as conductor of the souls had already entered popular religion. In any event, the dead Sarpedon is the first in a long iconographical line that includes Memnon being carried by his mother Eos, and the dead Meleager carried home from battle. It is at the end of this iconographical tradition that we see finally, in the Renaissance, those poignant pictures of the deposition of Christ and the Pietá.

The poignancy, of course, is already present in this picture of Sarpedon. Toward the end of the sixth century, even the Homeric battle scenes have become transformed. Where in the previous generations the emphasis had still been on triumph and victory, the painters and their public now prefer those episodes of the Trojan epics that are filled with an inner tragedy. In this picture of Sarpedon there is not a trace of the triumph of Patroklos or the temporary victory of the Greeks. All affection and sympathy lies with the prince of Lycia and his mourning father. War is not glorified, but rather its impartial cruelty is brought home. The picture also demonstrates most forcefully the difference between poetry and art, and the different approach to mythology in ancient and in modern art. No ancient painting or sculpture is ever an illustration of literature, like Botticelli's drawings of the *Divine Comedy* or Flaxman's *Designs,* and we are constantly surprised how many of the better-known Greek myths are either not shown at all in ancient art, or only very rarely. The greater our admiration for an artist who with only three or four lines in Homer could create so memorable a picture as this Sarpedon.

Including this krater and the unpublished cup, there are now twenty-seven vases signed by or attributed to Euphronios. His talent has always been recognized and, in the words of François Villard, he is the most brilliant representative of the great red-figure painters. When I first saw photographs of this vase three months ago, I realized that I had never seen a finer Greek vase. This first impression was fully borne out in seeing the object itself, and is still the same today. We have, in short, the finest vase-painting by one of the best, if not the best of all vase-painters, and it is my firm belief that this vase, if acquired by the Museum, would bring us the kind of recognition that is our constant aim to achieve. But since masterpieces speak in their own very strong language, I shall stop now and invite you instead to look at and be captivated by the object itself.

After the viewing, I introduced the question of the price:

The price of this fine work of art is very, very high. It is $1,000,000. I want to point out that the price started off at an even higher level; namely, $1,500,000. Ted Rousseau, Dietrich von Bothmer, and I have been bargaining with the dealer, the middleman in the possible sale, Robert Hecht by name, since the beginning of the summer. We have reached the present figure, which I firmly believe is one that cannot be lowered. I also believe that Hecht will be able to sell this object to a number of museums and perhaps also several private collectors.

We have the money in hand to pay for the Euphronios pot, if the Committee chooses to vote on behalf of its acquisition. As you will recall at the Board meeting earlier today, the President reported that, regarding the sale of Greek and Roman coins, the Museum has received an advance from Sotheby in the amount of $1,520,000. Since the majority of the coin funds, which we hope will increase as the results of the sale become final, can legitimately be assigned to the Greek and Roman Department, and since it can also legitimately be said that the bulk of these funds should be used for acquisition purposes since they accrue from the sale of works of art, in this case numismatic material, it is logical and correct, I believe, to use two-thirds of the amount we have in hand to gain this extraordinary work of art.

To put the price into the correct perspective, may I point out that comparable prices have been paid for decorative arts at the Museum. The Cloisters' *Apocalypse* cost $750,000. The Bury St. Edmunds cross went for over $600,000 in 1963. The so-called East Greek treasure came to $1,070,000. This work of art, in my opinion, falls into these categories with one significant difference; that is, that its quality is equal to, or superior to, the others named.

Now, I would like to address myself to the question of provenance and our legal right to purchase the piece under existing laws and in keeping with the spirit of the UNESCO Draft Convention dealing with the illegal or illicit movement of works of art, which, incidentally, is not yet operative.

The following steps have been taken:

1. The vendor has been identified. He is Robert Hecht.

2. The owner is identified. He is the dealer Dikran A. Sarrafian of Beirut, Lebanon, a well-known art dealer.

3. Sarrafian has stated to Hecht and has submitted in writing the fact that the Euphronios Sarpedon has been in his family's collection at least since World War I.

4. A further letter outlining this statement in greater detail will be forthcoming in the near future.

5. We have, in hand, a bill from Hecht which also refers to the fact that this pot has been in the Sarrafian collection since World War I.

6. The payment, if the Committee votes in favor, will be made to Mr. Hecht in Zurich.

7. The vase cleared U.S. Customs openly and legally with all participants identified by name.

To conclude this brief presentation, I would simply say that this is a great moment in the history of collecting at the Metropolitan Museum. I urge you to act affirmatively.

The members present at the meeting, Messrs. Dillon, Frelinghuysen, Gilpatric, Houghton, Payson, Meyer, and Schiff, voted unanimously and with great enthusiasm for the acquisition of the object. Mrs. Astor, not present, had seen the vase beforehand and cast an aye vote.

In due time, the krater was placed on special exhibition in a gallery within the Greek and Roman Department. An excellent article on the object by James Mellow was published in the *New York Times Magazine* of November 12, accompanied by a color illustration on the magazine's cover. We were all delighted with the vase's debut in print, but three months later everything came apart on the front page of the *Times,* where the krater received more lineage than the Christmas bombings of Cambodia and Hanoi. There followed stories on national television and in papers across the United States and throughout the world, and we almost wished we had never heard of Euphronios, Euxitheos, or Sarpedon. The

Metropolitan was accused of having purchased a vase which had been illegally excavated near the Etrusan town and necropolis of Cerveteri in late November or early December of 1971 and smuggled out of Italy shortly thereafter. Charge grew upon charge, accusations of a different nature appeared each successive day: The Metropolitan had been directly involved; Sarrafian did not exist; the vase was a clever forgery; one of the "night diggers," a man named Armando Cenere, had identified the piece by the figure of Sarpedon and had drawn the precise sherd in the presence of a *New York Times* reporter; two pieces from the rim of the Metropolitan krater had been sent to the Italian authorities, which found that they constituted "almost certain proof" that the vase had recently been in Italy. There were many other, lesser, allegations.

Anything we said during the controversy seemed not to carry any weight. A year later, in March 1974, we issued a "white paper" in the form of a written report to the Members of the Museum Corporation. This set forth all the facts as known to us, and concluded:

> As to its provenance—always the larger question in the swirl of rumor, press speculation, false clues, and freakish coincidence which attended the controversy—every fact that has emerged over the months has served to erode and discredit specific allegations that the krater came from an illicit excavation conducted in November–December, 1971, at Cerveteri, near Rome, and was subsequently removed from Italy to Switzerland.
>
> Thus we believe now, as we believed from the start of the rather weird series of events which called the acquisition into question, that the vase—then in fragments in Switzerland—was the long-time property of Mr. Dikran Sarrafian, a well-known Middle Eastern collector and dealer, who engaged Mr. Robert Hecht, Jr., of Rome, to act as his agent in the sale of the krater to the Metropolitan.

In James Mellow's story in the *Times Magazine* the issue of provenance had not been taken up except for our statement that the vase had been in the collection of a private individual since World War I. That was a mistake. We should have revealed that it belonged to a dealer-collector in Beirut whose father had acquired it around 1918–19, and that it had been sold by him to us through the dealer Robert Hecht. We did not do this for two reasons. These seemed important then, they do not today. For reasons of his own, which may have related to local tax regulations, or perhaps because in the Middle East it is not always wise to proclaim that you are wealthy, Sarrafian preferred that his name be left out of the affair. Traditionally, the Museum has kept names of vendors confidential. Added to that, it was assumed that Sarrafian might have had other important objects that would be of interest to the Museum, and we didn't want to advertise his name lest others approach him. If we had revealed his name at the outset, the controversial stories on provenance might never have appeared. One never knows.

In order to discover the provenance, the *New York Times* assigned its art critic and an investigative reporter with experience with the Mafia, Nicholas Gage, to come up with the facts.

As reported to me from inside sources on the *Times*, John Canaday made contact with several dealers and collectors in Europe and learned that a highly important discovery of a vase had been made by illicit diggers in Italy in late 1971. One dealer reportedly mentioned the name Robert Hecht. From this I have been told that the assumption was immediately made that this discovery and the Metropolitan's calyx krater were one and the same. A story was published to that effect; the Italian authorities moved to issue arrest warrants against four individuals who allegedly were involved in the illegal excavation. When Sarrafian's name was revealed by us, Nicholas Gage went to Beirut and conducted an interview with the elderly dealer. Sarrafian apparently attempted to pass himself off as a humble coin dealer of no account. This apparently aroused Gage's suspicion that he was acting merely as an intermediary. When Gage returned to Italy, by some manner of means, presumably through the authorities, he met the star government witness, Armando Cenere. Cenere stated that he had been a lookout for the group of grave diggers and had seen "a piece of the vase about the size of a man's palm with a figure of a man lying on his side with blood pouring out of a wound"; one handle; the rim of the vase, which was in many small pieces; and the cul, or circular base of the vase. Cenere drew upon a photograph of the krater that Gage had with him the precise shape of the fragment he had seen depicting Sarpedon. We were puzzled about these statements at the time because they did not tally with certain significant points about our vase. For one thing, the rim was not in many pieces but in five large pieces.

Then the Italian authorities announced that they had been sent two pieces anonymously from an individual who stated that the pieces belonged to the Metropolitan's vase, most certainly to the rim. That also puzzled us, for not the minutest piece was missing from the rim of the vase.

Shortly thereafter the Italian authorities said that they had received fifteen or so fragments of a Euphronios calyx krater from another anonymous source—pieces that were said by the sender to have been found with our vase. The Italian authorities issued a statement saying that these fifteen pieces had been sent in deliberately to confuse the investigation. Another puzzle.

Over a period of time, the situation began to clarify. Armando Cenere appeared on Italian television to recant what he had earlier stated. This time he said he could not recall a figure such as Sarpedon, and that he had seen instead parts of the rim, one handle, and the base of a vase.

An Italian expert in the field of Greek vase painting was appointed by the Italian court to examine the two fragments that had been sent in. He worked from the photographs of the krater we supplied, which showed all the breaks, cracks, and missing slivers. His report, in December 1973, stated that the two pieces did not appear to fit the vase. "Obviously," he added, "a direct examination would lead to an absolute certainty." On a number of occasions the Metropolitan officially invited the Italian authorities to send experts here to examine the vase. To date, they have not acted on this invitation.

From another phase of the investigation we received an affidavit from a photographer in Basel, Switzerland, stating that he had taken photographs of the fragments in August 1971. This, of course, would have been impossible if our vase had really been the object excavated in November–December 1971.

In the fall of 1973 we were in touch with Mr. Sarrafian in Beirut and received a second affidavit from him attesting to the fact that he had possessed the vase, in fragments, since the death of his father in 1926. Another affidavit from a Beirut lawyer, a former head of the Bar Association there, related that Sarrafian had consulted him regarding the vase and its export from Lebanon in the mid-1960s. Each of these later affidavits was shown to us in the presence of an American consular official in Beirut.

In July 1973 we received, out of the blue, a letter from a woman in Chicago who had read the stories about the vase and Sarrafian. She enclosed a copy of a letter she had written to Sarrafian, which said in part: "I recall your showing me, when my husband and I were in your apartment in 1964, a large box containing as you stated then, the shards of a Euphronios krater, which, as you said, your father purchased in 1920." We were pleased.

Finally we were able to see the drawing Cenere had made on the photograph of the fragment he claimed to have had in his hands in November–December 1971. The size, shape, and outline of the actual fragment showing Sarpedon is wholly different from the drawing by Cenere.

We also learned that some of the fifteen fragments sent anonymously to the Italian police, and by them set aside, were by Euphronios and were indeed part of a calyx krater. It seems likely that they are pieces missing from a krater depicting Hercules Struggling with the Nemean Lion. This krater was discovered by the Marchese Campana, near Cerveteri in 1859. The krater has been in the Louvre since 1862. The evidence suggests that what was discovered in late 1971 were pieces belonging to the Louvre krater. All the more so since the Louvre krater lacks pieces of the rim, which is indeed in many small fragments, has only one handle, and lacks its base.

In order to get those facts out, we have urged the Italian court to take judicial notice of the fifteen fragments, which were deposited by police authorities in the Villa Giulia in Rome. On February 28, 1975, the judge in Civitavecchia appointed a new panel of experts to replace the previous experts whose report had been declared null and void due to a legal technicality. The judge acknowledged that there are other fragments in addition to the ones examined previously and specifically instructed the new panel to consider in their report "all fragments seized by the police authorities." The judge also indicated he would recommend comparison of the fragments with the vase in New York if the experts so recommend in their report.

Certain immensely treasurable works of art, and sometimes entire collections, do not pass through the curatorial rehearsal process, nor are they studied by the Acquisitions Committee. These are major bequests or donations that are reviewed by the Executive Committee and the full Board and then accepted or not as the case may be. Typical of this category in recent years are the Temple of Dendur, the Robert Lehman Collection, the Nelson A. Rockefeller Collection, the Irwin Untermyer Collection, and the Lesley and Emma Sheafer Collection. It has been said truly that a curator collects individual works of art or, sometimes, groups of objects, while the Director and the President collect monuments and whole collections. The Temple of Dendur and the Lehman Collection are prime examples of this facet of the collecting mission.

The Museum has always collected architecture in a zestful manner. Our philosophy here was in great part promulgated by the genius in this field, James Rorimer, who with the then Curator of Western European Arts, Joseph Breck, worked intimately with one of the most generous and enlightened donors the Metropolitan has ever known, John D. Rockefeller, Jr., to establish The Cloisters. Large pieces of architecture, both exterior and interior are, however, not restricted to The Cloisters. Every time we have an opportunity to collect a period room or a great stairway, an entire patio, such as the one from Vélez Blanco given by George Blumenthal, a set of boiseries, a seventeenth century Islamic room from Damascus, an entire house by Frank Lloyd Wright, or a temple from ancient Egypt, we move with delight and alacrity.

Architecture explains the paintings hanging in galleries, the majolica amassed in vitrines, or the medieval sculptures on their pedestals. It also provides that invaluable change or relief of environment in a vast museum that would, without architecture and period rooms, consist of too dry and monotonous a series of exhibition galleries. The Temple of Dendur provides not only a massive building but an entire environment of its own and elucidates by its great and ancient presence much of the flavor of the Egyptian heritage.

I first heard of this temple when I was Administrator of Parks, Recreation and Cultural Affairs of the City of New York in the fall of 1966. Two members of the Museum's transitional team, Theodore Rousseau and Joseph Noble, then Chief of Operations, and the Curator of the Egyptian Department, Henry G. Fischer, consulted me, the legal landlord of the Museum, for help in obtaining the temple. Although late in date—it was of the time of the emperor Augustus, and thus far beyond the best period of Egyptian art—it formed part of an unchanging canon. Consisting of a large gateway and the temple proper, it was indeed an impressive late Nubian structure, almost totally covered with reliefs, raised inside the temple, sunken on the outside surfaces. I was fascinated. Imagine, an entire temple from the banks of the Nile! Carefully dismantled and moved from its original location because of construction in connection with the Aswan High Dam, the temple at present was a collection of 642 marked stone blocks awaiting shipment to the United States. For, in a most gracious gesture of thanks to our government for our participation in the moving of Abu Simbel, the temple had been presented to our nation.

In one of those rare moments of New York political history (times were not as stringent then), I was able to obtain the full support of the City

FIGURE 5. The Temple of Dendur in situ on the Nile

Planning Commission, the City Council Finance Committee, and the Board of Estimate, including the mayor, for a capital allotment of $1,400,000 toward shipping the stones from Egypt.

The Museum, meanwhile, made an application to the then President, Lyndon Johnson, to be awarded the temple. All seemed to go smoothly for a while until it appeared that President Johnson was going to award the temple arbitrarily to another city. Happily, this turned out to be a false rumor. However, a commission of public officials and Egyptologists was empowered to conduct hearings on the matter of placement.

At that point, December 1966, I had been appointed Director of the Museum and moved rapidly on our submission.

Our arguments were sound: we had an excellent financial commitment from the city, we housed the greatest collection of Egyptian antiquities in the United States, our study programs were extensive in the Egyptian field, particularly as they were related to those of our neighbor and colleague institution, the Institute of Fine Arts of New York University. I learned then that the most important factor was probably going to be how the dry, ancient sandstone blocks would best be preserved in the American climate. What I needed, obviously, was an instant comprehensive architectural plan for "our temple."

With the help of Arthur Rosenblatt, my chief deputy for architecture and engineering at Parks, I placed the temple over an unattractive parking lot at the north end of the Museum, adjacent to the Egyptian galleries. I "designed" the protective structure, essentially an enormous glass vitrine, some 200 by 100 by 50 feet. Rosenblatt, who soon became the Metropolitan's Vice Director for Architecture and Planning, observed that my conception looked like the product of a first-year architecture student who would soon flunk out. He made some changes to ensure that the building would stand up and suggested that we get the finest architectural renderer in the business to submit two large renderings of the "building," one showing it during the day; the other at night.

The renderings were made, our detailed proposal was drafted, and the package was sent to the President's Special Commission. At the same time, I solicited letters of support from Governor Rockefeller, Mayor Lindsay, and Senator Javits. They immediately sent communications to the Special Commission. After this promising start, it all seemed to fall apart. The Smithsonian Institution, I heard, was driving hard to land the prize, despite disclaimers from high officials of that institution. I asked

Senator Robert Kennedy for his strong support since he had given us a favorable letter about the project a year earlier. He was evasive about a new, stronger letter and suggested that I get in touch with one of his aides, Richard Goodwin. This I did. Goodwin told me the temple deserved to be in Washington, somewhere on Constitution Avenue, since President Kennedy had in fact been instrumental in obtaining Egypt's gift in the first place. I was flabbergasted and could only point to the Senator's earlier letter. It ought to be in Washington was the gist of Goodwin's answer. I once again reached Senator Kennedy and expressed my puzzlement. He told me to telephone his sister-in-law, Jacqueline Kennedy, who had views on the matter. I was even more puzzled when Mrs. Kennedy told me over the telephone that it was her wish that the temple be placed in Washington.

She expressed some inaccurate views about President Johnson's methods of making the decision of where to send the temple. I put the Metropolitan's case strongly, outlining the opportunities for scholarship if the temple came to us and pointing out the current work of President Johnson's Special Commission. It seemed to me that Mrs. Kennedy was unimpressed, but she called me later on to say that she agreed after all about the role of the Commission. She added that she would speak with her brother-in-law concerning his support.

I have no idea whether her change of opinion helped us, but I do know that Senator Kennedy did not write a second letter on our behalf.

In April 1967, we received this letter from President Johnson:

It gives me great pleasure to inform you that the Egyptian temple of Dendur is being awarded to the Metropolitan Museum of Art for its permanent location. As you know, my decision is based on the recommendation of a specially appointed committee, which reviewed many attractive offers from cities throughout the nation to display the temple.

I have asked our Embassy in Cairo to inform the Government of the United Arab Republic of my decision. I have assured them that the Metropolitan Museum will assume the full cost of removing the temple to this country and of ensuring its permanent safety.

I am deeply appreciative of the United Arab Republic's generous gift and I am convinced that the Metropolitan's plans for the temple will protect it and make it available to millions of Americans in a setting appropriate to its character.

FIGURE 6. Temple and gateway from Dendur. Egypt, early Roman period (late 1st century B.C.). Aeolian sandstone. Gift of the Government and People of the Arab Republic of Egypt to the Government and People of the United States, awarded to the Museum by a presidential commission, 68.154. Projected installation in a scale model by Kevin Roche, John Dinkeloo and Associates, architects

Today the reerection of the temple is completed. The great glass house for it, designed by the Museum's architectural firm, Kevin Roche, John Dinkeloo and Associates, is planned for completion in 1977. The temple, with its gateway and a symbolic River Nile in front of it will, no doubt, be one of the most spectacular exhibitions of ancient architecture in this country.

For many years Robert Lehman, a Trustee of the Metropolitan since 1941, had maintained an incomparable collection of art that he and his father, Phillip, had gathered together: trecento and quattrocento Italian masters, from pre-Giotto through Giovanni de Paolo, Botticelli, and Tiepolo, old-master Dutch and Flemish works, a fine series of French paintings ranging from Jean Fouquet, the Master of Moulins, and Ingres to the Impressionist and post-Impressionist masters. The collection was also rich in majolica and porcelain, enamels, textiles, tapestries, and furniture. And to cap it all off, the Lehman collection of drawings was one most distinguished private holdings anywhere.

In 1961, upon the completion of work that transformed the Lehman home at 14 West Fifty-fourth Street into a private museum, and under somewhat bitter circumstances which no one has ever been able to assess accurately, Robert Lehman removed all of his and his father's treasures from the Metropolitan and installed them for his own viewing and that of small, carefully selected tour-groups and individual scholars.

Arthur Houghton, Jr., the Museum's President when I was about to become Director, felt that one of our first tasks would be to secure the majestic Lehman Collection for the Museum. We both felt that it would be a severe, perhaps irreparable blow to the prestige of the Museum if this collection, in the possession of one of our principal Trustees, went to another city.

After discussions with Ted Rousseau, who, in the words of Lehman himself, "had been the only slim thread that held my interest in the Metropolitan," and with Louis Goldenberg of Wildenstein and Company, a long-time friend of Lehman's, I telephoned Lehman the very day I was designated Director, December 22, 1966, and requested an appointment. He was brusque. He obviously didn't want to see me, but his sense of politeness, which was legendary, forced him to say that he would—for fifteen minutes. I assured him I only needed ten minutes for the courtesy call.

One William Street, home of the investment banking firm of Lehman Brothers, projects an awesome aura of quietude and discretion. I was shown into a minuscule office just at the entrance of the partners' floor, precisely at three in the afternoon. It occurred to me at the time that this was the "quick visitor" office. I later learned that this was the private office of the Chairman of the Board of Lehman Brothers. Robert Lehman, entering a minute later, looked at me quickly. He appeared embarrassed. I remembered from my curatorial days at the Museum that Robert Lehman was a diffident man, but his attitude puzzled me. Within ten minutes I told him what I hoped to accomplish at the Museum in a number of areas, including management, working conditions, architectural planning, and collecting of art. I then made my move to leave. He motioned me to stay. Some three and a half hours later we were still talking. The conversation was animated with great, warm pleasure as we discussed the problem areas of the Metropolitan and fine points of collecting and connoisseurship. Finally, it was time to leave. With easy courtesy, Robert Lehman helped me on with my coat.

Delighted with the way the man had opened up and obviously enjoyed our discussion, I decided to take a chance. Why, I asked him, had he seemed to be so uncomfortable at the beginning of our meeting? Because he had been opposed to my becoming Director of the Museum, he said. Somehow he had failed to realize, until this afternoon, that I had worked in the Museum. Even less explicably, he had assumed that I was a politician from the Lindsay Administration who had no experience whatsoever with art. As he apologized for his misconceptions he said with a look of pure pleasure, "But it doesn't really matter, you see. Everybody will think you have won over, on the first meeting, a sour old type. They will think it's a triumph. You know, it is going to be marvelous being a Trustee of the Metropolitan once again."

Lehman and I became close friends. Every week I would meet him at his Park Avenue apartment and we would talk about art, management, finance, labor, politics, and of course, collecting. We would compare notes on our separate selections of the "three best" in every great museum of the world, and we would come pretty close to agreeing. His knowledge was considerable, his eye was practically a professional's.

Together, we visited exhibitions of many kinds. Routinely we each marked up a catalogue to indicate our choices of the best. Almost always we picked the same pieces. Together we scoured the art market. One pair of late fifteenth-century paintings stood out. They had been at Wildenstein's for some years: two exquisite panels, each the size of a playing card, painted superbly by the Venetian painter and miniaturist Jacometto da Venezia. On the principal side appeared two excellent portraits, one of a young man, probably Alvise Contarini, the other of a young woman of serene beauty, presumably his love, despite her dress, a nun's habit—which, I might add, showed a startling décolletage. On the reverse of Contarini's portrait was a beautiful little recumbent doe with a golden collar and a chain around her delicate neck, fastened to a roundel bearing an inscription in Greek: AIE ('Forever''). On the back of the woman's portrait, in golden monochrome, was a figure sitting in a landscape, perhaps a scene from Homer.

Bobby Lehman and I were enamored of these panels but not of the price: $500,000 for the two. He told me that if I could manage to reduce the price, he would support their acquisition by the Museum.

One day, several months after my initial visit to Lehman Brothers, when we were discussing private collections in general, I asked Bobby what he was going to do with his. With a smile, he told me that it would never come to the Metropolitan. He had made that decision long ago, and it was irrevocable. First, he said, the Board had not made him President of the Museum, even for a single day. Then, complaining further about the elitist attitude of the Board, he said that he had never been able to suggest anyone to be a member of it. Finally, when he had once considered giving his collection to the Museum, the Board had rejected his wish to keep the collection together. He had not wanted a separate area in the Museum because of personal vanity, he told me; he had wanted this because he felt that the Museum needed certain areas, adjacent to but somewhat separate from the main galleries, in order to provide a change of thought from the relative sameness of the Museum's chronological arrangements. Now, he invoked the name of Bernard Berenson. Years before, Berenson had advised Bobby to keep the collection together always and to keep it unconnected with any large institution. And since Bobby had just done over the family mansion, he had decided the best thing would be to keep the collection in the private house on Fifty-fourth Street forever. He offered to explain to the other Trustees that my being Director of the Metropolitan had nothing to do with his decision, which had been arrived at, in fact, before my directorship.

Thanking Bobby for his personal courtesy to me, I asked him what his course of action would be if I could overcome all of his objections. He cautioned me that it would take several miracles to make him change his mind, even though he admitted that he wished the decision really could be changed.

It took no longer than a month for us to present Lehman with our proposal. First, President Houghton agreed without hesitation to move, on a suggestion of Charles Wrightsman, to create for Lehman the title of Chairman of the Board of Trustees. He approved, in effect, the creation of a position above his own. Leadership of that caliber is rare but not with Arthur Houghton.

Then it was firmly established that the Metropolitan would keep the Lehman Collection together in its own area of the building. Finally, I pointed out to Lehman that his private home/museum simply could not function as a public institution. Additional space for the full collection was needed, there had to be access for the public, and certain technical facilities would have to be introduced to keep the great collection in good order. Furthermore, the neighborhood around the family mansion might change for the worse. Assuredly, the Museum was the only safe place for the long pull.

Bobby was pleasantly shocked by the Museum's leap to action. He would think it over, he said.

When the decision came, it was transmitted to me in such an odd manner that I wasn't sure exactly what Bobby had really said. After some effort I had persuaded Wildenstein to reduce its price on the two beautiful Jacomettos to a point where I felt able to offer them to the Acquisitions Committee. When I phoned Bobby to tell him of the price break and remind him of his promise of support, he took me aback by saying that he himself had just bought the panels—at the price I had negotiated. He went on to say that, if I thought it was acceptable, he would offer the panels to the Museum as a gift, something he had rarely done. But there would be a condition. The two gemlike panels would have to go into the building that would house his entire collection when it came to the Museum. He spoke of these matters offhandedly, inconclusively. Since my call had been put through to him as he was undergoing examinations in a hospital, it hardly seemed the moment to press for clarification.

Not long afterward, Bobby gave me the go-ahead for the preparation of an architectural master plan for the Museum and for the structure that would contain his collection. I mentioned that I would have to ask the Finance Committee for the money. He asked me not to submit the request, since, for a time, he wished to keep his changed decision a secret. He handed me his personal check for $100,000 and told me to put it in my bank account so that I could pay the architect directly. After the awkwardness of such an arrangement was explained to him, he allowed the money to be presented to the Museum as a gift from an anonymous donor who was interested in the architectural future of the place. And this is the way the entire comprehensive plan of the Metropolitan was begun. The plan, I might point out, will complete the building of the 105-year-old institution.

Lehman was keenly interested in the planning of the edifice for his collection. He came to the Museum several times a week to walk through the galleries and study the existing plan of the building and the preliminary ideas of the architect, Kevin Roche. Presently he concluded that the best way to house the collection would be to make an exact reproduction of his private house, façade and all, somewhere on the Museum grounds. I told him I thought it would look crazy but Kevin Roche, quite sensibly, said he would develop a plan. He made a large model of the Museum and a movable model of the house. We shifted this from one location to another to show Lehman all the possibilities. With the choice narrowed down to the south parking lot, Roche prepared a large, finished model of the ensemble. But he had developed at the same time a gem of a structure of octagonal form with a spacious central court, two levels of surrounding galleries, and reconstructions of seven rooms from the Fifty-fourth Street house. Both models were set up in a presentation room, the former in the prime position.

It was clear that Lehman knew instantly, when he saw the model, that to try to adapt a piece of street architecture to the vastness of the Metropolitan's neoclassical architecture would be absurd. I could see that he wanted to laugh, but was restraining himself out of politeness for Kevin Roche. Then, eyeing the other model and seeing the rooms of his house reproduced precisely, with the paintings and even a selection of the drawings done in small scale and placed perfectly, he said, simply, "I approve."

Shortly thereafter, Bobby Lehman entered a hospital for an ailment from which he never recovered. I saw him at his apartment whenever I could, once bringing with me a suitcase containing some beautiful drawings, manuscripts, and small works of art in the Museum's collections. I didn't have to say a word, nor did he. When I held one of the treasures up for him to see, his eyes would burn with pleasure.

The last thing he said to me was that he was deeply happy with his changed decision, and that the officers of his foundation would work out the details. He assured me they would make certain that everything was in a formal contract. As it turned out, it was one of the most amicable agreements we have ever entered into, for one of the most important gifts in our history. The Museum put up the funds for the building and the Lehman Foundation put up the full endowment for the maintenance of the building, the guardianship of the collection, and all the curatorial functions. The Robert Lehman Collection, housed in a building which was constructed on budget, opened on May 12, 1975, to enthusiastic acclaim.

A reading of these pages might lead one to think that the staff of the Metropolitan has experienced only success after success throughout a century of collecting. Not so. Our annals record occasional lapses, failures, and losses. It is often said in the field of collecting that you remember more vividly and far longer the works of art you miss than those you secure. That's a bit exaggerated, of course, but it is not without truth. So the Metropolitan will remember vividly and always certain great prizes that it failed to secure: the Chester Dale Collection, now in the National Gallery, Washington; the Karolik Collection in the Museum of Fine Arts, Boston; the finest Rubens in the United States, *The Adoration of the Magi,* in the Toledo Museum of Art; the splendid *Saint George* by Vittore Carpaccio in the private collection of Baron Thyssen-Bornemisza in Lugano; a monumental stone *Madonna and Child* by Tilman Riemens- chneider, now in the museum at Würzburg; the Rothschild Cameo, with the cameo of the late antique emperor Honorius and his spouse, Maria, still in the Rothschild Collection; a marvelous group of the *Rape of Helen,* by Pierre Puget, now in the Palazzo Bianco in Genova; a superb bust of Urban VIII by Bernini, now in the Galleria Nazionale in Rome; and a majestic, life-size, marble head of St. Paul, of around 300 A.D. in the Museum of Fine Arts, Boston.

I shall personally never forget this head of St. Paul, dating back to my assistant curatorship in the Medieval Department. One day the main Information Desk called to say that a man was there who had something Early Christian in a large cardboard box. The man came to my office with his heavy box. As he undid it, he told me he was an ex-G.I. who had been stationed in Greece in the late 1940s. There he had married a Greek girl. Imbedded in the stones of a well on her family's property, near the ancient town of Corinth, he had found a fine marble head of a bearded man. Lifting the head from the box, he said the Museum could have it for $2,000. Remarkable, simply remarkable, I thought, and I explained to this welcome visitor our study process. He told me to keep the head for a month or two. As it turned out, it never reached the Board, for a member of the staff, not in the curatorial ranks, for some reason took a dim view of the head and discouraged the Director about it. That was that. I passed

FIGURE 7. Interior of the completed Robert Lehman Collection wing. Photograph: Norman McGrath

my thoughts about it on to Cornelius Vermeule, of the Museum of Fine Arts, Boston. The head was purchased immediately. Vermeule's research later revealed the strong likelihood that the stone head was the cult image of the Apostle Paul. In the early days of Christianity it was probably enshrined in the great Basilica of Saint Paul in Corinth. When I am in Boston I never fail to pay it curatorial homage.

The chase and capture of an important piece of architecture such as the Temple of Dendur or of a great collection like the Lehman is an exciting business. Nevertheless the excitement somehow cannot equal the tracking down and winning of a single work of art in a purely curatorial manner. That offers the highest excitement of all—as I have said, something, despite efforts to remain calm and dispassionate, like the excitement of a love affair.

Every curator has his or her own classic tale of the rooting out, tracking down, study, and—with luck—capture of an important work of art. Mine concerns one of the preeminent works of art in the entire collection of the Metropolitan and its subsidiary, The Cloisters: The magnificent twelfth-century ivory crucifix called the Bury St. Edmunds Cross. Although this powerful object has been in the public eye for a decade now, the full story of the competition for its acquisition has not been told before.

I first heard of the cross in 1959, several months after I joined the Metropolitan Museum as a junior curator at the completion of my Ph.D. at Princeton University. A colleague who had moved on to bigger things at the Museum of Fine Arts, Boston, came to dinner one evening and was trying to soothe my anger at having been turned down for the second and final time on the purchase of a large silver-gilt cross of the early thirteenth century.

"The Board should certainly have bought it," he said, "but you can't get everything. Anyway, why worry about the silver cross when the prize of all art history, as crosses go, is waiting in the possession of a remarkable collector named Mimara or Matutin or Mimara-Matutin, who is a Yugoslav by birth, Austrian by citizenship, lives in Tangiers, Morocco, stays at cheap hotels in Zurich, and keeps most of his junk in the vault of the Unione Banque de Suisse—and I think he's an arms dealer."

Comforting, I thought. The cross in question, my friend continued, was of walrus ivory, about two feet high, carved fantastically on both sides with dozens of scenes and figures and inscriptions in Latin and Greek.

It was supposed to be English or French and of early to mid twelfth century. It was superb—but a superb *fake,* he finally burst out, laughing good-naturedly. He urged me to see it if only to sharpen my eye for distinguished forgeries.

I asked him what was wrong with it. Everything. The style was ambiguous. There were errors in the iconography. But most telling of all—the prime tip-off of the forgery—was the curious inscription. The "titulus," or placard carved into the cross above Christ's head, did not carry the rubric I.N.R.I., Jesus Nazareus Rex Iudeorum, which is the canonical formula listed in the biblical texts and displayed on literally millions of works of art. This "titulus" read, incongruously, Jesus of Nazareth, King of the Confessors. Most strange. I remember remarking that this was so incredibly bizarre as to be a double puzzle. Why would a forger, normally a cautious type, take such an unusual liberty with the Bible? Could it not, by its highly unusual nature, be a mark of authenticity? Unlikely! The subject was dropped.

But this "great" ivory cross kept sticking in my mind. Eager to show my boss, James Rorimer, the then Director of the Metropolitan, that I left no object unstudied in my deep desire to collect the finest medieval works available, I decided to double check.

The departmental file was meager. The piece had been examined in 1956 in Zurich. The examiner's handwritten notes stated simply: "Large walrus ivory cross, fantastic work (f) $2-million only." The (f) indicated forgery. The letter to the owner in Tangiers was as clipped as a curatorial turn-down can possibly be: "Dear Monsieur Topic: Thank you for showing me the objects in Zurich. None of them are of interest to the Museum for acquisition. Sincerely yours, _____"

Also in the file was a letter from a certain Harold W. Parsons, praising the cross. This Parsons was one of the most intriguing individuals in the art-dealing trade at the time. Highly cultivated and urbane, "marchand amateur" or gentleman agent, he lived most of his months in the choicest of Europe's watering places or on his yacht in Venice, dabbling from time to time in—as he himself once put it—"the delightful art of making the perfect marriage arrangement between a collector, a great work of art, a wealthy museum in America—and yours truly." Parsons letter in the file, urging Rorimer to see the cross, was fastened to the curator's memo saying "This is hogwash. The cross is one of the worst forgeries (or best) that I have ever seen. Unquestionably wrong. The price was one million dollars, which gives you some idea of Mr. Matutin-Mimara's mental arithmetic. Everything else we saw was either fake or fussed up."

With this, the door had been closed. Rorimer had put the cross, Matutin-Mimara, and Parsons out of his acquisition plans forever. Or so he thought.

I tried to locate the mysterious owner of the large fake cross by letter. None of the five or six addresses I had, worked. The clue to Topic-Mimara's whereabouts came finally five months after the start, thanks to a brainstorm of Marjorie Baucom, the secretary of the Medieval Department. She remembered somebody once telling her that the Austrian National Police would track down any Austrian citizen if the proper request were made. Thus, a slightly amazed Topic-Mimara answered my letter of June 1961 from a hospital in Munich, where he was recovering from a spinal operation. He wrote that he would be pleased to show Rorimer and me his "great" cross and that henceforth he would appreciate having our registered letters sent to his home in Morocco. He was not happy that I prevailed on the Austrian police to determine his whereabouts.

Several weeks later Jim Rorimer received a feverish letter from Harold Parsons:

> I hope that your vacationing steps will be bringing you to Italy this summer and that I shall see you. I plan to stay in this charming little hotel until October.
>
> The purpose of this letter is to inform you that Mr. A. Topic-Mimara, the rich owner of that fabulous Winchester ivory cross, which you have never seen, came to Rome a month ago to consult me again about "placing" that object, as he invited me to do some three years ago. He is in no great haste to cede the piece; and he knows quite well it could be bought by only one of three or four museums in the world. That, I am convinced, is precisely what will happen, and probably at the staggering price he is now asking for it; for as we all know, and as the greatest specialists in the field have all agreed, this is an incomparable mediaeval objet d'art, the masterpiece of all known Winchester ivories.
>
> Before elaborating the sequence of events which have transpired since I first brought this remarkable object to your attention, let me say, once and for all, that the professional fee which Mr. Topic-Mimara has agreed to allocate for my services would not have any real significance concerning the price which he demands and will, in my opinion, ultimately obtain, or one very close to it. He paid a large sum for the cross many years ago, making great personal

sacrifices to secure it over a period of time, with installment payments. He was not as rich then as he has subsequently become. But for years he has studied the piece, as has his collaborator, Dr. Hildrith Mersmann, a scholar of some renown in the field of Mediaeval art. He has lately married Frau Dr. Mersmann, the mother of his twelve-year-old son; and they are now in Tangier for the rest of the summer and autumn, where he has a large apartment and keeps the greater part of his extensive collection of paintings, sculptures and decorative arts; but his objets d'art are in the vaults of the bank in Zurich. I have today written Robert Lehman[1] that a remarkable mediaeval object, of which you are aware but have never seen, exists in a private collection in a country of Europe from which it can be legally exported at any time; and that if he intends coming to Venice, as he usually does during the summer, I shall be glad to give him full particulars concerning this remarkable object and could, in all probability, arrange for him to see it while on his travels. I am sure that Mr. A. Topic-Mimara would fly to Zurich for a rendez-vous with you and Robert Lehman, if you could let him or me know well in advance.

The sequence of events is as follows: Mr. Topic-Mimara, knowing that I was a retired American museum art adviser and occasional consultant of one or two private collectors, information given to him by his old friend Dr. Fritz Volbach,[2] came to Rome to make my acquaintance, some four years ago, and invite me to see his collection in Zurich, the ivory cross in particular. I did so and, incidentally, advised the Nelson Gallery, although no longer officially their art adviser, to acquire a certain painting from his collection, which they did. I then reported the Winchester cross almost contemporaneously to you, to Milliken,[3] who was still Director at the time, and to Kenneth Clark;[4] also to Swarzenski.[5]

Kenneth Clark immediately sent Pope-Hennessy[6] to see the object. Then came Milliken, then Swarzenski, then young Randall sent by you, then Sherman Lee[7] who had just come to the Directorship, accompanied by Severance Milliken, later William Wixom, recently appointed curator of mediaeval art; finally Bruce-Mitford.[8] The latter, equipped with books and photographs, came to Zurich for five days and spent all of those days in the vaults of the bank,

[1] At the time, Vice President of the Metropolitan Museum.
[2] Of Berlin and Rome, one of the world's leading medievalists.
[3] Robert Millikin, then recently Director of the Cleveland Museum, responsible for acquiring part of the famed Guelph Treasure of medieval antiquities.
[4] In 1961, Director of the National Gallery, London; now Lord Clark of Saltwood.
[5] Hanns Swarzenski, Curator of Decorative Arts, Museum of Fine Arts, Boston.
[6] John Pope-Hennessy, Director and Keeper of Sculpture, the Victoria and Albert Museum, London; now Sir John Pope-Hennessy, Director of the British Museum.
[7] A specialist in Far Eastern Art, Director of the Cleveland Museum.
[8] Ruppert Bruce-Mitford, Keeper of Medieval Antiquities, the British Museum.

studying the cross. Our American museum men, as is their wont, had only a brief time to spend; we have so little time in America, alas! But Wixom remained for a day. All were enthusiastic; all expressed a desire to acquire the cross for his museum, but Swarzenski was involved with the French wooden statue; Cleveland with other things. All were staggered, and still are, by Mr. Topic Mimara's valuation. It was half a million dollars for Cleveland, last year, when he had undergone a serious spinal operation which kept him in plaster for six months and the surgeons of Munich had told him frankly that his days might be numbered. Now he has recovered and the price to England is 200,000 pounds. I have seen, in confidence, Bruce-Mitford's reply; and I know you will also keep it confidential; it was to say that they want the cross at *any* price, but *that* sum would require an act of Parliament. Who knows what some title-seeking, newly rich English magnate might not do, at the behest of Lord Crawford, Kenneth Clark and the Director of the Museum? It happened with the great Rubens we had hoped to have for Kansas City; it has happened with many other important works of art lately. Personally, I hope to see the cross permanently housed in the C.M.A. or in the Cloisters. For it is the masterpiece of English mediaeval objets d'art and the finest Winchester ivory in existence; all the rest are minor or but fragments. It is one of the greatest masterpieces of art extant. In beauty and importance, it would dwarf the Antioch chalice to insignificance. I hope you will have the courage to charge for it, as you have for other battles you have won. Such things will never come again.

Frau Dr. Mersmann is publishing the cross, over which she has been working for years, in the autumn. The inscription alone is of the greatest interest and significance. The owner has recently bought an estate of some hundreds of acres near Vienna, where he will live as soon as the present political atmosphere clears, giving up Tangier. He is a very prudent man. He has never returned to his native Jugoslavia, since it went Communist, and has become an Austrian citizen, having served in the Austrian army during the first world war. If you were to pass by Tangier, or wing your way there from Spain, he would be glad to meet you and show you his collection there, which seems to contain one very important painting; but I still have it under study. If it is what I at present believe to be the case, it is a museum masterpiece of the very highest order. But the evasive matter of definite attribution is ever with us. My suggestion would be for you to make a date with him for Zurich, as soon as you conveniently can. He states that he does not wish to appear to play, through me, one American museum against another; and the C.M.A. is *profoundly* interested but have allocated their 1961 funds completely; but hope with all earnestness that it can be acquired in 1962, and have so stated to the owner; but the matter of price remains a hurdle. It appears to me to be a case of first come first served. I frankly believe he will never cede the cross for less than half a million dollars. His argument relating it to the present values for paintings is, I think, unanswerable. The cross, in mediaeval art, is a world-important masterpiece, which you will realize when you have a chance to study it,—not too hastily I hope.

Rorimer was pleased that I had reopened the issue but not at all interested in an object at that price. Also, he seemed a bit put off that I had written to Topic that he, the Director, wanted to see the object.

I requested photographs of the cross. Neither Parsons nor Topic would send us any. Topic told us what Parsons had already told us, that his wife was preparing a study of the object, and he added, somewhat churlishly, that one could, after all, see the object itself in Zurich.

Rorimer went to Europe but had no time to see the cross. I made arrangements to see it in the fall. Meantime, I took the normal steps to develop a dossier on the man and his object. Few scholars, I discovered, had seen the cross. Those few either thought it was a "real problem" or avoided expressing any firm opinion.

Our competition for the object came into focus as Cleveland and the British Museum. Seeking opinions elsewhere, I queried Hanns Swarzenski. "*If* good," he said cautiously, "it must be a truly great prize." Kurt Weitzmann of Princeton, the world's leading authority on ivory carving, my teacher and adviser, and himself the pupil of, and collaborator with, Adolph Goldschmidt, the compiler of the standard study on medieval ivories, had heard only vaguely of the object, and this in terms of a forgery. There was no reference to the cross in Adolph Goldschmidt's files, which led Weitzmann to observe, "this does not bode well for its authenticity."

Several months passed. I asked but again Topic refused photos. In October 1961, in a private underground room in the Unione Banque de Suisse, Zurich, I saw the cross for the first time.

For a trained scholar, the first look at a great and moving work of art is a tense experience. You try to prepare yourself for objectivity, you try to be as passive as you can, to allow the object itself, not your eyes or your preconception, to speak. You are, or should be, like a blotter, neutrally soaking up the multiple images. But if something is truly grand, it has a kinetic effect. Something akin to being physically impelled. It is, frankly, a charge, both cerebral and viscerotonic, not unlike a sexual experience. But it is rare. In the all-surpassing number of times there is nothing but flaccid disappointment.

The cross was none of that. Although small in size, slender, almost thin, it loomed far larger as a presence. Golden and buttery in color, every surface and part shone and glistened with tiny, delicately formed figures. They seemed to be silently conversing one with another by means of artfully held scrolls. It seemed to me to be an intimate, very personal work of art, a magical object. To the touch it was smooth and oily with age yet rock hard and unyielding at the same time. My God, we simply had to have it! With me in the vault was a colleague from the Medieval Department, Carmen Gomez-Moreno. Later she told me that she had experienced an instant and exceedingly comfortable sense of confidence in the cross. To her, as well as to me, it couldn't be wrong.

We spent a long time in Topic's vault, writing down some of the difficult, greatly abbreviated inscriptions. We made some sketches of the scenes, identifying a number of them. We counted sixty-odd figures, seventeen separate subject matters. We tried, in short, to devour the piece, peel it like an onion, examine it coldly, skeptically, even with disdain. Our studied contempt was shattered time after time. The strength and beauty of the work prevailed and became more assertive.

It was necessary to try an act of deception. Topic-Mimara had to attend to a minor bank affair and said he would leave us alone with the work. I said that would be fine because it would give me a chance to take pictures with a Rolleiflex I had brought in the hope that something would work out. Topic said, always in Italian, which is the language we used throughout the years of negotiations, "Take all the photos you wish"—as he picked up the Rollei and took it with him. I had, however, also brought a Minox, and as Carmen Gomez-Moreno nervously stood by the door listening, I measured with the chain and clicked off five shots. Topic entered the room as I was on the last. Luckily my frantic attempts to conceal the camera under my belt went unnoticed.

When I left Zurich I knew a little more about the mysterious Topic. He described himself to me as simply an art collector, a humble man always on the move looking for treasures. I learned one thing about him during the session in his vault—that he was rich and wanted to be richer. In one of the vault chambers, there were three stacks, each half a meter high, of tightly bundled 1000 Swiss franc notes. I gauged the hoard at between a quarter of a million and half a million dollars. The price of the cross was, at present, he said, $600,000. It would not go down a penny and he would not sell it a day before January 1, 1962. After that day

FIGURE 8. Cross. England (Bury St. Edmunds). 1150–1190. Walrus ivory. The Cloisters Collection, 63.12, 63.127

the price would increase. He showed me a letter from Bruce-Mitford of the British Museum that confirmed what Harold Parsons had reported to Rorimer months earlier—that the British Museum wanted the cross at *any* price.

I now wrote two letters about the cross, one to Rorimer, "This cross—all walrus ivory—60 cm. high with literally dozens of inscriptions, is unquestionably one of the most beautiful and exciting ivory works of art I have ever seen—and those words are not to be taken lightly," the other to Margaret Freeman, curator of The Cloisters and my immediate boss, "The Zurich operation was exciting but bizarre. Topic is a hearty hail-fellow, well-met, with a face like a crowd, who, thank God, spoke Italian so communication was easy. French and even German seem beyond him. The cross is one of the most thrilling objects I have ever seen. Carmen agrees. The style, it seems to me, is around St. Albans and ca. 1120 or

FIGURES 9–13. Five hastily made photographs of the cross in the Unione Banque de Suisse, Zurich, October 1961

1150? The price for this beauty is also a beaut!—for him, not us. It rests at a comfortable 600,000. To me it's worth it, but I know Jim will not be at all interested."

In Munich I had my Minox film printed. Although the shots were not very stimulating, they were sufficient for study purposes. I was swept up at once in the joyful Munich scene. Here is a city rich in music, opera, excellent food, and fascinating night life of a particularly satisfying lowly and earthy nature. I made the rounds with a host of wild and eager museum friends, artists, and students, in particular Erich Steingraber, the brilliant curator of decorative arts at the Bayerisches Nationalmuseum. Erich, it will be remembered, had been my mentor at the Metropolitan in 1960. During a night crawl in Schwabing, I filled his ear with my impressions of Topic's great cross. Was it a fake? Erich didn't think so, but he was naturally cautious just on the basis of the photos.

We went together to see his chief, Theodore Muller, the Generaldirector of the great Bavarian museum. "Topic-Mimara?" he said. "Oh, do I remember that one!" At the end of World War II, Topic, wearing a flamboyant uniform of some high rank in the Yugoslav army, had suddenly appeared at the collecting point in Munich where hundreds upon hundreds of looted works of art had been gathered by the Allied Art Recovery unit. "He appeared to be *some* sort of a general with a marshal's baton," Muller said. "He claimed he was a museum custodian. Very amusing. But he never did much but look around. Very few of the looted objects were Yugoslavian."

Muller remembered that the scholar Hermann Schnitzler, in Cologne, had seen at least part of the cross. I called Schnitzler at once from Muller's office and learned that in 1947 or 1948 Topic-Mimara, wearing what Schnitzler recalled as a Moroccan costume, had shown him the upper part of the cross. Schnitzler thought the man was slightly addled, but he remembered being impressed with the piece, sensing that it was probably genuine and probably of about the twelfth century. Topic had promised to show Schnitzler the rest of the cross as he secured it, piece by piece. Apparently he was buying them in lots on a time-payment plan. When pressed for an opinion on the cross, Schnitzler begged off, saying that he couldn't remember clearly enough.

I next tried to reach Fritz Volbach, the medievalist whom Parsons had called an old friend of Topic's. No luck. In fact, my repeated efforts to obtain information from Volbach about the cross's origin all failed. Topic himself had told me that he would "guarantee" the legality of the cross and would place the entire information in an envelope which would be delivered to the Museum upon his death. From this time on, through the difficult months that followed, the issue of title and provenance menaced our negotiations.

Before returning to New York I visited the Bargello in Florence and examined a small ivory that appeared to have some of the stylistic characteristics of the cross. It was part of a group that Adolph Goldschmidt has published in a category he called English-French, twelfth century. Topic-Mimara's mysterious cross was beginning to be pinpointed.

In New York I prepared an extensive memo for Jim Rorimer on everything discovered so far. Rorimer, although more interested than before, doubted that further action was warranted. My next problem was how to capture Rorimer's interest sufficiently to get him to look at the piece. I knew there was no hope of acquiring it until the Director had personally examined it and recommended its purchase to the Board.

Looking at the ground rules, I had to admit it was unlikely that the piece would ever end up at The Cloisters. The high price for an unknown, unpublished, "wandering" ivory whose authenticity was already seriously questioned made the collecting situation almost laughable. Topic-Mimara's restrictions seemed deliberately calculated to make everything more difficult. No photos were available for study. (My Minox shots helped with Rorimer but were not good enough for the Board.) Under no conditions would Topic-Mimara allow the cross to be sent to New York for the normal intensive examination. No information on the provenance would be given until the purchaser handed over his payment. Practically the only helpful information I had elicited from Topic-Mimara was that, if proof ever came that the piece was a forgery, he would take it back and give the purchaser full compensation.

Meantime, my dossier of outside expert advice was growing in size and importance. The statement I obtained from George Zarnecki, the brilliant medievalist associated with the Courtauld Institute in London, had a substantive effect on Rorimer's coolness: "The institution that acquires this work can consider itself the most fortunate in the world."

The cross became an obsession with me—*the* vital element of my professional existence. In my mind's eye, I would analyze and reanalyze every element of the work I could see from my photos and sketches. I would start from the powerful circle at the center with its depiction of

Moses raising the brazen serpent in the desert, an allusion to the Christ raised on the cross, through the complex cycle of the Crucifixion and entombment depicted on the right square, over to the left with its scene of the Three Marys at the tomb and the Resurrection, to the scene at the top of the High Priest before Pontius Pilate, then to the Ascension above, in which, in typically invigorating English style, Christ was shown half-transported into the clouds of paradise. I dwelled upon the inscriptions that I had been able to transcribe. All were chosen from the Old Testament and referred to acts and moments of the Passion of Christ. I dwelled on the two large inscriptions on the front and sides of the upright piece of walrus ivory, astonished by the power of their brutal significance: "Earth trembles, Death is conquered and bewails. From the opening grave Life surges forth and synagogue is crushed by its disgraceful stupidity." And on the side half-hidden by the shape of the cross: "Just as Cham laughed at the shameful nakedness of his father, the Jews mock the agony of the dying God." Nowhere could I recall such violence expressed on a religious object. For this reason, from time to time the delicate, still beauty of the magnificent cross seemed to be crushed and the splendor filled with an awful taint of some kind of sickness. But then the crystalline beauty, the harmonious grace, the perfection of the object would win out, and the object would once again in my mind be restored to full stature.

For the next year my efforts were spent on research, enlarging my dossier, and trying to persuade Rorimer to go and see the object. A breakthrough came early in 1962 when Topic-Mimara wrote that if Rorimer were to come to Zurich, he would not deny him a set of photos to take with him. But no persuasion on my part, it seemed, was going to prod the busy Director into going. Frustrations mounted. Some of my memos, in retrospect, were models of coolness and objectivity, but the hand that wrote them was shaking in rage and incredulity at times. One reads: "It seems to me that this cross could not be a more perfect object for The Cloisters. It is indeed expensive. But all great things are. As you say, we are looking for the best. If authentic, this cross *is* the best and worthy of our utmost consideration. With the danger of being called the proponent of the 'hardsell,' I must state my feeling that we should begin the consideration of this object. This does not mean that I feel we should rush out and purchase it with a flamboyant gesture. It means, on the contrary, that we should at least *start* the consideration as soon as feasible, realizing that it is going to be a long, difficult road to travel. Long, careful study is necessary."

Of course, if I had had my way, I probably would have made the totally flamboyant gesture, gone to Zurich, paid the man his money, and brought the cross back in my arms. Months passed—an impasse. Meanwhile our most determined competitor, the British Museum, prepared its case. Gloomy letters came to me from Harold Parsons, describing the progress of the campaign to petition Parliament for money to purchase the cross.

Finally, in June 1962, Rorimer and Margaret Freeman examined the cross in Zurich. Peg's letter from Zurich gave me one of the most thrilling moments in the long chase:

> Dear Tom, James and I are really quite excited about *that object*. (I am not to mention it by name even in a sealed letter.) We spent a good part of yesterday examining it and the rest of the day trying to borrow an ultraviolet lamp. James finally secured a lamp this morning and we studied the piece again under ultraviolet. I must say that it looks *very good*—although there are a few questions still remaining. We do want Weitzmann to see it when he can. James says to tell you not to talk about it because of the interest that the British Museum has in it.
>
> I have Mrs. Topic-Mimara's list of all of the inscriptions, some of which I checked on myself . . . .

I replied at once:

> We're all very thrilled with the news. After Weitzmann I really do think we should move *fast*. Anyway, I have a suspicion that James thinks the same. What about photos? And, of course, I'd be delighted to nibble on some of those inscriptions.

I was sent a nearly complete record of the inscriptions. It was a heady moment, for I had always felt that these were the clues to the cross's complete authenticity and possibly its origin. I decided to examine the texts first, not as unconnected passages from the Old Testament, but as a group that could perhaps be linked to a known series of writings. How? It was really rather simple. There exists a compendium of church or patristic writings from earliest times through the early Renaissance. Compiled in the nineteenth century, it is known as the *Patrologia Latina* and the *Patrologia Graeca*. The *Pat. Lat.*, as it is known in the field, consists of two hundred and twenty-one volumes, each containing about 1,500 pages of the Latin texts in double columns of small print. Mercifully there are four volumes of indices to the *Patrologia*. I went to the set with my inscriptions listed both as they appeared on the object and as they appeared in the Old Testament. It was boring, rather mechanical work—until I had cross-referenced about 15 of the 39 inscriptions and sat back to reflect upon a possible pattern. It was then apparent that all the texts I had traced appeared in a series of writings called the Disputations or Argumentations between Christians and Jews over the divine nature of Christ and the legitimacy of the Christian church. In many instances, particularly at moments in history when the battle lines between the two factions were harshly drawn, these disputations were of extremely violent nature. My initial 15 inscriptions appeared in one eighth-century Disputation. Eventually 25 of the 39 appeared in one of the late twelfth century, and all were found in a series of two or three which themselves were very closely associated. I checked further and found no more than one of the cross texts in any of the other patristic writings of the *Patrologia*. The meaning of this was clear: The cross was not only an object made to glorify the Christian faith, like any cross, but in addition, was something unique in crosses—a polemic, a sometimes bitter denunciation of Synagogue, a scathing condemnation of the Jewish people not only of antiquity but of the twelfth century as well. I became depressed and puzzled. How could it be that such a beautiful object, with its lacelike concatenation of serene figures, bore such a bleak and embittered message?

Along with the discovery of the link with the Disputation, I found evidences that dispelled whatever lingering suspicions I had about the ivory. If forged, one would have to assume that the forger had made the most daring tour de force possible, for he would have had to know the Disputations as few scholars of patristic literature had ever known them. And he—the phantom forger—would not have been able to work after an existing work of art but from nothing. Forgery was additionally ruled out when one of the inscriptions, differing from the Old Testament version, turned up in a disputation of the first half of the twelfth century in which the writer explained that in this one case the Bible had been changed, possibly by a Jewish writer attempting to sabotage the text.

Rorimer was elated at the discovery of the true nature of the inscriptions. Reading them as if they formed a polemical sermon, he told me all I had left to do was find out when the "sermon" was spoken and under what terrible circumstances. That discovery came much later, almost too late.

At last we received Professor Weitzmann's report from Zurich. His long-awaited and crucial analysis reached the Museum in late September 1962. Knowing it was in the building, I could hardly contain myself until Rorimer phoned me and said that all was well. This is Weitzmann's letter to Rorimer, dated September 16, 1962:

The day before I left Switzerland I went to Zurich to see the cross. Mr. Topic had sent me a telegram that he would come from Tangier for that day and so he did. He and his wife, whom I had met previously in Bonn, were waiting at the entrance of the Bank. After Mrs. Topic had shown me the photos at Bonn as I wrote you—a preview, so to speak, at which I could judge the piece only iconographically and could find nothing wrong—I now looked at the piece more from the technical point of view and again I can't find anything wrong. The way the pieces are put together is in agreement with English miniature painting and especially the rubbing of the surface in those figures at the lower stem where a priest would hold it and therefore cause a certain amount of surface rubbing, look thoroughly convincing. In one word: I have convinced myself that the piece is genuine. But aside from the details I cannot conceive of a faker with that amount of inventiveness and not making a single slip in such a complicated program for which there is no direct model. If certain details in the program cannot be explained at this moment it only means that art history has to do more research on this piece and I have the impression that eventually there will be plenty. To restate: I have no reservations as to the genuineness of the piece.

Mr. Topic told me of course that you and Miss Freeman had looked at the piece and furthermore he showed me a letter of Bruce-Mitford. If he had the letter already by the time you were in Zurich, then he surely has shown it to you. If not, this is the content: Bruce-Mitford is going to present the case at a meeting of the Trustees of his museum in November and is going to recommend the acquisition of the cross. So there may be a time factor involved!

Mr. Topic then showed me quite a lot of his collection, i.e. as much as he has in the tresor of the Zurich bank, but I suppose you saw other pieces too, some of which seemed to me quite remarkable. May I mention one piece (at the risk that I repeat what is all known to you): a rather huge glass vessel with painted enamel: rinceaux work exactly in the style of the Aethelwold Benedictional. Of course, I cannot judge glass. But if it is genuine it would be a very remarkable and unique piece. I mention this piece because Topic told me he would sell the cross only together with the glass. Well, from here on it is your problem.

The last line sounded ominous indeed.
As if on call, a letter came to me from Harold Parsons with more

depressing news about the progress of the British and with some chatty observations about Topic-Mimara, which later turned out to be rather far from the truth:

> This is just a line to tell you that I heard, in a very round-about way, that the Trustees of the British Museum have given their sanction for the purchase of the early English ivory cross and that all that now remains to be done is to raise the money. That may not be as difficult as it sounds.
>
> Having been at considerable pains to do what I could to save it for one of our American collections to which it would add the greatest kudos—either the Cleveland Museum or The Cloisters—I would doubly regret its going to the British Museum; . . . we may all have missed the bus. I am told that the matter will probably be accomplished at the British Museum at the end of the month of October.
>
> By the way Topic told me that whichever of the two museums, yours or the British, is the first to meet his terms regarding the ivory cross will be given the opportunity to acquire his other English treasures.
>
> Topic was amused that Rorimer—to whom, please, my warmest regards—had thought him a "merchant of death" like Buehrle of Zurich who manufactured precision anti-aircraft and guns. "Armatore," in Italian, means an owner of cargo ships, like Onassis, et al. The Topic family are rich "armatori" with their base at Monte Carlo; they are Yugoslavic in origin. Topic himself is an Austrian, and strongly anti-communist, which is why he cut all ties with his native country years ago. He lived for twenty-five years in Germany; now in Tangier and has recently bought property in Austria to which he is about to retire. He is a rich man.

To which one might have added—and soon to become richer.

This letter from Parsons and the information from Weitzmann put James Rorimer into a minor panic, and the Director and I now had one of the few flaming fights we ever experienced together. He blamed me for not alerting him to the danger of the British "threat." I left his office, returned with the file, slammed it down in front of him, and shouted that it contained plea after plea, entreaty after entreaty, to go, to do something, to see the cross, to make a decision. It was a sorry moment, forgotten soon enough in our mutual worry about Topic's legal title to the cross. Rorimer stated flatly that The Cloisters would never acquire it without evidence of ownership and a proper bill of sale. That became an issue of almost daily significance for the next ten months.

Immediate preparations were made to present the cross in the form of a scale model to the Purchase Committee (as it was called in 1963) in special session as soon as possible. Once convinced and charged up, James Rorimer was not one to give an inch. He was wonderful to watch.

Curious things now began to happen. Confidential sources in Britain reported to Rorimer that the British team was making continual progress in their effort to raise money from Parliament and "a highly interested donor." Then a strange new communication filtered in from Britain to the effect that the consortium of some 50 renowned scholars said to be backing the importance and authenticity of the cross had come apart at the seams. This turned out to be a ruse. Other rumors had it that an unnamed scholar in East Germany knew of the forger's name. We, in our turn, seeded a story to the British that we had an unnamed American scholar who could prove that the cross was Saxon or Westphalian of the mid-twelfth century and therefore of no interest to the British Museum. Our material was as ineffectual upon them as theirs was upon us.

Among the mysterious letters sent to me in 1962 was this gem:

Dear Thomas:
    What happened to the $1-million cross? The world awaits reports and retorts of the supposed summer visit of a certain important gentleman to a bank vault in an international country. How's your beautiful wife?

                          Yrs. (in secrecy)
                          Mr. Topic-Mimara
                          Allah Ben Ahmed
                          Grand Mogol.

Acting on Rorimer's instruction, I dispatched a letter to Topic, attempting once more to get from him a piece of crucial information:

    There is at this final moment one *very difficult* problem regarding the purchase of the cross. With such a large price involved the Trustees are going to be extremely hesitant unless proof of title is forthcoming. A solution to this problem would be if you told Mr. Rorimer, and Mr. Rorimer alone, in the strictest confidence, where you purchased the object. If you did this Mr. Rorimer would give his word and promise that no one else would learn this information—not me, not any of the Trustees. All we ask is indication of former ownership or your clear title that would hold the Museum harmless in the event of a claim, however absurd, by a third party. This information would be placed in a sealed envelope in the Museum's safe and would not be opened for x number of years.

Late in October, this answer arrived:

You again raise the question about the provenance of the cross. Of course I can understand your hesitations. But I have answered this question already and will never be able to give you a different answer.

In a few weeks the publication of the cross will come out. This fact alone should give you a complete assuredness.

In the case that one should reach further negotiations, a way doubtlessly could be found, which would protect you against any third party claims of which you seem to be afraid.

But, should you have any fundamental hesitations to buy anything from my collection, it would be better not to have any dealings at all.

Again Rorimer became anxious. A letter like this was not from a man who was burning to sell the object—at least to us. A special session of the Purchase Committee was convoked to study the model of the cross we had fabricated from the photographs Rorimer had brought back from Zurich. Rorimer and Margaret Freeman asked me to make the presentation. I rested my case on these points: one, the piece was unquestionably authentic, based upon Weitzmann's expertise; two, I was convinced that we would discover a very specific origin for it, since we had already narrowed the style to a series of illuminated manuscripts that were known to have come from the Abbey of Bury St. Edmunds; three, that it was a unique work of art of international importance—here I quoted the statement I had elicited from George Zarnecki; and, four, that this was a great spiritual object, a surpassingly beautiful masterwork that was not a price tag but a unique work of art. My summation to the Committee was emotional. I spoke of how I had lived with the object for more than two years, of how my period of doubt had evolved to a period of no doubt at all. And I expressed my deep belief that the eccentric owner would not come down one penny from his price. Go for it, I pleaded. If you do not, this will constitute, without question, one of the darkest, most lassitudinous moments in the history of a great institution, one that has continually pledged itself to the acquisition of the finest works of art available in the world.

I recall none of the questions that followed. Then it was time for the Trustees to speak. Henry Luce expressed himself as convinced. "Let's take the opportunity," he said. "Don't throw caution to the winds, but let us not, on the other hand, descend to hair-splitting. It's a summation, this cross, of an entire epoch of man's achievement, both good and bad. It's an honest and splendidly frank thing. I'm for it." (Hurrah!)

Roland Redmond, then President of the Museum, stated that he, too, agreed that the object was great, a masterpiece, certainly, but the Museum, he added, must be prudent. There would be other works of art, surely. (Groan!)

Irwin Untermyer spoke in favor of acquiring this unique object. (Ha!)

Robert Lehman stated that he was for it, if some means could be worked out on the legal title. (Maybe we're in!)

And so it went. The Committee went into executive session. Peg Freeman and I were excused. I waited nearby for the decision—and when I read the resolution I felt sandbagged. An amount not to exceed $500,000 from The Cloisters balance would be available to purchase Topic's cross, subject to negotiations and final approval by the Director after legal approval of a proper title of sale and guarantees to be included therein.

The British Museum, I thought bitterly, might as well go to Zurich and pick the cross up.

Next day, Rorimer cabled Topic that he was now in a position to make a definite offer to buy the cross. Then he suggested something new, a trip by Topic to New York to make the final deal. Topic rejected the suggestion of coming to New York in a return cable, claiming illness. (It would take years for me to learn his real reason.)

Then, in a letter following the cable, Topic dropped a bomb:

"Furthermore, I must insist on your buying, besides the cross, several other objects from my collection, because otherwise one cannot find a justification in connection with the promise I have already given to the British Museum. Should the payment for the additional objects be impossible for you at this moment, I would agree to a later payment as well.

Thinking this one through, Rorimer and I suspected that the British Museum had not offered to buy anything else. How could they, we reasoned, since they were trying everything in their power just to raise the money for the cross alone? Still, one could not be sure. On Rorimer's instruction, I prepared a list of Topic's works of art that would be acceptable to us. The list was small. Most of his objects were heavily doubted by me. We dispatched a letter to Topic stating that the sudden

mention of "other objects" threatened the whole affair. We were interested in the cross and that alone, and with a legal title and bill of sale
guaranteed. If Topic were not willing to talk on those terms, forget it.

By return mail, Topic held firm to his refrain that he would in some
manner guarantee the title. In a confusing passage he seemed to allude
to the *loan* of other objects, not their purchase. Had his bluff been called?
Was he backing down?

I again wrote to him to find out his precise state of mind concerning
the other objects and then went into detail about the title:

> What our lawyers and Trustees might consider adequate title is still a prob-
> lem. You must understand that as an internationally famous institution The
> Metropolitan must act with the same circumspection as similar institutions
> must also conduct their affairs. We have offered one solution to the problem;
> namely, that you inform Rorimer alone, that he tell no one else, and that the
> information be placed in a sealed envelope not to be opened for a long time.
> We've tried to think of other methods. I have the feeling, however, that *you*
> might be able to think of something that would satisfy the needs of us both.
>
> I personally feel that we can come to an arrangement in this affair and that
> as intelligent people with much in common when it comes to a deep apprecia-
> tion about art, we will, in time, do so.

I suppose I thought at the time that flattery would get us everywhere.
It did not. The next week, the day before Christmas, I received a discouraging letter from Parsons stating that Topic had practically decided
to cede the cross to the British Museum and that *all* English scholars
had signed an enthusiastic letter to the Chancellor of the Exchequer. Too
bad, Topic had said to Parsons, that "Sig. Rorimer marcia con piedi di
piombo"—walks with leaden feet.

It was now Rorimer's turn to inform Topic that negotiations could not
proceed without his clarification on the key points of whether we would
have to buy other objects and whether we would get assurance on the
title.

We did not receive a clear answer on the first point. On the second,
Topic said he was *certain* something could be worked out to the advantage of both sides. I wrote to Parsons, who seemed to have some effect
on Topic. "We are not being hyper-difficult about the title," I said.

> An institution like ours simply has to have some protection against the outsider

suddenly popping up—even years hence—and claiming that this object is a great national treasure and was improperly sold out of such-and-such monastery and so-and-so town, let's say, Yugoslavia, even if the outsider is a fraud. Understandably when Topic-Mimara purchased the piece (or rather pieces—for he says he bought it piece by piece over several years) he had to commit himself to certain promises not to reveal the source. All right—but sources do not live forever, nor does the jeopardy continue to eternity.

In this letter I referred rather despondently to a new decision of Rorimer's: not to go to Zurich to meet Topic at all. The *Mona Lisa* was on its trip to America and the Director felt, quite rightly, that his presence was essential at the Metropolitan. Things seemed to be rapidly slipping away.

Rorimer decided to probe the British situation directly. He sent John Phillips, the curator of Western European Arts, to speak to Sir Frank Francis, the Director of the British Museum. Phillips's report came to us on the eight of January 1962. He had talked both with Francis and Ruppert Bruce-Mitford:

1. The British Museum was going after the cross. The Director had applied officially to the Exchequer for the funds. The decision was expected in a few weeks, certainly by the first of February.

2. A group of scholars was unanimous in its opinion that the cross was one of the most important medieval objects to have survived and was without question of English origin. All felt it should be acquired by the British Museum.

3. Although the cross was believed to be surely English, no specific evidence had come to light to prove this.

4. Topic had refused to supply Francis and Bruce-Mitford with any information as to its history.

5. The fact that Topic's wife was about to publish the cross in a special edition of the *Walraf-Richartz Jahrbuch* as belonging to Topic was considered to be a certain indication that he had legal title (the magazine would finally appear in January 1963).

6. The British Museum had *not* been asked by Topic to purchase any other objects as part of the proposed deal.

Upon receipt of Phillips's letter Rorimer dispatched me to Zurich. "Try to bargain," he said. "Be sure to get the legal title and bill of sale drafted by the Museum's attorneys *signed,* and head off the British." In a letter to Topic, assigning me as the Museum's emissary, he wrote: "It would be my proposal, in view of other options the Museum has, that an elegant solution to our problems would be that we send money to a Swiss bank and you transfer the object to Mr. Hoving."

My plane was scheduled to land me in Zurich on January 12. The plan had been worked out with Topic by telephone. We would go to the bank, make the final arrangements, sign the bill of sale and title, and I would take delivery of the cross. Although I was still deeply concerned that the Trustees had voted only $500,000 for the cross, I felt confident that the lack would not present a difficulty. After all, Topic had told us that he would accept payment over a period of time.

The plane, buffeted by one of the worst snow storms of the year, could not land in Zurich. After one pass over the airport that had the passengers gasping in fear, it flew on to Geneva. Total chaos at the airport. A hundred or more airplanes from all over Europe had come to the only port in the storm. Communications were out. Trains were solidly booked and running hours late. I arrived at the Hotel Central in Zurich ten hours late. A highly incensed Topic awaited me in the lobby. "I have come to purchase the great cross," I told him. "That will not be possible," he said. "The British are coming for it tomorrow." He seemed to relish my look of shock. "I had no idea that you would really come," he said, "since the Metropolitan always walks with feet of lead, so I spoke to Bruce-Mitford today and gave him until January thirtieth to raise the money. You must remember that the British saw the cross before you did. They respected it. Your other man rejected it. Rorimer took so long. He was difficult when he came to see it. The British asked me to delay until February tenth. On the ninth they will have a meeting with the Trustees of the Museum and the Chancellor of the Exchequer to make the decision on the money. But because of my regard for you I will not grant the delay. I will hold them to the thirtieth of January. After that the suitor that has the cash gets the girl."

Crushed by the news, convinced that if I had come with the full amount I might have been able, somehow, to clinch the deal then and there, battered by the grueling trip, I spent a miserable night. I was too exhausted to sleep. In the early hours, just in time for the streetcars to start clanking by under my window, I dozed off to a rest bothered by vicious dreams and the blackness of total disappointment. As I told my wife in a letter that early morning, my sorrow was so deep that I could hardly breathe.

The next evening I went out to dinner with Topic and the British team, consisting of Ruppert Bruce-Mitford and his assistant, Peter Lasko. When we met, Bruce-Mitford smiled confidently, and with that special brand of warmth reserved for losers like me, said, "Mr. Hoving, I imagine you feel somewhat like Paul Revere."

Put up a show of utter confidence, I thought, and did. After all, we *had* the money—or almost the money. They didn't yet have theirs.

This was my first report to the Museum:

The British Museum gets an option until midnight January 30th. Topic has sworn that no matter what price we try to offer and no matter whether the British Museum doesn't get the money, the price to us will never come down a single dollar from $600,000—no 10%—nothing less. After the end of January, Topic swears that if ever we want to discuss the purchase of the object, the price will be *more,* not less.

I have tried every argument and means of persuasion at my disposal. Believe me it has been going on hour after hour—over and over. Topic is obdurate. He has not changed one iota from his original stand. He simply will not break. He refuses to listen to any bargaining. So this is it.

Time is growing short. I met Bruce-Mitford and Lasko this evening for dinner with Topic—but no business was discussed. My distinct impression is that they do not have all the money yet but have an excellent chance for it.

I want to confirm in writing that Topic has read the bill of sale and legal title in both German and English and has agreed to sign it before the U.S. Consul.

A few days later, on January 15th:

The British government is willing to go to 150,000 (Sterling). The team will try to get the rest from a donor. They begged for a delay until the 10th of February but Topic said no, since I'm sitting in this back pocket.

Next day:

Was with Topic from 8:30 a.m. to 6:00 p.m. I tested him out all day. No change. There is one very important point the English don't know, nor does Topic; namely, that we have *not* all the money voted. If he knew this for sure he would cut us out of our chance that the English can't make it. I have thus been forced into a difficult and extremely wary position.

He then said if we were thinking at all of bargaining he would give the English all the time they needed—since he wants to make it absolutely certain that we *know* the price to us is $600,000 and to the English £200,000. I have gotten around this blunt question: "Are you willing to pay now?" by twisting the conversation to reply: "Yes, I, Hoving, know your full price to us is $600,000."

I have two alternatives:

1. If you *do* decide to vote extra money which I firmly believe we *must* do, I must have a check certified at the Leu Bank in Topic's name as far as possible before the witching hour of midnight 30 January. If the English say *no* early (a remote possibility) he will expect prompt payment which I can stall only so long. I am fine now for a week more or so.

2. If you do *not* vote the extra money, I suggest our immediate indication to the English. This gesture will put us in good light. I can explain to Topic by saying we cede owing to fact that English need English cross more than we—who have a variety of other important offers. This will put us in a good position for him in the future—for there are other things of his that might come up (God knows why I would want to go through this again!). It would also be an honest and responsible thing to do for the British.

But, of course, *I* feel alternative #2 would be a sorry decision.

On the same day I wrote Peg Freeman:

Peg—please *push* Jim. But don't annoy him. We *must* have this thing. We *must* go to $600,000. Any idea you might have that will influence the raising of the $100,000, which we have in the bank, *use*. But *don't* say you know that's the difference.

At this point, living in Topic's hip pocket was becoming a terrible strain. How many straight days can you have breakfast, lunch, tea, dinner, and an evening beer with a "Yugoslav by birth, Austrian by citizenship, [who] lives in Tangiers, . . . and keeps most of his junk in the vault of the Unione Banque de Suisse"—and all in Italian? But among his dozens of anecdotes, several were spectacular: How he had met Adolf Hitler in a beer hall in Munich in the earliest days of his climb to power and had told him to his face that he was indeed mad. How he had been imprisoned during the war because of his opposition to the Nazi regime and how, just after the war, with the connivance of an unnamed American colonel in Berlin, he had managed to escape from the eastern sector with all his art treasures carefully loaded into an American army train. How his friend Marshal Tito had, after the war, begged him to run all the museums in Yugoslavia.

Most intriguing of all, how he had seen the first piece of the cross.

It was, Topic related, in 1930, when he was a poor art student and an apprentice restorer, traveling throughout Europe. While in Mons, he had visited an art dealer. He could remember the exact place but no street names. The dealer showed him a solid square block of golden walrus ivory. It had on one side the angel, symbol of Matthew, and on the other "a complicated scene with two tiers and many figures."

I realized with astonishment that he actually *must* have seen the cross's missing bottom square. The three existing blocks had on the front the symbols of the Evangelists. The angel of Matthew was the sole missing piece. The complicated two-tiered scene had to be the Harrowing of Hell, when Christ descended into the bowels of the earth, and breaking the doors, pulled out Adam and Eve and the blessed souls. The bottom of the cross would have been the appropriate place for the scene. And on the side just above the missing block the prophet was Jonah, whose experience in the belly of the whale was the standard Old Testament reference to the Harrowing of Hell.

Topic told me that years later, after the war, when he had come upon the cross, he instantly remembered the block he had seen in Mons. He went back to the same street, to the same shop, but the art dealer was gone. He never saw the piece again. "Perhaps, if you are lucky enough to purchase my great cross," he said, "you will chance upon the missing piece." Almost, but not quite, as it turned out.

The tension of waiting for the English decision, my own Board's decision on the additional $100,000 to complete the deal—if the English were unsuccessful—and being constantly with Topic began to debilitate me. Zurich became a depressing trap—cold, distant, gray. It was the worst winter in seventy-five years. The lake was frozen over. Nobody could quite remember *that*. I took off for four days to Engelberg to ski. I saw monks from the local monastery skiing in their habits, feet wide apart, going like mad, with their black dresses snapping like a hundred flags in the wind. And in the historic monastery itself, I saw a golden cross with the depiction of Moses Raising the Serpent in the Desert. The cross! Suddenly, halfway down a slope, I pulled up—what if I broke my damned leg and couldn't make the final meeting with Topic on the 30th of January! I returned to the Hotel Central. A cable from the Museum awaited me. I carried it unopened to the Stuberl of the hotel, ordered a whisky, bought a fine cigar, and put the cable in front of me for a while, looking at it like a high-roller in a seven-card stud game begging for a king to my straight flush. I opened it with closed eyes and laid it out. O.K., hit me! REQUEST GRANTED. DETAILS FOLLOW. RORIMER.

Rorimer had gone immediately to the Purchase Committee by phone upon receipt of my fish-or-cut-bait letter. His notes state that within three hours he obtained a quorum of ayes from Elihu Root, Jr., Charles Wrightsman, in Florida ("Essential for a thing like that"), Walter Baker, Irwin Untermyer, Arthur Houghton, and Roland Redmond, the President.

In the detailed letter that came the next day Rorimer wrote: "Our funds are sufficient for me to have what I want and I am a spoiled boy. You can be that later on when you grow to be my age."

I considered it a coin toss. At least we had tried our very best. Several days passed. The check did not arrive. I telephoned Ken Loughry, the Museum's treasurer. There would be no check. The decision had been made to transfer the funds from Morgan Guaranty to the Unione Banque de Suisse. I thought it idiotic for the Museum not to trust me at *this* point. Was I really going to fly off to Brazil? The certified check would have cost nothing. The transfer of funds cost $2,300.

January 30. I met Topic for a late dinner. "Well, you may have won," he said, "but if the British telephone and give me their word that they have the money, it is theirs." As we were finishing dinner he was called to the phone. "They have asked me for a two-day extension," he told me. "Do they have the money yet?" I asked. "Not yet."

Topic told me that he hoped I would not win the cross. "It would be so easy for me to see it in the British Museum," he said. "But surely your health will improve so that you could come to see it at The Cloisters," I said. "It is not a question of my health," he replied.

We waited. At midnight Topic shrugged "I believe my cross is yours," he said, "but I believe you should buy one or two other objects in my collection, too." "Look, my friend," I said, "in the Unione Banque de Suisse there is a transfer of funds in your name for $600,000. One more word on any other object and you'll never see it. I will walk out of this place, and you will never see me or anyone else from the Metropolitan again." He laughed, said that it was all in jest, and ordered champagne. We shook hands and signed the cork for old times' sake.

February 1:

> Dear Peg, What a squeaker! The agonies of that last day! I read five mystery stories (and I don't remember a word of any). Let me say one thing: *Vive de Gaulle!* If Common Market hadn't collapsed—thus making Chancellor of Exchequer Maudling extremely busy—they might have gotten it."

A cable from the Medieval Department: HURRAH.

Topic and I first went to the American Consul to sign and have witnessed the guarantee of title and bill of sale, then to the bank where a poker-faced official handled the transfer of funds as if it were a bus ticket. But then he asked if he could see the work of art. Down in the vault, watching the head of the art-shipping firm, M.A.T. Transport, himself carefully cut the special box and wrap the object, the bank official said, "Now I see that it is surely worth this large sum of money!"

I saw Topic once again after that experience. It was conveyed to us that he had a portfolio of drawings by Goya that he might wish to sell. The drawings were not by Goya.

Just last year I was in bed late at night reading the fascinating tale of the exploits of General Reinhard Gehlen, the twentieth-century Nazi superspy, THE GENERAL WAS A SPY by Heinz Höhne and Herman Zolling. On page 158, I noted the following with great amusement: "The Czechs were still trying to replace their arrested agents when the ORG discovered another network—a spy ring run by the Yugoslav secret service. . . . head of the Yugoslav intelligence service in Germany is a certain Topic, alias Mimara, a museum custodian by profession. He is a member of the Yugoslav Restitution and Reparations Commission in the U.S. Zone. In 1947 Topic was expelled from Säckingen by the French for currency offenses; he went first to Berlin and thence to Frankfurt-am-Main; he is now in Munich."

Soon after we had the cross at the Museum, Kurt Weitzmann showed us an old photograph he had found in the files of Adolph Goldschmidt. It was of a square piece of walrus ivory carved with a scene of Christ being brought before the High Priest Caiphas. The piece was unquestionably part of the cross. On the back of the photo, in Goldschmidt's hand, was the information that a Mrs. Fuld of Frankfurt had shown the ivory to Goldschmidt in Berlin in 1932. Goldschmidt had added the notation: "English, 12th century (?)."

Our inquiries in Frankfurt did not take us far. The Fulds, before World War II, had been the principal stockholders and managers of several telephone companies. There seemed to be no members of the family left in Frankfurt.

Rorimer suggested that I show a copy of Goldschmidt's photo to Saemy Rosenberg, head of the firm of Rosenberg and Stiebel. He had sold The Cloisters some of its finest treasures, and his eye and knowledge were such that any time he telephone me to say, "I believe I have just received something that would be perfect for The Cloisters," I would go at once to his gallery on Fifty-seventh Street. Invariably we bought the piece.

Rosenberg, as Rorimer had anticipated, recalled the Fulds. In the early twenties he had sold the family a few modest items, though not the ivory. He had never seen the ivory, and he was not impressed by what he could see of it in my photograph. I had been sworn by Rorimer not to reveal why we wanted the piece. Rosenberg did not know if any of the Fulds were still alive, but he said he would try to track down the ivory for us. His lack of interest in the photograph suggested that he did not consider the ivory a worthy item for The Cloisters.

With this phase of the chase begun, I sent some fifty form letters and copies of the photo to colleagues and medievalists around the world.

The news was negative for several months. Especially discouraging was the word from Saemy Rosenberg that he had scoured all his European contacts and found nothing. I was then deep in the research, finding strong relationships between the cross and the Abbey of Bury St. Edmunds under its great and energetic abbot, Samson de Tottington. Full of excitement about my work, I disregarded Rorimer's instructions and told Rosenberg the full story of the cross. As I did so, I showed him the very fine photographs we had made of it in the Museum. As I had hoped, Rosenberg felt the spur. Within a month he had found the ivory for us. It was owned by a niece of the original owner, an elderly woman in Frankfurt. Not a collector herself, she had kept the piece for sentimental reasons. She was willing to sell it to us for $12,000. How had Saemy done it? By direct approach, he said. Since the woman was by no means a connoisseur, he had told her that the mighty Metropolitan Museum coveted her ivory and she should name her price. She had settled on a sum she considered astronomical. Unorthodox methods are sometimes the best.

But there is still more to tell about our cross—and one more example to mention of our new way of collecting extraordinary works of art.

Nearly six years after we acquired the cross, Florens Deuchler, then director of The Cloisters, on a visit to the Kunstindustrimuseet in Oslo, spotted a splendid walrus-ivory figure of Christ that seemed to be a possible candidate for the missing corpus of the cross. The figure was lent to us, and it was found to fit quite neatly in the empty place. Most experts today believe that we found the original corpus, made at Bury St. Edmunds around 1150. We and the museum in Oslo now share in the benefits of our mutual collecting and scholarship, in that each institution takes its turn in exhibiting, for a term of three years, the reunited elements of the cross.

Appendix 1

Dear

1. The Metropolitan Museum of Art in New York is considering the purchase of the following work of art which, to the best of our knowledge, is unpublished (photograph attached as Appendix I).

    a) Subject _____

    b) Material _____

    c) Dimensions _____

    d) Condition _____

2. In this form letter we should like to ask whether you, your ministry or service, have any information concerning the provenance or previous ownership of the described work of art.

3. We would appreciate hearing from you at your earliest convenience. If after 45 days we have received no reply from you, we shall assume you have no information concerning the above mentioned work of art.

4. At your early convenience, we would appreciate the return of the enclosed photograph.

Very truly yours,

Ashton Hawkins
Secretary

Appendix 2

CONVENTION
BETWEEN
INSTITUTO NACIONAL DE
ANTROPOLOGIA E HISTORIA
AND
THE METROPOLITAN MUSEUM OF ART

1. WHEREAS both the Instituto Nacional de Antropologia e Historia (here-inafter referred to as "the Institute") and The Metropolitan Museum of Art (hereinafter referred to as "the Museum") are engaged in developing and spreading the knowledge of art on a world-wide scale as a means of peaceful coexistence;
2. WHEREAS the Institute and the Museum, the former a Governmental legal entity and the latter a private legal entity, are the custodians of artistic resources, collections, and other manifestations of art, culture and history, and use these exclusively for scientific, educational and cultural purposes by exhibiting them publicly and conserving them for posterity;
3. WHEREAS full scientific understanding and a full exchange of information and ideas, as well as the wisest use of the artistic resources in their custody, is of mutual interest for the peoples of the United States of America and México;
4. WHEREAS under Mexican law and the Charter, Constitution and By-Laws of the Museum there are practical means for advantageous international negotiations and transactions, which do not impair the sovereignty of México nor contravene the Charter, Constitution and By-Laws of the Museum; and
5. WHEREAS, after a careful review of all the legal, moral, technical, scientific, cultural and artistic aspects without finding any objection of any kind, the

Institute, in full exercise of the powers granted to it by Articles I and II of its Ley orgánica on the one hand, and the Museum, in conformity with its Charter, Constitution and By-laws on the other, have agreed to conclude a Convention for artistic, scientific and cultural exchanges based upon the following

CLAUSES:

FIRST. The Institute and the Museum mutually agree to lend works of art to each other for public exhibition, as well as to exchange artistic, scientific and educational information and knowledge in the fields of art and art history. The loan of objects by the Institute will be subject in every case to compliance with the provisions of Mexican law; and the loan of objects by the Museum will be subject in every case to the rules and policies of the Board of Trustees of the Museum. Those objects which because of their fragility might suffer irreparable damage or deterioration are not included within the terms of this Convention.

SECOND. The term of the present Convention shall be for twenty-five years, subject to renewal by mutual agreement.

THIRD. The Institute and the Museum agree to pay all the costs which full exercise of the rights granted to each under this Convention requires. However, as regards insurance, neither the Institute nor the Museum shall have an obligation to insure works of art received on loan, but both the Institute and the Museum in their discretion may insure their own property provided that the policy of insurance shall contain an express waiver of subrogation in favor of the borrower and that the insurance carrier shall give a certified copy of such waiver to the borrower.

Notwithstanding the foregoing, each of the parties hereby grant a reciprocal release to the other from any responsibility arising from the loss, deterioration or damage which the art works, belonging to the lender, may suffer for any reason during the life of this Convention.

FOURTH. The Institute and the Museum agree to exhibit publicly, with all the security measures which the case may require, objects which they may mutually lend, informing the public that such exhibition is made possible as a result of this Convention for reciprocity.

FIFTH. The Institute and the Museum agree to establish a practical *modus operandi* to facilitate normal operations, selection of objects, and documentary legal formalities arising out of this Convention.

SIXTH. The Institute and the Museum agree to discuss and settle any matter which has not been foreseen in this Convention.

SEVENTH. The Institute and the Museum agree that as this is a cultural Convention for reciprocal benefit it may be cancelled when either of the two parties desires, provided that no such cancellation shall take place before the expiration of three years from the date upon which the Convention is signed. A period of one year, commencing from the date of cancellation of the Convention shall be allowed for the return of objects mutually lent and for the cessation of scientific services or exchanges which have been established.

EIGHTH. In all matters relating to the present Convention, both parties expressly agree to submit to the jurisdiction of the competent Federal Courts of México, the Museum hereby expressly waiving any right it may have to appeal to any other forum by reason of its nationality or domicile, and the Institute hereby waiving any right it may have to plead sovereign immunity by reason of its being an agency of the Federal Government of México.

NINTH. The parties agree to sign this Convention in México City and to carry it out commencing the 30th day of January, 1968.

TENTH. This Convention shall become effective on the date upon which it shall be ratified by the Constitutional Secretary of Public Education of the Government of the United Mexican States and registered according to protocol before the authorities of the Secretariat of Foreign Affairs.

México, D.F. 30th of January, 1968.

signed:

_____

Agustin Yáñez,
Secretario de Educación Pública.

_____   _____

Jorge Enciso,
Sub-Director Administrativo
Instituto Nacional de Antropología
e Historia.

Thomas Hoving,
Director
Metropolitan Museum of
Art

_____   _____

Ignacio Bernal,
Sub-Director Técnico
Instituto Nacional de Antropo-
logía e Historia

Dudley T. Easby,
Secretario
Metropolitan Museum of
Art

_____

Dr. Daniel Rubín de la
Borbolla
Special Representative
of the Metropolitan
Museum of Art

Appendix 3

The Department of American Paintings and Sculpture
by John K. Howat, Curator

1. It is generally agreed that the collection of this Department, comprised of American paintings, miniatures, drawings, and sculptures of the eighteenth and nineteenth centuries, is the largest, most comprehensive, and best such collection in the nation. Collections in Boston, Brooklyn, Philadelphia, Washington, and Detroit have similar value, but are less comprehensive.
2. Aims of the Department with regard to the collections:
   A. Curate and acquire objects of highest quality by artists of genuine interest.
   B. Collect and display American art in a comprehensive manner, aiming to show its various and most important manifestations, including the individual development of the most important artists. The collection is regarded as an important art-historical reference tool, in addition to its primary value as a collection of esthetically important individual objects. The study collection concept is embraced in plans for the new American Bicentennial Wing.
   C. Provide objects for display in "period room" context in the new American Bicentennial Wing, in addition to gallery and study collection installations.
3. Present character of the collection.
   A. Sculpture. The collection of 205 pieces of American sculpture (43 statues, 88 statuettes, 54 busts, and 20 reliefs) is one of the largest and finest in the country. Especially well represented in the collection are Hiram Powers, Thomas Crawford, William Wetmore Story, William H. Rinehart, Randolph Rogers, John Quincy Adams Ward, Frederick MacMonnies, Augustus Saint-Gaudens, Daniel Chester French, Olin Warner, and Frederic Remington. There remain the following weaknesses in the collection: folk

sculpture, early wood and stone carving, and works by Horatio Greenough, William Rush, Hezekiah Augur, John Frazee, and Thomas Eakins.

The high esthetic quality and the comprehensive scope of the collection is largely the result of the efforts of Daniel Chester French, the noted American sculptor, who was the Chairman of the Trustees' Committee on Sculpture for the Museum from 1905 until his death in 1931. This rich collection, when exhibited in the American Bicentennial Wing, will play a major role in the continuing revival of interest in the field of American sculpture.

B. Miniatures. This collection, acquired primarily through gift and bequest, is excellent and sizable, containing approximately 260 items, the large majority of which were executed before 1860. Works by over 90 artists are represented including strong representation by Robert Field, Charles Fraser, Robert Fulton, Sarah Goodrich, Edward Greene Malbone, Charles Willson Peale, James Peale, John Ramage, Walter Robertson, Benjamin Trott, and James Wood. It is an excellent display and reference collection.

C. Watercolors and Drawings. This collection, which is housed and available for study in the Drawings Department, contains approximately 1,500 objects, the great majority of which are of the nineteenth century. Included are large and important holdings of works on paper by Mary Cassatt, John Singleton Copley, Arthur B. Davies, A. J. Davis, Thomas Eakins, Winslow Homer, John LaFarge, William Trost Richards, John Singer Sargent, Thomas Sully, William Guy Wall, and James A. McN. Whistler. Also there is the Edward W. C. Arnold Collection of New York Prints, Maps, and Pictures, which contains numerous drawings and watercolor views of the city and environs. There are also a sizable number of American naive drawings and watercolors given to the Museum by Edgar William and Bernice Chrysler Garbisch. The Department hopes to continue adding fine examples to the collection, with particular emphasis on drawings and watercolors of the late eighteenth and first half of the nineteenth century.

D. Paintings. This collection is extraordinarily fine and comprehensive, a leader among such collections representing approximately 950 paintings by 350 artists of the eighteenth, nineteenth, and early twentieth centuries. It contains sizable groups of paintings by Ralph Blakelock, Mary Cassatt, William Merritt Chase, Frederic E. Church, Thomas Cole, John Singleton Copley, Jasper Cropsey, Arthur B. Davies, Asher B. Durand, Thomas Eakins, Ralph Earl, Charles L. Elliott, William Morris Hunt, Daniel Huntington, George Inness, John Wesley Jarvis, Eastman Johnson, John F. Kensett, William Sidney Mount, Charles Willson Peale, Albert Pinkham Ryder, John Singer Sargent, Gilbert Stuart, Thomas Sully, John Trumbull, Samuel Waldo and William Jewett, Benjamin West, James A. McN. Whistler, and Alexander

Wyant. The collection is strongest in portraiture of the late eighteenth and all of the nineteenth century and landscape painting of the nineteenth century. The collection has weaknesses in portraiture of the late seventeenth and early eighteenth century, early nineteenth-century landscape and history painting, still life and genre painting of the nineteenth century, certain mid-nineteenth century landscapists, and "Western" and non-East Coast subjects. In recent years pictures by Matthew Pratt, John Durand, Francis Edmonds, Martin Johnson Heade, Fitz Hugh Lane, William Bradford, and Robert Duncanson have been added to the collection to strengthen some of these areas, but there remain many artists who should be represented in the collection by important works. Among them, to name but a few that vary in rarity, are Cosmo Alexander, Thomas Birch, Winthrop Chandler, James Clonney, Charles Deas, George Durrie, Seth Eastman, Henry Farny, Alvan Fisher, John Francis, John Greenwood, Francis Guy, Charles Bird King, John Krimmel, Alfred Jacob Miller, Rubens Peale, William Ranney, William Rimmer, Charles Russell, Robert Salmon, John Mix Stanley, Pieter Vanderlyn, and Richard Woodville.

The Acquisition of a Jewellike Sphinx

CHRISTINE LILYQUIST

Curator, Egyptian Art

Perhaps no single object in the Egyptian collection illustrates a department's persistent interest in a work as much as the blue faience sphinx of Amenhotep III acquired in 1972.

This exquisite sculpture has a brilliant blue glaze, a fineness of detail, and a sleekness of modeling that give it a jewellike appearance. It is small (9⅞" long), but the detail and care exhibited in it give it extraordinary presence. The king wears a pleated linen headcloth, bracelets on his arms,

FIGURE 14. Sphinx of Amenhotep III. Egyptian. 1417–1379 B.C. Faience. Purchase, Lila Acheson Wallace Fund, Inc., Gift, 1972.125

and offers jars of wine or milk to a god. The sculpture was perhaps made as a New Year's gift for King Amenhotep III, whose name is incised on the chest. It may have been a dedication by that king for a temple—or an item for the king's own tomb.

The sculpture came to the attention of the Egyptian Department in January 1936 through a Cairo banker who occasionally alerted the department to important objects. The banker wrote to then curator Herbert Winlock that a unique item "of finest workmanship" would be available for inspection in London the following summer; the price was considerable in view of the current market in Egyptian antiquities. During that summer the department learned that the owner of the sphinx was Howard Carter. It did not pursue the matter, however, perhaps because the original provenance of the sphinx seemed problematic, despite the banker's word that Carter had bought the object in Cairo. Howard Carter died in 1939, and left his house at Thebes and its contents to the Metropolitan Museum; Harry Burton, the Metropolitan's expedition photographer, was named one of two executors of the estate. At the time, there still seems to have been a question as to the provenance of the sphinx. However, the object was probated, whereas some items in Carter's London house were not, and nothing in Carter's house at Thebes gave a clue as to the provenance of the sphinx. The executors pressed the Metropolitan to buy it, one executor setting a high price on it in order to benefit the estate, and Mr. Burton (the only member of the department who had seen the object) sincerely wanted it to go to the Metropolitan. However, before other members of the Museum staff or the Trustees could see the object, the London dealer Spink was able to find a client willing to pay its price, and the sphinx found its home at the Cranbrook Foundation in Bloomfield Hills, Michigan.

One would have thought the matter settled then. But forty-two years later, in 1972, the Trustees of the Cranbrook Academy of Art decided to focus efforts on their art school and to dispose of part of their collection. Important objects were put up for auction at (Sotheby) Parke-Bernet in New York, and once again the blue faience sphinx appeared. This time it was the star attraction of a major sale, and museum curators, private collectors, and dealers excitedly discussed the questions of who might acquire the sphinx and how high the bidding might go. One of the Metropolitan's own trustees, Charles Wrightsman, was keenly interested in acquiring the sphinx, but stepped aside when it became clear that the Museum itself wanted it.

By this time it was not only the quality of the object that was desirable; the sphinx would make a magnificent contribution to the reinstallation of the Museum's Egyptian collection. This installation (the first part of which will open in February 1976) was to be a chronological arrangement in which pictures of specific people in specific periods were to be brought together to create a sense of Egyptian time and culture. For Amenhotep III there were to be wall paintings, pottery, glass, bronze, and faience objects from his palace; statues of Sekhmet from his temple for Mut; a life-size quartzite head of him and a fragment in jasper of his wife, Queen Tiye; representations of his officials; and funerary equipment of his father-in-law. The Museum had a major collection of art from this glorious and elegant period and the sphinx would not only highlight that array, but the array was seen as a meaningful setting for the sphinx.

Theodore Rousseau, Curator in Chief in 1972, bid on the object for the Museum one Thursday afternoon in April, but when the auction was concluded it was learned that the sphinx had gone to a mysterious art-world personality who had plans for founding a new museum. The Metropolitan had been third-highest bidder. The highest bidder's available funds were apparently less than his expectations, however, and thirty days elapsed without the sphinx being claimed. Parke-Bernet, with Cranbrook's consent, then approached the second-highest bidder, and although this party was initially interested in paying a sum close to its bid in the auction, it cancelled its offer after several weeks. The gallery then entered into discussions with the Metropolitan Museum. At that point we had our fourth chance to acquire the sphinx, and the Egyptian Department's great friend, Lila Acheson Wallace, graciously offered to purchase the sculpture for the Museum. Since then it has had the preeminent place in the Egyptian Gold Room, and of course will be starred in the new installation.

A Curator's Choice

DIETRICH von BOTHMER

Chairman, Greek and Roman Art

The Greek and Roman Department traces its history back to the very beginning of the Museum, since the first numbered object in the official register is a Roman sarcophagus from Tarsos. In the early years the Museum's growth in Greek and Roman art was impressive, though fortuitous: large collections were acquired by gift or purchase, but curatorial participation was not initiated until seventy years ago. With the appointment of Edward Robinson in 1905, a period of systematic collecting began that has brought about a balanced collection on a broad base, in which almost all the recognized categories of ancient art are well represented by hundreds of masterpieces of Greek and Roman art, now forever linked with the Museum and known to every student and connoisseur.

Acquisition is perhaps the most compelling instinct of a curator, and his aim to see his collection grow contributes toward the enrichment of an entire museum. Success in these matters, however, is not predictable and cannot be measured on graphs and charts. It depends on many factors, chief among them the availability of an object, the persuasive power of the curator, and the strong support of the Director at the crucial meeting of the Trustees' Acquisitions Committee. Money, which in the popular mind assumes an exaggerated role, is seldom an overriding consideration.

A curator of Greek and Roman art is by definition a classical archaeologist. A training in the classics, Greek, Latin, and ancient history is joined to a knowledge and understanding of ancient art. A Greek and Roman collection imposes the added task of illustrating all aspects of an ancient civilization. A Greek helmet or a Roman safety pin, not to mention lamps and loom weights, are legitimate components of the collection, and the boundaries between "utensils" and "works of art" are not always marked. This, from the outset, separates us from other departments but does not bring us into conflict with them.

An equally important consideration is the history of survival. Much of the classical past is irretrievably lost, and most of what we now possess has been recovered from the ground or from the sea. The condition of these objects ranges from "intact" to "fragmentary," but we have become reconciled to the ravages of time and do not reject outright a statue that lacks its feet or a vase that has been broken.

There remains the question of preferences, which is often governed by prevailing taste or fashion. A curator who is concerned with the future of a museum and its collections must have catholic taste and cultivate historic impartiality. In the classical field, first place was accorded for several centuries to the "classic," which is to say objects of the fifth and fourth centuries B.C. A hundred years ago, "archaic" art became recognized and gradually even appreciated, and in this century the even earlier civilization of the Bronze Age has come into its own. Modern art has contributed to a reappraisal of Cycladic marble sculptures, and other trends have restored the art of the Hellentistic age to a position of great esteem.

Many European museums, through government allocations or by active participation in excavations, have secured great bodies of ancient art: the Campana collection of vases in the Louvre, the Pergamon altar in Berlin, the Aegina pediments in Munich, or the Elgin marbles in the British Museum. Most of our acquisitions, however, have been made by seizing the limited opportunities on the art market and by gifts and bequests of private collectors. Every one of our objects has a story behind its acquisition: how it was found, and why it was chosen for recommendation by the curator; taken together, the works of art reveal some of the principles that govern the growth of the collection.

A favorite phrase often heard in the board room was that such and such a purchase would "fill a gap in the collection," and, indeed, the bigger the scope of a department, the more gaps there had to be. If, for example, a certain shape of Greek vase was not yet represented, it was natural to be on the lookout for such a form and to acquire an example of it when it appeared on the market. By the same token, in so rich a field for

FIGURE 15. Bronze hydria with lid. Greek. 3rd century B.C. Rogers Fund, 66.11.12

collectors as Greek vases, a constant watch had to be kept for representative works by the great vase-painters. No detailed lists are kept of
our gaps, but we are reminded of them every time we visit other great
museums or keep abreast of publications in the field. Only a small percentage of objects appear at public auctions, the catalogues of which can
be studied beforehand. Many more change hands privately and can be
spotted only by seeking out dealers and collectors here and abroad. If
we have been able to fill some of our gaps, it has not always been through
sheer dogged determination; luck also enters into it.

A Hellenistic bronze hydria was obtained at Sotheby's in 1966 for the
incredibly low price of £50, mostly because the auctioneers, unfamiliar
with its provenance and past publication, had taken it to be a modern
reproduction, did not illustrate it, and described it in the special code
employed for forgeries. Because of its low price, the U.S. Customs officials
doubted its authenticity and were reluctant to let it in duty free; discreet
inquiries among New York dealers for an expert on bronze hydriai,
however, revealed to the Customs service that I was the authority to be
consulted, and with this the examination was concluded in our favor. On
another occasion we were offered the fragmentary leg of a bronze tripod
with an engraved plaque showing Bellerophon and the Chimaera. The
object was examined in Basel, and, as it was of the seventh century B.C.,
executed in an unusual style, it was recommended for purchase. A week
later a dealer in Geneva showed me another plaque in the same style; this
time Peleus and Thetis were depicted. As I had carefully traced the
contours of the Basel plaque, I perceived at once that the Geneva plaque
joined it; this was further confirmed by the position of the ancient rivets
that had attached the plaques to the tripod leg. The Geneva plaque, too,
was recommended for purchase, and both were bought by the Trustees
at the same meeting. That today they bear two different accession numbers
reflects only the excessive accuracy of our registration system; one plaque
arrived at Christmas time, and the other did not clear customs until after
the new year.

Keeping together antiquities that belong with each other is, of course,
one of the sacred duties of an archaeologist. At the Metropolitan we have
not always been lucky. In the fall of 1965 a unique pair of Attic vases
was offered for sale. They complement one another, and, as there are no
other Attic parallels, it may be assumed that they were not only found
together but in all probability were made that way. One lacked its foot
and stem and repeated its painted subject, a sphinx, on obverse and

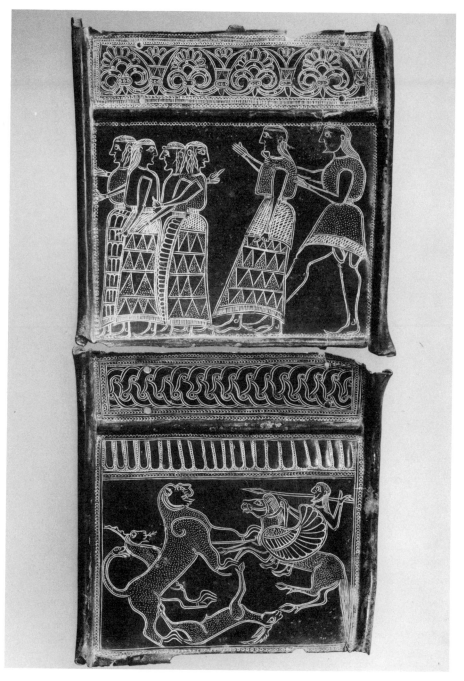

FIGURE 16. Bronze tripod leg. Greek. Mid-7th century B.C. Purchase, Huntley Bequest,
58.11.6a–d, 59.11.1

FIGURE 17. Vase: side A, iris; B, sphinx. Attic. About 520 B.C. Louis V. Bell Fund, 65.11.14

FIGURE 18. Group of bronze and silver objects. Greek. 4th and 3rd centuries B.C. Bequest of Walter C. Baker, 1972.118.88, 161–164

reverse, whereas the other was more complete and had two different subjects. Since the price for both was considered high, the Trustees authorized the purchase of only one—the "better one." The vendor would not agree to this, and for a time it looked as if this extraordinary pair would be lost to us. Fortunately a friend of the Museum, Norbert Schimmel, bought the less complete piece. The two vases are now separated, but at least they are in the same city.

There are other instances when the Museum benefited from the enlightened attitude of collectors. In the fall of 1951 a Munich collector offered us, for only $3,000, a famous hoard of silver vases found with a bronze situla in Prusias. For some reason—not clear then and less so now—the curator's recommendation was turned down. But all was not lost: Walter C. Baker, a collector who remained a friend of this department for forty years, acquired the group. Thanks to the munificent bequest of his classical collection, this group is today in the museum to which it had first been offered. This is only a small part of what the department and the Museum owe to Mr. Baker.

The close relations that curators develop with collectors are an integral part of their activities. Often a collector knows that a work of art is available long before the curator hears of it and will tell the curator what he has seen or show him what he has bought. In each case the Museum profits from the open exchange of information. Moreover, a collector does not need an authorization from a Board of Trustees to buy: he can act quickly. When the vast collection of the late Joseph Brummer was privately offered to museums and a few collectors before its public sale in 1949, the Metropolitan could not possibly acquire all the objects it desired. Moreover, when the lists of our preferences were drawn up, several departments found themselves competing for the limited purchase funds. The list of Greek and Roman objects was drastically reduced, and many a good piece was reluctantly deleted. But again, thanks to private help, my department did not lose everything.

At just about that time, Alastair Bradley Martin began forming a collection and selected objects the Museum liked but could not buy. In the Greek and Roman field Mr. Martin acquired a splended Attic vase—a black-figured plate with the moving scene of an Amazon carrying a dead comrade from the battlefield—and a rare red-figured vase in the shape of an egg that has for its subject the abduction of Helen. Both objects were on loan to the Museum for more than a quarter of a century and were recently given to us along with a Cycladic statuette.

Cycladic art is an area of collecting that has been difficult for the Museum. Before the Second World War, it was only occasionally offered by dealers and seldom appeared at public auction; during this period the Museum acquired a few statuettes, but after the war interest grew and prices soared. Yet the Museum did succeed in acquiring the superb seated harp-player from the estate of Joseph Brummer. With so many private collectors—many of them in New York—competing for Cycladic art, the need to develop this particular area did not seem to be quite so urgent; much of the Cycladic sculpture in the Museum today came to us as a gift or bequest or is here on loan. In addition to the gift from Mr. Martin, he has lent us a large marble head; three statuettes are the bequest of Mr. Baker, and a very large statuette, as well as a head, are the gifts of Christos G. Bastis. A close friend and supporter of the department for almost thirty years, Mr. Bastis began lending us objects from his collection in 1948; for many years he regularly donated money to the curatorial purchase fund. He has also given us several of his vases.

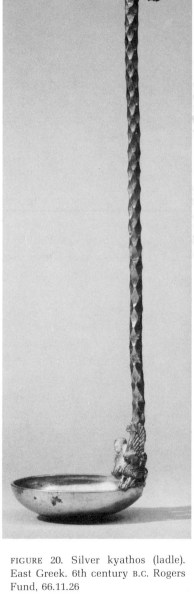

FIGURE 19. Silver oinochoe (jug) with handle in the form of a youth. East Greek. 6th century B.C. Rogers Fund, 66.11.23

FIGURE 20. Silver kyathos (ladle). East Greek. 6th century B.C. Rogers Fund, 66.11.26

It is against this background and the climate for collecting that our acquisitions must be judged. Every year has brought new challenges, and in spite of occasional setbacks, progress can be reported on all fronts. The obvious quality of many recent acquisitions requires no special explanation, let alone justification, but one large group stands apart and should be introduced properly.

In the summer of 1966 I was shown by a New York dealer a dazzling assembly of silver vases, gold ornaments, and personal jewelry, all said to have been found together, and all certainly of the same style and period. Nothing quite like it had ever come on the market before, and no other museum had anything comparable in scope and quality dating to the same period. In fact, many of the shapes had not been encountered before in silver, though ancient authors often wrote of silver vessels, and temple inventories, recorded in inscriptions, list such treasures in great quantity. The opportunity presented more than the normal challenge to negotiate successfully for an expensive purchase: a new chapter in our knowledge of ancient art seemed to have opened up. The presentation of these objects proved difficult, for the very novelty of such a group precluded comparisons with other purchases. This group came up twice before the Acquisitions Committee, and the second time I had eloquent help from Pierre Amandry, then at Princeton, and an expert on gold and silver. Amandry, who had catalogued the Stathatos collection in Athens—one of the few that contained objects comparable with some of the vases in our group—answered the committee's questions with authority and enthusiasm, and, thanks to him, neither the value nor the age of the objects was doubted. At the close of the second session there remained only the obstacle of price. This was speedily overcome by the prompt and generous help of a large group of friends of the department who understood the significance of the proposed purchase. Their enthusiastic response to our needs highlights the close relations between the Museum and the public.

This purchase was followed by another in 1968, similar to the previous one in period and style, but introducing many new shapes and ornaments. The 1968 purchase was made in New York; in the years that followed, other groups appeared on the European market and were likewise purchased—most recently at Sotheby's in 1972. In the meantime some smaller lots had been acquired by the Ashmolean Museum, Oxford, and by the Antikenabteilung of the Stiftung Preussischer Kulturbesitz in Berlin, but the more than two hundred items now in the Museum and exhibited here

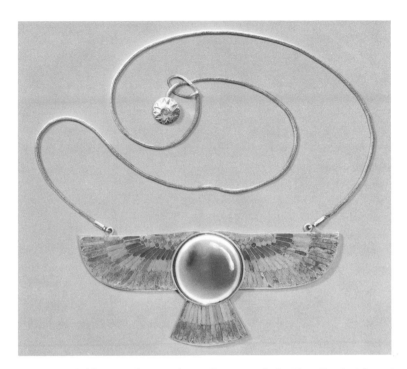

FIGURE 21. Gold pectoral: winged sun-disc on a chain. East Greek, 6th century B.C. Rogers Fund, 68.11.26

FIGURE 22. Calyx krater: Sleep and Death lifting the body of Sarpedon. Attic. About 515 B.C. Signed by Euxitheos as potter and Euphronios as painter. Bequest of Joseph H. Durkee, Gift of Darius Ogden Mills, and Gift of Mr. and Mrs. C. Ruxton Love, by exchange, 1972.11.10

for the first time as a group are easily the best illustration of what collecting for a museum is all about. It would have been easy to select only the more spectacular objects, but such selectivity would have been misplaced, as it would have destroyed most of the knowledge we gain from having reasonably intact groups. Instead of creating more gaps that would eventually have to be filled, we have acquired something that will aid scholarship and appreciation of ancient art for a long time to come.

Though many lament that the golden age of collecting is over, our own experience has been that opportunities continue to arise. Only three years ago the finest vase by Euphronios was bought by the Museum, and I do not believe that this will be the last vase we will acquire. A liberal policy of long-term exchanges among American public collections has at last begun. Last year the Museum of Fine Arts, Boston, agreed to lend us the nozzle of an archaic marble lamp. The lamp is in our collection and the pieces had become separated more than seventy years ago. In exchange, we lent the Museum of Fine Arts two Cypriot sculptures. Exchanges of vase fragments are under way with the Musée du Louvre and with the Vatican Museum. We hope that in time the jealous rivalries of the past will be replaced by the more enlightened attitude that treats art—no matter where it is housed—as a universal heritage to be shared and enjoyed by all.

The Lure
of the
Carpet

RICHARD ETTINGHAUSEN

Consultative Chairman, Islamic Art

Every art lover knows that many works of art contain a special inner force. It cannot be defined in the usual esthetic terms because it goes beyond the representational, symbolic, and decorative aspects. In "primitive" civilizations this force is the so-called magic content. Or if the term "magic" is too strong, we might speak of this indefinable force as the mysteriously enticing power in the object: the peculiar appeal that it makes, causing a person to feel that he must possess it, just as he is possessed by it.

The art of the Islamic world is on the whole rational and of such a harmony that, in general, it appeals to our esthetic senses rather than to our emotions. Yet one has to admit that there are certain Persian miniatures, such as some in the Houghton *Shah-nameh,* where we immediately feel the seductive emotional pull, along with the peculiar effect it has on our proprietary urges.

There is, however, a category of Near Eastern art that has been widely believed to be imbued with magical qualities. This is the category of the carpet, especially the type used by Muslims to perform the five daily prayers. This belief in the carpet's magic can be found not only in western folklore, as in the flying carpets of fairy tales and magazine cartoons, but also in the Muslim world. The twelfth-century Iranian mystic Attar told of the ascetic Hasan al-Basri, who placed his prayer rug on the water of the Euphrates and invited the woman saint Rabia al-Adawiyya to join him there in prayer. She then threw her rug into the air and asked Hasan to join her in prayer up there. Such Iranian stories have been illustrated by Persian miniaturists from the late fifteenth century on.

Of course, aside from their magical qualities, oriental carpets have always had a strong esthetic appeal. In the Near East, carpets have, since the thirteenth century, challenged the artistic ingenuity of master weavers, who have given us some of the world's most fascinating patterned and colored compositions. It is a constant marvel how imaginative these weavers were in decorating a limited rectangular field in so many different and appealing ways. The Iranians, creators of some of the most sophisticated designs, developed two particularly satisfying themes: the royal hunt and the garden. The royal hunt carpets reminded the king of kings daily of his courage, strength, and superiority. And while an actual garden can only be enjoyed in spring and summer, the flowers on the knotted surrogate give constant pleasure, blooming all year round.

In the West, Islamic carpets have always been honored. Transported to Europe, despite their considerable weight, as early as about 1300, they soon exerted their special spell. They are prominent in Italian and other paintings in which they are usually set in a place of honor, or at least in a central position, for example, under the feet of saints or the Madonna's throne. They were hung over window sills and banisters on feast days. Coronations took place on them. In well-to-do homes, they were used as table covers. With the rise of the middle class, they became the ideal status symbol, and decorated the mansions of merchant princes and robber barons, as well as the homes of the otherwise thrifty bourgeoisie. Their attraction continues to this day. While there are only a handful of collectors of Persian or Indian miniatures, and a few more of Near Eastern pottery, there are comparatively large numbers of proud carpet owners. Visible proof of this situation is provided by the many rug societies in America, each with an astonishingly large and active membership. These were not founded, like Alcoholics Anonymous, to combat their common urge, but rather to encourage the condition. In their enthusiasm and happiness, the members are like fervent believers who know they have found the true path. Thus the evils that can threaten the blissful state—questions of cost, decay, and damages—are either ignored or heroically dealt with.

It is only natural that a person so mysteriously affected would never forget the circumstances of his first encounter with a particularly beautiful piece that subjected him forever to the magic appeal. In my case such an event occurred in the late nineteen-fifties in Vienna's Museum of Applied Arts, where the treasured carpets of the Hapsburgs are housed. Even more fascinating to me than the beautiful Persian, Indian, Turkish, and Caucasian pieces was an Egyptian carpet of the late fifteenth or early sixteenth century. It was a particularly large one, knotted with silk threads in twelve shimmering colors. Its kaleidoscopic arrangement of stars, medallions, octagons, squares, and triangles made it seem to me more like a fantastic dream than a fabric to cover a floor. Its basic layout seemed clear enough, yet the manner in which secondary units were combined and interlocked created a bewildering and enticing spectacle. Continued viewing and later study only reinforced my initial impression. Added to the esthetic impact was the mystery that has always surrounded the origin of the Mamluk carpets. They were traditionally associated with Damascus, although every student of the subject knew they had nothing to do with the Syrian capital. In 1921, they were correctly identified by Friedrich Sarre, one of the grand old masters of carpet research, who recognized the group as being of the late fifteenth or early sixteenth century and of Cairene manufacture.

Other perplexing aspects of these carpets have never been explained. Was this group inspired by earlier indigenous Egyptian art, especially Coptic fabrics, by marble floors in opus sectile technique, or by Mongol carpets? What was the relation of these carpets to Mamluk embroideries, the only contemporary medium with similar geometric elements? Was the small, common motif, a stemmed umbrella leaf, an updated rendition of the ancient Egyptian papyrus motif, or was it an Egyptian version of the Chinese brocade scroll? And why were these carpets created with the Persian, or Senna, knot if, during the preceding two hundred years, Egyptians had imported and admired Anatolian carpets knotted in the Turkish, or Gördes knot?

But these art-historical concerns paled into insignificance when I beheld the Mamluk masterpiece in the Vienna museum. I became sensitized to its type, unique in Islamic art, and now its magic began to work. My first wonder was whether there might be another outstanding piece of the same type, not in a museum, waiting to be discovered and enjoyed. Then—under the delicate promptings of the possessive urge—a second question arose: if such a carpet existed, could it be acquired for an appreciative museum? The answer to the first question, it turned out, was yes. There was, or at least there had been, such a piece. In the first comprehensive exhibition of Muslim art, held in Munich in 1910, a great Mamluk carpet was exhibited. It was at the time owned by the Galleria Simonetti, a firm in Rome. Although knotted only in wool, like most Mamluk carpets, it was even larger than the Hapsburg piece. And it was unique in that its composition was in five parts, instead of three, as in the Vienna and other large carpets. To judge from the illustration in the exhibition catalogue, the overall rendition of the field and border seemed clearer, although the interplay of primary and secondary motifs and colors still formed a fascinating aspect.

I made inquiries. Nobody seemed to know where the Simonetti carpet was. It had last been sold after 1937 when the owner, Luigi Pisa, being Jewish, had had to sell his treasures. Since the carpet seemed to have dropped from sight, the question of which happy museum might acquire it appeared of little importance. The Freer Gallery of Art, of which I was then head curator, was not a prospective owner anyway, since out of respect for another local public collection, The Textile Museum, it did not collect carpets. On the other hand, The Textile Museum, of which I was (and am) a trustee, would probably not be able to afford such a fine, hence expensive, piece.

In 1967 I left the Freer Gallery to become a professor at the Institute of Fine Arts of New York University. One day, on a possible buying visit to French and Company with the director and a trustee of a major museum, I was invited to look at a large carpet. It was unrolled for us: a Mamluk of unusual size and proportions, long and narrow, and of the finest quality, the colors pristine and beautiful. My first thought was that it looked much like my memory of the Simonetti. Then, in a flash, I realized that I was looking at *the* Simonetti.

As so often happens, the first encounter with an original, known previously only from black-and-white illustrations, brought some surprises.

FIGURE 23. *Carpet*. Egyptian. Probably 1460–1490. Wool. Fletcher Fund,
1970.105

Quite apart from my sudden awareness of the large size, the first strong impact was caused by the brilliant colors. In this huge piece, as in smaller rugs of the type, there were only three major colors: a claret red, a light green, and—less important—a light blue, with touches of yellow, gold, a darker green, white, and black. Yet in spite of the limited range, the effect was anything but restricted. On the contrary, possibly due to the sheen of the wool, the rich colors seemed to glow and even to vibrate. It was fascinating to see how the two principal colors balanced one another perfectly. Most of the patterns were formed by the green on a red ground, but a good deal of the design was in red and green. The border, made up of forms related to those in the field, showed the same treatment of green on red, and red on green. A curious aspect of these colors was that from one side, the lay of the lustrous pile made the greens look stronger, while from the other side the reds appeared more prominent. And I was struck by another difference between the photograph and the carpet itself. Certain parts—particularly the eight small stars around the center—seemed more important in the black-and-white version than when the rug was laid out flat on the floor. Only later did it become clear that the stars appear more distinctly when the carpet is suspended on a wall and specially lighted, as it would be for making a photograph.

My next impression was of how subtly the juxtaposed geometric forms avoided what might have been a hard and rigid design. It appeared that there were two principles used in organizing and unifying the design. For the larger units, an "encapsulating" scheme was employed. The large central figures consist of no less than six eight-pointed stars, one within the other, with octagons interspersed between them. The same arrangement was used with the two lateral figures, which are mainly combinations of circles as well as rounded and flattened polylobed shapes. The smaller end units consist of series of encapsulated octagons. The second compositional scheme is that of satellite arrangements framing the five focal elements. These forms are unified through a dense, repeating overall pattern, and also through the similarity of their shapes: all are either eight-sided, eight-rayed, or eight-lobed. With its limited but well-balanced color scheme and its intricately interlocked geometric configurations, the Simonetti carpet was obviously unique.

I examined it closely for wear. Despite its nearly five hundred years, it was in remarkably good condition. Only in a few black areas, where the iron dye mordant had eaten away the wool—as it always does—had repairs been made with a white wool that stood out too strongly. Much of the old pile—the very soul of the carpet—was well preserved.

But alas, even at this unexpected, happy juncture, there was another hitch. Robert Samuels, the head of French and Company, informed me that the carpet, which was jointly owned, could not yet be purchased, since one of the owners had not agreed to sell. While this appeared to represent only a temporary delay, a second factor was more serious: in spite of all my enthusiastic praise and thorough explanations, the museum trustee did not seem to have fallen under the spell of the carpet or at least had successfully resisted it and, in view of the price, there seemed to be little hope that his museum would acquire it. Sad as I was at the time about this disappointing situation, all that could be done by me in the following months was to go and see the carpet again and again as a kind of private indulgence. But enjoyable as these visits were, they were done with a heavy heart as one owner was still holding out and the carpet continued to be unavailable. We had come closer to a solution, but not yet close enough.

In April 1969 I joined the staff of The Metropolitan Museum of Art as Consultative Chairman of its Department of Islamic Art. Knowing of this treasure and its possible availability and also that the Metropolitan Museum had only a small and not too distinguished group of Mamluk carpets (the best piece having been given by its former President George Blumenthal in 1941), the chances for a happy ending seemed more promising. The only difficulty was that "the fish might get away." The visits to French and Company continued, but I could obtain from Mr. Samuels only a promise that the Metropolitan would at once be informed as soon as the Simonetti carpet was available at a given sum.

One day that happy hour did arrive, but the purchase had to be made within a week, as another buyer, offering a higher sum than the one quoted to the Museum, was lurking in the wings. An immediate decision was required, and there was no time to submit the object to a regular meeting of the Acquisitions Committee. Fortunately, the Director of the Museum and its President were as excited about the carpet as I, and a procedure existed for just such an emergency. Each Trustee could be approached directly with the proper recommendation and forms to obtain their consent. This was done quickly by messenger, and happily nobody was beyond our reach. The jinx had finally been broken and without further complications the old, famed Simonetti carpet entered our splendid collection of oriental carpets. Today, in accordance with its superb quality and historical importance, it is the centerpiece of our new Mamluk-Moorish gallery. The oldest complete carpet in our collection, it is also one of the finest.

One mystery, however, remains: the identity of the recent owners. All we learned is that the vendor had been a Swiss bank. In former times, individuals took pride in the possession of great works of art. Nowadays, regrettably, anonymity and depersonalization reign, and a work of art is too often a commodity, bought and sold by a corporation.

There is an epilogue. A short time after the purchase I met in Europe an old friend, a great and highly astute collector—one of those few who know all the secrets of the market and of the collecting world. I was warmly congratulated by him on this particular purchase. But then I also learned that a famous major museum had been anxious to acquire just this piece and that it had been willing to do so at a much higher price than we had paid because the Simonetti carpet was considered so outstanding as to represent alone the whole field of oriental carpet weaving. That statement left no doubt about the importance of our purchase.

The long hunt had indeed come to a happy ending.

Asian Art for the Metropolitan Museum

WEN FONG

Special Consultant for Far Eastern Affairs

More than any other major art museum in this country, The Metropolitan Museum of Art is primarily a museum of great collectors and their collections. Asian art at the Museum began with the New York collectors' fascination with Chinese and Japanese decorative arts in the late nineteenth century. Until World War II, many great New York collectors—the Havemeyers, the Altmans, the John D. Rockefeller, Jrs., and others—collected Chinese and Japanese art as a matter of general interest, but not as specialists. Their generous gifts and bequests, supplemented by the Museum's own purchases, made the Metropolitan a significant repository of Asian art, with superb Chinese ceramics and decorative jades, Japanese prints and Chinese Buddhist sculptures, as well as outstanding ancient Chinese bronzes, Japanese screens, and Indian sculpture.

The earlier interest in Asian art in this country had resulted in two preeminent collections: in the Museum of Fine Arts, Boston, and the Freer Gallery of Art in Washington, D.C., which grew out of the private collection of Charles Lang Freer. In the 1930s, the Nelson-Atkins Gallery of Art in Kansas City, Missouri, began to build an Asian art collection of the finest quality. But it was not until the post-World War II years that widespread interest in the collecting of Asian art developed, contributing immeasurably to the general growth and cultural enrichment of art museums across the country. Great Asian art collections, besides those already mentioned, are found today in Cleveland, San Francisco, Chicago, Los Angeles, Seattle, and many other places.

Compared with other leading museums, the Metropolitan was relatively inactive in Asian art in those exciting decades of the 40s through the 60s, at a time when New York City was the undisputed center of the post-World War II Asian art market. A generation of New Yorkers who had collected since the 1930s took full advantage of the new stimulation and discoveries provided by the exciting archaeological activities in China in the 30s, the massive exodus of private Chinese art from mainland China in the late 40s, and the increased commerce and travel to Japan and other points in the Far East in the 50s and 60s. In this remarkable new enterprise of bringing the finest Asian art to America, dealers, scholars, and collectors each played a significant role. Many played it magnificently well—and it was a role that, especially in the earlier years, required great sensitivity and devotion but promised uncertain returns. To the unfamiliar eye, a Chinese scroll, a Japanese screen, or an Indian statue looks just like any other seen in ordinary antique shops. It is no accident, therefore, that serious collectors of Asian art today frequently aim for public exhibitions of their art with scholarly (and educational) catalogues. Through collecting many have found the opportunity to introduce to the American public entire new important chapters of the history of art of the Asian half of the world. For these collectors it was understood that art collecting was no mere random accumulation; their collections, being historical and comprehensive in character, have each a significance that far exceeds the sum of its parts.

Though theoretically an "encyclopaedic" art museum, the Metropolitan has been under constant attack for already being too big and unmanageable. One might ask, Does it need more Asian art? Can it provide the necessary scholarship and expertise for interpreting and caring for such new art? The fact is that, unlike European art, Asian art in America lacks a cultural context; it needs to be seen among the contemporary arts of its time and considered in its cultural milieu; it needs to be discussed and interpreted by scholars and collectors who devote lifetimes to that study. In the end great art must be destined for public edification rather than the private delectation of a few—and this is especially true for Asian arts in America; without proper presentation and scholarly interpretation they remain as mere exotic curios, but when gathered in a significant context can represent a magnificent record of the Asian mind and sensibility. This is the task of a great center for Asian art.

In 1971 the Metropolitan Museum, in planning for an enlarged Department of Far Eastern Art, began to make new acquisitions and to plan a Center for Asian Art Studies. Two of its most significant recent acquisitions were a group of twenty-five important Sung and Yüan paintings from the C. C. Wang collection, purchased in 1973 with the help of the Dillon Fund, and the purchase in 1975 of the Harry C. Packard collection of Japanese art. These two acquisitions are of the greatest importance not only to the Metropolitan Museum but also to the study of Asian art in this country.

The importance of our acquiring the paintings from the C. C. Wang Collection can best be appreciated when we consider the remarkable progress that has been made in the study of Chinese painting in this country during the past twenty years. From a position of timidity and confusion, connoisseurship in the field has advanced to a point where it now not only satisfies the most rigorous standards of Western art history, but also contributes new methods and insights to Western art historians. American museums and private collectors now possess Chinese paintings that not only compare with the finest in China, but also rank among the noblest masterpieces of the world's art. Long-neglected artists and schools have been rediscovered, as traditionally established masters and art theories come under critical reevaluation, and spirited arguments over traditional attributions have generated intellectual ferment both here and abroad. In universities across this country, graduate study of Chinese painting has become the most important among Asian art topics; the influence of recent American scholarship and museum acquisitions has been clearly felt in Japan, and even in conservative circles in Taiwan, there has been talk of a "reconstruction" of Chinese painting history.

This whole experience has been rewarding in a way in which only the study of a great subject can be rewarding. To study Chinese painting is, in fact, to learn about the cultural history of the Chinese of the last one thousand and more years. As the art of the so-called scholar-official class—the educated men and women in traditional China—Chinese landscape painting, which has been the dominant subject since the tenth century A.D., reflects not only the artist's view of the world, his culture and lifestyle, but also his innermost emotional state—thoughts on, and responses to, the crises and exigencies of human life and history.

If it is true that the discovery of a new art form is one of the most important things that can happen to a civilization, then the creation of the monumental landscape in tenth-century China must count as one of the most significant events of the Eastern world—something comparable perhaps to the creation of the Byzantine Pantocrator in the history of the Christian world. Retreating to the mountains to escape the turmoil and destruction at the end of the T'ang dynasty, the tenth-century hermit painters rediscovered moral striving and the pursuit of truth in landscape painting. In the Metropolitan Museum's *Summer Mountains* (attributed

FIGURE 24. Ch'ü Ting (active about 1023–1056). Detail of handscroll: Summer Mountains. Chinese, Northern Sung dynasty. Ink and light color on silk. Gift of The Dillon Fund, 1973.120.1

to Ch'ü Ting and datable to about 1050, we see a climax of the grand manner of Northern Sung landscape art. The great, imposing mountain, reinforcing the Sung neo-Confucian view of the world, is like "a ruler among his subjects, a master among servants." Continuing to uphold eremetism as a pure way of life, the Sung Chinese saw landscape painting—of "the heart of forests and streams"—as an antidote for material concerns and worldly ills.

A second landscape style appeared during the next national catastrophe, the Mongol (Yüan) conquest of the southern Sung in the late thirteenth century. This time, the entire Chinese intelligentsia became social outcasts, and landscape painting turned into an art of personal expression. Wang Meng's *Red Cliffs and Green Valleys,* of the late 1360s, epitomizes the emotion-filled calligraphic style; the tremulous brushstrokes fairly throb with inner excitement. Many critics today have compared this Yüan kinesthetic calligraphic drawing with modern abstract expressionism; it is as if Jackson Pollock had lived fully six hundred years before his time. Tao-chi, a seventeenth-century follower of the Yüan style, put it this way:

Beating drums with a cypress-wood stick,
Or writing calligraphy with a sheep-hair brush,
What matters most is the satisfaction of the moment,
So never mind success or failure in the eyes of posterity.
But without a hand
like General Kun Yü's
who kills all his opponents,
How dare one play around with a painting brush!

Painting as a physical act was thus likened to hand-to-hand combat, and painters like Wang Meng and Tao-chi were artist-heroes. While the moods and concerns of their landscape paintings are primarily secular, the respect for nature and for the traditions of the artist's own past approaches a religious feeling. We modern viewers easily sympathize with the former while—unconsciously perhaps—harboring a longing for the latter. Small wonder that Chinese calligraphic painting strikes a response in us today.

Ch'ü Ting's *Summer Mountains* and Wang Meng's *Red Cliffs* are part of the Metropolitan's recent purchase from the C. C. Wang collection, which in one single stroke lifted the Museum's holdings in early Chinese painting from a position of weakness to one of eminence. Heir to a long tradition of great private Chinese collectors, such as Hsiang Yuan-pien (1525–1590), Liang Ch'ing-piao (1620–1691), Kao Shih-ch'i (1645–1704), and An Chi (1683–after 1742), C. C. Wang began collecting in the late 1930s

遠上青山十萬重丹崖翠壑
杳難通松風送瀑來天際花氣
和雲出洞中漁艇緩時來到此
奏人何處空相逢春光易老花
易落流水年年空向東黃鶴山
樵王蒙明為原東賣芹題贗
詩於上

黃鶴山樵丹庄翠壑圖

FIGURE 25. Wang Meng (1310–1385). Hanging scroll: Red Cliffs and Green Valleys. Chinese, late Yüan–early Ming dynasty. Ink on paper. Purchase, Gift of Darius Ogden Mills and Gift of Mrs. Robert Young, by exchange, 1973.121.7

FIGURE 26. Detail of Figure 25: shoreline with rocks

when he undertook a systematic study of Ming and Ch'ing paintings while compiling (with Victoria Contag) the valuable reference work *Seals of Chinese Painters and Collectors of the Ming and Ch'ing Periods* (Shanghai 1941; second edition, Hong Kong 1966). After World War II, when much of the Mukden (Manchurian) portion of the former imperial treasures was dispersed and came on the art market, he bought brilliantly, concentrating especially on Sung and Yüan paintings. He moved to New York in the late 1940s and lived frugally; for some twenty years he was in a unique position to add to and improve his collection. While other refugee collectors sold, he simply waited, bought, and bought more.

In retrospect it seems incredible, even outrageous, that one individual in New York in the mid-twentieth-century, strife-filled world should acquire so much of the "bones and marrow" of Chinese civilization. And why did the American museums not take full advantage of this treasure trove long ago? A simple reason is the fear of forgeries and copies, which abound in Chinese paintings. A powerful Western contribution to the study of Chinese painting during the past decades has been the development of stylistic analysis; the notion that a structural analysis of styles can provide independent clues for dating has served as a useful corrective to a picture of random growth through imitation and copying. Yet such notions of "period styles" as we have today are merely theoretical concepts to be continually refined, expanded, and corrected by long intimate experience with actual paintings.

Meanwhile, it is through different, or even conflicting, perceptions and opinions that great collections are made. To illustrate that collecting Chinese paintings is not for the fainthearted, I shall relate one recent incident. Just before the Metropolitan went ahead with the purchase of the Wang paintings, the Museum's Director, Thomas Hoving, in the presence of the Museum's President, Douglas Dillon, was greeted by a fellow museum director, a notably successful collector of Chinese painting, with the remark that one of the Metropolitan's recent acquisitions, bought as an early fourteenth-century painting, was really a modern forgery. "But relax," said he to Mr. Hoving, "my own first purchase in Chinese painting many years ago also turned out to be a copy!" Although I was totally surprised by a such an observation, I simply assured Hoving that, after due consideration, I would not only stand by my judgment, but would also be happy to answer any scholarly query about said painting, if the challenge were presented in print. I confessed to Hoving that I, too, on occasion, have been equally forthright about other people's paintings, and I can only hope that no one would accept my pronouncements without due consideration.

It was lucky for me—and for the Metropolitan Museum—that neither Dillon nor Hoving was discouraged by such apparent lack of consensus among experts, and the Museum goes on buying important Chinese paintings.

The acquisition of the C. C. Wang Collection was prefaced by a unique event. It is not unusual for the Museum to seek the advice and counsel of scholars and experts outside the institution prior to making a major purchase, but in the case of the C. C. Wang Collection general comments were not only solicited from scholars in the field, but three eminent experts were asked to study each object destined for purchase and to grade each work from A, the highest category, to D, unacceptable. In addition, each expert was asked to supply specific written comments on individual works and to make a general observation on the overall importance of the collection to the Metropolitan. At the time that the purchase of the C. C. Wang Collection was announced to the public, the Museum made available to the press the entire file of comments and revealed the identity and credentials of the experts consulted.

Given the inevitable subjectivity of connoisseurship and the variety of personal preferences, our outside experts were extraordinarily unanimous in their high appraisal of the individual paintings. The A classification was almost universal, and the experts found it necessary to add the subtle gradations of A + and A − to this topmost level of quality. The greatest variation in individual opinion was the evaluation of a handscroll variously graded A +, A, and B.

The importance of the collection as a whole to the Metropolitan was summarized in the opinion of Dr. Richard Barnhart of Yale University: "The overall quality and range of the paintings compare favorably with the finest collections of Chinese painting in the West. . . . In terms of quality and importance . . . it would be difficult to improve upon this selection for its fundamental significance to scholars of Chinese painting. . . . It would be a shame to let so irreplaceable a collection get away."

There is no doubt that one of the reasons that the C. C. Wang collection did not "get away" was the unique manner in which the most able scholarship in the world was placed at the disposal of Trustees to aid them in assessing the importance of the collection and its meaning to the Metropolitan.

In contrast to the general feeling of distrust for dealers' attributions in collecting Chinese paintings, the collecting and selling of Japanese art seems to proceed in relatively simple and untroubled waters. This does not mean that there are no problems of attribution in Japanese art—in Japanese painting it is as difficult as in Chinese painting—but in general, thanks to modern Japanese scholarship, much of Japanese art is better documented and its problems better defined.

The remarkable story of the Harry C. Packard collection of Japanese art can now be told. Born in 1919 in Utah, Harry Packard learned Japanese in Navy language school and at the end of 1946 found himself in Nagasaki in charge of a repatriation camp processing Japanese from Soviet-occupied areas. After the U.S. occupation of Japan ended in 1950, he studied at

FIGURE 27. Haniwa bust of a warrior. Japanese. Late part of tomb period (about 300–600 A.D.). Clay. The Harry G. C. Packard Collection of Asian Art, Gift of Harry G. C. Packard and Purchase, Fletcher, Rogers, Harris Brisbane Dick, and Louis V. Bell Funds, Joseph Pulitzer Bequest, and The Annenberg Fund, Inc., Gift, 1975

Waseda University. About this time he met the eminent Japanese art scholar Shujiro Shimada, who was then the curator-in-chief at the Kyoto National Museum. Years later, Shimada would recall: "Harry was the most devoted American student of Japanese art I ever met. Whenever there was a lecture in Kyoto, he would come from Tokyo by the night train, sleeping on some newspapers on the floor of a third-class coach, then go back to Tokyo the same way on the following night. He did this consistently for several years, sometimes twice a week."

Once he started collecting, he went about with a similar persistence and Spartan discipline. His first purchase was conventional enough—a group of excellent Ukiyō-e prints. From the very start he learned to do things the Japanese way: speaking Japanese fluently, he befriended scholars, traveled with them to remote countryside to seek out art, and always tried to buy from the source. He once commented: "I learned the Japanese rule of personal obligation well; you don't let them down, and they won't let you down. Now I never made decisions without consulting others." But above all else, he did his homework thoroughly. The moment a major work became available, he traveled all over the map to study comparative materials in museums and temple collections, learning all about the subject in the process. Once he wanted something, he pursued it with a knight-errant's zeal in seeking a lady's hand. There are stories about his selling his house to buy art and about his camping out at art owners' doorsteps until they finally relented.

In the 1950s there were, besides Packard, several other resident Americans in Japan who had made fine collections, ranging from Chinese bronzes to Japanese art to Korean pottery and ceramics. Blending a unique American breadth of vision with a Japanese studiousness and precision, which they learned from their scholarly Japanese friends, these men collected, within each subject, comprehensively and art historically, placing equal emphasis on the quality of the object as well as its historical importance. This art-historical approach to collecting had stimulated an earlier generation of Americans to buy European art on a grand scale. As a cultural phenomenon it reflects our educational system—from encyclopaedic museums to the college omnibus survey course, Art 101. Packard's collection, now numbering 412 items, covers the entire history of Japanese art, from the neolithic age to the twentieth century. It is as if, from the very first piece he ever bought, he had a grand survey course of Japanese civilization in mind.

From the Museum's point of view, here was a unique opportunity to fill a glaring gap in the collections. Although we possessed some important Japanese materials—the Soami and Korin screens, the Ledoux prints—in contrast to our magnificent holdings from most of the major cultures of the world, the Japanese collection had been sadly inadequate. Both Dillon and Hoving had wanted to see something done in this area, and now their interest was spurred by the enthusiasm of Mrs. Vincent Astor who, as a Museum Trustee and Chairman of the Visiting Committee of the Far Eastern Art Department, was determined that the Metropolitan should have great Asian art. Together, Dillon and Hoving and Mrs. Astor decided that a special effort would be made to bring the Packard collection to New York—by raising fresh funds, if necessary.

In late spring 1974 a complete set of photographs of all the objects in

FIGURE 28. One of four guardian kings on a rock dais. Japanese. Late Heian period (897–1185). Wood with colors. The Harry G. C. Packard Collection of Asian Art, Gift of Harry G. C. Packard and Purchase, Fletcher, Rogers, Harris Brisbane Dick, and Louis V. Bell Funds, Joseph Pulitzer Bequest, and The Annenberg Fund, Inc., Gift, 1975

the collection was assembled. Although many of the fine ceramics and paintings in the group were well known to students of Japanese art through publications (more than fifty of the paintings were included in the *Japanese Art in Western Collections* series), the range and quality of the whole collection astonished all of us who saw it for the first time. Divided into categories (archaeology, sculpture, painting, ceramics) the photographic albums showed surpassing strengths in archaeology, early Buddhist iconographic scrolls, screen paintings of the Momoyama period, ceramics, and a number of exceptionally fine and exceedingly rare sculptures. It was evident that this material, combined with the older holdings of the Museum, would in one fell swoop place the Metropolitan's among the top-ranking Japanese art collections in the Western world.

There had been long-standing rumors that the Japanese government was uneasy about the export of such a collection to America. Upon inquiry, it developed that Japan's Agency for Cultural Affairs had for years kept a close watch over Packard's activities. But the ranking members of the Agency now expressed feelings of relief and satisfaction at the possibility that the collection might be destined for the Metropolitan, which is regarded in Japan as one of the three leading art museums—the other two are the Louvre and the British Museum—in the Western world. The Metropolitan, on its part, promised and gave full cooperation to the Japanese Cultural Affairs Agency. The job of documenting some four hundred twelve pieces of art, collected over a period of some twenty-five years, kept Mr. Packard and the staff of the Museum busy for more than a year, but in the end the Japanese authorities requested further examination of only two objects—an outcome no daring optimist would have predicted a year earlier.

Meanwhile, the long and laborious task of bringing the project through the various meetings of curators and Trustees began. Normally, each object proposed for acquisition is first shown and ranked with other proposed objects at a meeting of the eighteen curatorial heads of departments, before it is formally presented to the Trustees' Acquisitions Committee, which makes the final decisions. Because of the unusual size and complexities of the Packard project, two sets of curatorial and Trustee meetings took place. At the very first of these meetings, something wonderful—and quite unexpected—happened. As a preliminary presentation, four pairs of screens, half a dozen scroll paintings, a like number of sculptures, and a dozen or so archaeological objects and ceramic pieces

FIGURE 29. Detail of pair of screens: Cranes in Bamboo and Pines by Ogata Korin. Japanese. Edo period (17th century). Colors on paper. The Harry G. C. Packard Collection of Asian Art, Gift of Harry G. C. Packard and Purchase, Fletcher, Rogers, Harris Brisbane Dick, and Louis V. Bell Funds, Joseph Pulitzer Bequest, and The Annenberg Fund, Inc., Gift, 1975

were displayed around the walls of a storeroom; hundreds of wooden boxes, with their lids open but scrolls and ceramics still within, were laid out on long tables in the middle of the room. The scene resembled a small-town antiques auction more than the immaculately prepared presentation (usually taking place in the Metropolitan's board room) such an occasion normally would have dictated. As the curators gathered, one by one, they began to browse and look closely at the objects; there was suddenly excitement in the room, followed by a hushed silence. "What is this all about?" someone whispered. At Mr. Hoving's signal, I gave a short speech, describing as well as I could, in summary statements, what I thought the Museum's needs were, what I thought of the collection before us, and what I thought such a collection would do for the Museum and for the study of Asian art as a whole. Since I was told that it would take several meetings to deal with the project, I secretly hoped that the problem of financing would not have to be discussed right away.

"But how do you propose that we finance the purchase?" someone asked. I began slowly: "My duty is to present the facts and inform the Trustees of the opportunity. We will all have to work hard to see if at least half of the needed money couldn't be raised from outside. . . ."

Suddenly, Hoving tore a sheet from a large note pad. Drawing a line down the middle, he wrote "Yes" on one side and "No" on the other side, then waving the sheet of paper in front of his assembled curators he said: "Suppose we don't raise any new money, would you vote 'yes' or 'no' to committing, for a period of five years, a great portion of our annual unrestricted acquisition funds to this extraordinary project?"

I was dumb-struck. There were questions and answers between the curators and Hoving as the paper was passed around the room. Eventually, it came back and everyone left. I looked hard at Hoving, as he handed me the folded paper and said stiffly: "Well, I have never seen such a vote in all my years at this institution." The vote was thirteen yeses, three nos, and one abstention.

Of course, this extraordinary vote of the curators by itself did not commit the funds to the project—only the Trustees could do that. But its symbolic significance was enormous. It meant that the curators of American art, western European arts, medieval art, prints, drawings, Egyptian art, musical instruments, and others—whose traditional responsibility is to guard their own interests—decided that the rounding out in good style of an important area in the Asian art field was worth their giving up most

of their own shares in the unrestricted acquisition funds. For the much-beleaguered Far Eastern Art Department, this gesture alone was worth almost as much as gaining the Packard collection.

After the Trustees' Acquisitions Committee met for the first time with the display in the storeroom, a selection of some one hundred twenty objects was installed—this time properly, with cases and lighting—in a closed exhibition area. There, the curators as well as the members of the entire Board of Trustees were invited to view the objects and ask questions. At the Acquisitions Committee's final meeting on the subject, more hard questions were asked: Can the Museum afford to do everything? Why Japanese art? But the overriding consideration, along with some very practical and responsible discussion, was a simple one: it is important today that first-quality Asian art should be represented at the Metropolitan.

FIGURE 30. Kano Sansetsu (1589–1651). Four sliding door panels: Aged Plum. Japanese. Momoyama period (early 17th century). Colors on gold. The Harry G. C. Packard Collection of Asian Art, Gift of Harry G. C. Packard and Purchase, Fletcher, Rogers, Harris Brisbane Dick, and Louis V. Bell Funds, Joseph Pulitzer Bequest, and The Annenberg Fund, Inc., Gift, 1975

At the signing of the contract in August 1975, Harry Packard announced his plans to use the proceeds of the sale to support Western-Japanese exchange fellowships and publications devoted to Japanese art studies. This proposal fits well with the Metropolitan's own planned Center for Asian Art Studies. In the years to come the public display and scholarly publications of the Packard materials at the Metropolitan will not only bring to the nation's leading museum something it has long lacked—an exciting and comprehensive collection of Japanese art—but will also be a great general stimulus to the study of Asian art.

Our Finest Hour

OLGA RAGGIO

Chairman, Western European Arts

Every curator knows that, to add to his collection, he needs more than mere tenacity in pursuing and securing well-known works of art on the market and in private collections. As an art historian, he is aware of the vast number of works that have fallen out of sight over the centuries. Artists' biographies, inventories of collections, and all manner of historical records are full of descriptions of lost works. But experience shows that, strange as it may seem, and except for works in precious metals, comparatively few objects have really been destroyed or fallen prey to fires, wars, or revolutions. Many more have simply lost their identity, engulfed in the successive changes of taste, rejected by one generation, misunderstood by another. Frequently, they have been removed from their original locations and then simply forgotten. The art historian's most challenging and fascinating task is to serve as Fate's retriever. He questions the works of art that surface before him to understand their true nature and their original context, and to uncover their genesis and their influence. If he happens to also be a curator, the search is not purely academic: it acquires a pressing reality, in which discovery and acquisition become interdependent. As the work of art ends its travesty existence

149

and is acquired for its true identity, he can proudly feel that he is living his finest hour.

I had the good fortune to identify three major works of sculpture, all of which were still unrecognized when they were offered to us between 1963 and 1970. The acquisitions themselves were the fruit of a collaboration with John G. Phillips, then chairman of the department. It is he who carried the responsibility of the financial aspects and who recommended the purchases to the Trustees. The happy outcome was a success for us both. Each of us played a clearly defined role, yet we shared at all stages the effort and the excitement of each of the adventures.

Early in January 1963, a stranger, Mildred Centers, came to the Museum seeking my opinion about a wooden sculpture she owned, a standing figure of Saint John the Baptist. She believed it could possibly be by Michelangelo. I looked at the snapshots she had brought. Two showed the saint three-fourths down from the front and in profile, one was a close-up of his legs, and one showed the entire figure from the back, standing on a flagstone pavement alongside a clapboard house. I could easily identify the carving as a sculpture of Spanish flavor, with characteristic painted eyes and traces of polychromy over the surface. Quite probably, I thought at first, a nineteenth-century devotional figure. Yet, in scanning with a magnifying glass the small, misty prints, I saw details that seemed unusual: the sculpture was quite large, the drapery on the back fell with great nobility and breadth, and the pattern on its surface appeared to have a fine baroque design. Especially striking was the detail of the left arm: powerful, throbbing with life, with a superbly carved hand, long, noble fingers, and flat nails pressing into a bunch of cloth gathered under it. To my eyes, trained on sixteenth- and seventeenth-century sculptures, this arm and hand seemed certainly carved by a Renaissance artist.

I explained to Mrs. Centers, who had come to New York from Jacksonville, Florida, that her sculpture had nothing to do with Michelangelo and that it seemed to be Spanish. Then, since she seemed anxious to learn more about it, I suggested that she take her snapshots to the Hispanic Society, where the curator of sculpture would probably confirm my suggestion and possibly give her some further information. When she left, I thought the matter closed. Many such inquiries by outsiders come to no more than this. But this turned out to be only the beginning.

Two months later, quite without warning, Mrs. Centers telephoned me from the Museum's information desk. She had brought the statue to the Museum, hoping that I would look at it. Remembering the extraordinary hand with its lovely fingers, I excused myself from my concern of the moment and went to the Great Hall. There I found Mrs. Centers and her husband, both a bit weary from their long drive from Florida. But where was the statue? Oh, it was much too big for them to bring it into the Museum. It was in their car, and perhaps I could go out and look at it there. I suggested that they drive around to the delivery entrance. There, a few minutes later, I saw the *Saint John* comfortably reclining on a bed of blankets in a station wagon. At once the carving of his rich brown hair appeared masterful, as did the surface of his face, painted with great subtlety, and that of his dark red cloak, superbly picked up in gold, in the typical Spanish technique of *estofado*. The entire polychromed surface seemed almost untouched and unblemished. Hardly believing my eyes, I asked that the sculpture be taken out of the car and brought into our receiving storeroom. As the statue was carefully removed by our men, placed on a dolly, and then raised onto one of our large examining tables, it traveled easily and swiftly, its weight hardly a problem. The wood was old and dry. Standing before me in its full height, the statue had a monumental presence. This was Saint John standing by the River Jordan, shown in the moment in which he points toward Jesus and says: "Behold the Lamb of God, which taketh away the sin of the world." It was not an ascetic, emaciated image of the prophet preaching in the desert but a strangely serene youth with an almost magnetic power in his gaze.

As I looked at the sculpture intensely, experiencing that kind of direct, intimate dialogue that is immediately established between a great work of art and oneself, I knew that it was by a great master of the seventeenth century—perhaps by Gregorio Fernández (about 1576–1636) or Juan Martínez Montañés (1568–1649), whose works I had admired in Seville. Mr. and Mrs. Centers waited quietly for my verdict. I felt I had to act prudently, but also quickly and effectively. First of all, I had to get John Phillips to view the sculpture immediately. And we would have to ask the owners to leave the statue with us for a time. While we waited for Mr. Phillips to appear, I hurried to my office and leafed through a book on Montañés: the photographs of several works by this artist were indeed astonishingly close. I knew I had not been dreaming.

When I returned to the storeroom, Jack Phillips was scrutinizing the

FIGURE 31. Detail of Montañes's *Saint John the Baptist*. Snapshot submitted by Mrs. Centers

FIGURE 32. Montañes's *Saint John the Baptist* seen from the back. Snapshot submitted by Mrs. Centers

sculpture. I stood close to him and studied his expression: I was afraid he would perhaps not warm up to the statue. As he continued to stand silent, I whispered to him, "Montañes." "How do you know?" he whispered back, almost motionless, perhaps irritated by what seemed to him an imprudently rash attribution. No matter, I now knew that he was impressed.

We asked the owners to leave the statue with us for a few days. They agreed. Since the statue was apparently not for sale, and because we could not tell what it was, we waived the usual valuation clause when the Registrar issued a receipt.

The investigation began at once. I showed the Montañes photographs to Jack Phillips. His enthusiasm quickly caught up with mine. We both knew that if I had indeed discovered a work by Montañes, the Museum should not miss the chance of acquiring it. We had often talked about our need to acquire some great example of Spanish sculpture to add to our fine but all too meager group of sixteenth-century works. Among those we had always been proud of was a relief that came to us in 1945 with the bequest of Helen Hay Whitney: an *Adoration of the Magi,* carved around 1567–68 by Diego de Pesquera for a retable in a church near Granada. A spirited example of mannerist design, Pesquera's relief is admirable for the superb quality of its polychromed and gilded surface, where the opulent brocades worn by the figures vie with the exuberant grotesques of the background, in a glorious display of *estofado* technique. But nothing in our collections could even start to suggest the world of intense spirituality that is one of the great achievements of such seventeenth-century masters of religious sculpture as Fernández, Montañes, or Alonso Cano, whose works are parallel to the paintings of Velázquez, Murillo, and Zurbarán. Sculptures by these masters have almost never left Spain. They are often still in the churches for which they were first made, and almost none are in private collections or come up on the market. Our need for caution, therefore, was obvious. To claim to have discovered such a work, unrecorded and unknown, would be even less believable than the claim of coming across a totally unknown painting. We sought the opinions of three colleagues, Murray Pease, our Conservator, Ted Rousseau, then Curator of European Paintings and a long-time connoisseur and admirer of Spanish art, and Carmen Gomez-Moreno of our Medieval Department, whose knowledge of Spanish sculpture and painting is extensive. All three examined the work in the storeroom and agreed that it looked astonishingly close to the works of Montañes. The figure had all the majesty and serene classicism that are characteristic of the creations of the great Sevillian master. Painterly details such as the delicate handling of the saint's face, the muted reds of his embroidered cloak, and the leaves and tendrils covering the rocky ledge at his feet recalled the beautiful naturalism of other works, whose surfaces were painted in oils by Francisco Pacheco, the master and father-in-law of Velázquez.

I addressed myself to the task of finding some reference to a lost *Saint John* by Montañes. No list of missing works seemed to have been compiled, and the literature on Montañes was dispersed in many rare Spanish publications not available in our library. At the same time my stylistic analysis, in my effort to arrive at an approximate dating, progressed swiftly. Careful comparison with other dated works by Montañes suggested that this *Saint John* was especially close to the retables he undertook in the latter part of his career, between 1620 and 1640. These were the years when the Sevillian master, famous for his great works for the Cathedral of Seville and the large retable of Saint Jerome in the Carthusian monastery at Santiponce, was given many commissions for religious congregations and churches both in Seville and in the surrounding provinces. Two figures of Saint John the Evangelist and of Saint John the Baptist, made for the convent of Santa Clara between 1622 and 1624, offered the closest similarities in conception and handling. Other, perhaps even more convincing similarities appeared in the two retables undertaken by the master in 1638 for the Sevillian convent of Santa Paula. The design of these helped us to understand the context in which our *Saint John* was originally conceived. Since it was finished all around and made to be seen at considerable height, the sculpture had been most probably made for the central niche of a simple tripartite retable, with late mannerist or early baroque ornamental details. It became more and more likely in my mind that the *Saint John* could once well have been in a Sevillian convent or church secularized in the nineteenth century. But if the convent did not exist any longer, and no written mention of it survived, how were we to find out about it?

I was also puzzled by another point: it was difficult to believe that this sculpture had been allowed to leave Spain in recent times. If we were to assume that it had had a fairly long existence in exile, its unusually good state of preservation showed that it probably had been in a private collection. (Wooden sculptures in churches are often disfigured by later repainting.) But which collection? Connoisseurs and collectors of Spanish sculpture in this country hardly exist. Perhaps it had come from Latin America. Carmen Gómez-Moreno reminded me that Montañes is known to have sent some works to the Spanish colonies, especially to Lima. As the hours passed, it became increasingly clear that the immediate thing to do was acquire the sculpture. Later on we surely would discover its origin.

We learned a bit more about Mr. and Mrs. Centers the day they returned to the Museum. Mildred Centers owned an antique shop in Jacksonville, and her husband handled the gun and coin division of their business. They accepted our attribution to Montañes and agreed to sell the sculpture for $16,000. They then gave us a baffling fragment of information, which was that they had acquired the sculpture the year before in Cincinnati. With their offer in hand, we could at least start the buying process.

The time before the next meeting of the Acquisitions Committee was short. Discarding hope of writing a lengthy report, I embodied my thoughts on the sculpture in a terse but enthusiastic memorandum in which I unhesitatingly attributed the sculpture to Juan Martínez Montañes and urged its acquisition for the Museum. Jack Phillips's own evaluation of the sculpture, written on the recommendation blank addressed to the Director and the Trustees, reflected the same feelings.

As the papers were delivered to the Director, James Rorimer, the *Saint John* was wheeled into his office. Impressed by the majestic beauty of the saint, he agreed to support our recommendation.

The day before the meeting of the Acquisitions Committee Mrs. Centers reappeared and showed us a telegram from a man she identified as a Jacksonville attorney, stating that a client had authorized him to double his offer for the *Saint John*. This offer, according to Mrs. Centers, had been $10,000, for which reason her price would now have to be $20,000. This sort of development could be fatal, not only with the Director but with the Trustees. We renegotiated and finally settled at $18,000, provided the purchase was approved within 48 hours. Jack Phillips, deeply worried, sent Rorimer this note:

> I would like to make a special plea with regard to the painted wooden statue of Saint John. Further study of it convinces me that it is a piece we simply

FIGURE 33. Juan Martinez Montañes (1568–1649, Spanish). *Saint John the Baptist*. Second quarter of 17th century. Cedar, polychromed and gilded. From the Church of the Convent of the Conception, Seville. Purchase, Joseph Pulitzer Bequest, 63.40

cannot afford to lose. It is a commanding figure, and has in an unparalleled way, in my experience, aroused the enthusiasm of a number of the members of the curatorial staff who are concerned with European art. They, like myself, are impressed with its unique qualities which make it an outstanding example of Spanish sculpture. Montañes is perhaps the greatest of the post-medieval sculptors, and virtually all of his works remain in Spain. By some fluke—how, we don't know—the Saint John came to this country. If it were still in Spain and in the hands of a dealer, it seems unlikely that permission could be secured to export it. Now, therefore, is the time to act. If what I say here is generally correct, the price—$18,000—remains a reasonable one.

The Acquisitions Committee met in Rorimer's office. The saint was present. Both Jack Phillips and Ted Rousseau extolled its beauty and put Montañes's achievement as a sculptor in a class with that of Velázquez, who greatly admired Montañes's works and painted his portrait. The following morning Jack wired Mrs. Centers in Jacksonville:

> Purchase of Saint John authorized at final price quoted in your offer dated March eleventh. Please immediately send bill so that payment can be made. Request that there be no announcement of sale until Museum announces this acquisition. This follows our usual custom. Congratulations and best wishes.

The last request was added by the Director. We were then in the final stages of reinstalling the Vélez Blanco Patio, a major monument that had come to us from the Blumenthal collection, and we were planning a grand opening. An adjoining gallery of Spanish art was under construction and the Montañes, shown in that context, would be one more added glory.

While the saint waited quietly for its official unveiling, we tried to find out more about it. The microscopic and chemical examination of its surfaces in our conservation laboratory confirmed that the structure of oil paint was partly upon a gesso priming, as Murray Pease had determined when he had first examined the sculpture. Now we received a report on the wood samples we had sent to the Forest Laboratory of the United States Department of Agriculture. They were identified as Spanish cedar—a very good sign indeed, since this wood was often used in Andalusia for important religious works, Montañes's *Christ of Clemency* in the Cathedral of Seville being one of these.

My inquiries about a Cincinnati collection of Spanish art yielded nothing. Then, unexpectedly, news of our purchase appeared in the *Jacksonville Journal* and was picked up by the New York papers. In these stories we learned that Mr. and Mrs. Centers had bought the sculpture for $65 and then for months had tried to sell it for $1,000. In view of the price that we had paid, this was a sensational item, but even more interesting to us was the name of the previous owner, Walter Johnson, an antiques dealer, owner of The Trivet Shop in Cincinnati. According to the papers, Johnson claimed that he had had the piece for several years and had no recollection of where or how he obtained it. In due time Jack Phillips met with Walter Johnson and learned that the sculpture had been bought at an auction many years before, probably in the 1920s.

To follow this up was a bit like searching for a needle in a haystack, but the records of the firm of French and Company, to which we went first thing, gave us the answer. Our sculpture had been in the Henry Symons Sale, held at the Anderson Galleries from January 23 to February 3, 1923. At lot 1025 the sales catalogue illustrated our *Saint John* and offered the description:

> Sixteenth century Asturian carved and polychromed statue of St. Juan the Baptist by Juan Martinez Montañes . . . . The sculpture stood in the convent of La Nuestra de la Concepción in Seville.

Now that I knew the name of the convent, all I needed was to find it in the old guides of Seville. The most helpful was one published in 1844. In it, after a description of the convent, I read this:

> Under a big moulded arch with pilasters supporting a cornice, on a high pedestal placed over the base of the retable, stood the most beautiful figure of Saint John ever made by the celebrated Martinez Montañes. One can hardly explain the beauties of the design and the treatment of draperies and body of this famous image, the honor of its author and its country . . . . Everything was simple and in good taste in this unusual retable which, when in 1837 the convent was suppressed through the merging of its congregation of nuns with those of El Soccorro, perished with the rest of the contents of the church. Now the building has become a carriage-house for the stage coaches of the Kingdom and that of the convent is occupied by various establishments and workshops.

The riddle of the mysterious *Saint John* was solved. We still do not know how and when it left Spain, nor how it came into the hands of Henry Symons, a British dealer who is mainly known for the important furniture he included in the sales he organized in New York in the 1920s. But some day, I am sure, we may discover even that.

The second instance in which discovery and acquisition were closely linked is that of the purchase of one of our finest Italian late Renaissance marbles: the figure of Temperance by Giovanni Caccini that now graces the Vélez Blanco Patio. The sculpture belonged to a well-known Florentine dealer, Ugo Bardini. While I was in Italy in the fall of 1962, I learned that Bardini was offering us a statue attributed to Pietro Francavilla. The Museum wished me to take a look at the figure and report on it.

I visited Bardini in his palatial house in Florence, near the museum established by his father, the antiquarian Stefano Bardini. Ugo was a tall elderly gentleman, kind and polite, with the worldly manner of a merchant long accustomed to dealing with English and American clients. The statue was in a crowded storage area, standing next to an eighteenth-century coach and some pieces of Renaissance furniture. The view I had of it was mainly from the right profile: I saw a strongly classicizing, Junoesque figure of a woman holding a horse's bit and bridle in one hand, a ruler and pair of dividers in the other. These symbols of restraint and measure clearly identified her as an allegory of Temperance. I was struck by the sharpness and precision with which the marble was cut and the extraordinary cascade of flat folds on the back of the figure. Such a melodiously composed statue, with its handsome head with well-rounded features and elaborately braided hairdo, had a compelling way of recalling Giovanni Bologna's works. Large patches of moss and lichen were encrusted on parts of the drapery, indicating long years of exposure to the elements. I asked about its original location. "It comes from a Florentine garden," is all Bardini would tell me. The price was $80,000.

In the days that followed I found myself thinking over and over again of the statue. It was certainly a sculpture of great beauty, superbly controlled, serene and yet enigmatic. But by whom was it, really? The attribution to Francavilla did not make sense. True enough, Francavilla was a close follower of Giovanni Bologna and this would, apparently, justify the attribution. But the more I tried to reconcile it with the style of this artist's works, the more the stately classicism of its lines seemed to be at the opposite pole from the nervous, linear mannerisms of the sculptor of the *Primavera* on the Florentine Bridge of Santa Trinita. Actually, Bardini's *Temperance* appeared to be astonishingly close to another figure of Temperance: a large bronze statue in the University of Genoa, executed about 1579–1585 for Luca Grimaldi after a model by Giovanni Bologna. Could it be that it was carved not by Francavilla but by another

FIGURE 34. Caccini's *Temperance*, encrusted with moss and lichen, in a photograph by Ugo Bardini

prominent sculptor in Florence, perhaps Giovanni Caccini? Caccini was famous for his ability in handling marble and for his knowledge of antiquities. Perhaps there was a connection. In checking the photographs of Caccini's statues I noticed that their opulent garments, arranged in flat angular folds, with incredibly sharp undercuttings, were strikingly close to the draperies of the Bardini *Temperance*. But here the evidence ended.

There was still another avenue of research: to look into the writings of two Florentine authors of the sixteenth and seventeenth centuries, Raffaello Borghini and Filippo Baldinucci. When, in 1584, Borghini was writing his book *Il Riposo,* Caccini was a promising but still very young artist. Therefore only a few lines were devoted to him on the very last page. But they ended with this remark:

> He is now working on an over life-size marble figure for Monsignor Giovambattista del Milanese, Bishop of Marsi: it is meant to represent *Temperance*.

The statue must have been finished and delivered to the bishop, inasmuch as a hundred years later, about 1680, Baldinucci mentioned it as standing in the bishop's garden in the Via Larga. It was a statue so close in style to Giovanni Bologna that for a while Baldinucci even mistook it for a work of this master, later correcting himself.

There the puzzle was solved. Not only did Caccini work on a *Temperance,* but his figure looked astonishingly close to a design by Giovanni Bologna. Rarely do old records answer our questions so quickly and so accurately.

Upon my return to New York, I reported the results of my examination and pleaded for the acquisition of the rediscovered Caccini. The opportunity to acquire a great Italian Renaissance marble comes rarely. I had the good fortune to discover a documented work of one of the best mannerist sculptors of Medici Florence. Jack Phillips seemed to be much impressed by the statue and fully persuaded by my arguments. He took it upon himself to convince the Director. But to no avail. Whether Jim Rorimer could not warm up to the cool elegance of Caccini's work, or whether there were other pressing matters, I do not know. But our recommendation was shelved. Sadly disappointed, I was determined not to forget about the piece.

The following year, when I was again in Florence, I set out to find

FIGURE 35. Giovanni Caccini (1556–1612, Italian, Florentine). *Temperance*. 1583/1584. Marble. Made for the garden of the house of Giovanni Battista del Milanese, Florence. Harris Brisbane Dick Fund, 67.207

the house of the Bishop of Marsi. The only record I had found said that in the seventeenth century it had become the property of the Covoni family. On an eighteenth-century map of Florence I could clearly see a small garden behind the house, divided by a central alley. Pressed by curiosity, but without much hope, I went for a walk on the Via Cavour, once called the Via Larga. And there, right in front of the Medici Palace, my eye caught the coat of arms of Giovannibattista del Milanese, surmounted by his bishop's miter, high over the façade of an elegant *palazzetto*—a small but impeccable late sixteenth-century façade, accurately designed in the taste of Giovanni Bologna. Here was the perfect match in architecture to the style of Caccini's statue. And in the back there was indeed a small garden, no doubt the very garden mentioned by Bardini.

Four or five years later, we learned that Ugo Bardini had died. Then, in April 1967, a letter landed on my desk with an offer of sale. Attached to it was a snapshot of Caccini's *Temperance*. The letter was from an individual writing from the Italian Riviera, offering the statue as a "Francavilla" on behalf of a relative who had inherited it from Bardini. The price was $60,000, subject to negotiation. This time I was determined not to lose the opportunity. Thomas Hoving, to whom I had once spoken about my discovery, was now Director, and we could start afresh. Two months later he saw the sculpture in Florence, liked it, and agreed to support our recommendation. The purchase was authorized by the Trustees at their next meeting.

Unrecognized, unidentified, the so-called Francavilla, which had already been issued an export permit, had no trouble leaving Italy. Still covered with its Florentine moss and lichen, but with not a speck of its delicate marble missing, Caccini's *Temperance* was uncrated in the Museum a few weeks later.

My third story concerns the identification of two large bronze reliefs representing scenes of the martyrdom of Saint Daniel, by the late sixteenth-century Paduan sculptor Tiziano Aspetti. In November 1970, while I was doing research in Rome, Jack Phillips telephoned me from New York. Two months earlier he had seen in Munich two totally unknown bronze versions of the two stories of Saint Daniel made by Aspetti for the cathedral of Padua and illustrated in all histories of Italian sculpture;

now he had recommended their purchase to the Acquisitions Committee. Their price was about $68,000, and the Trustees had agreed to authorize this expenditure subject to my inspecting the bronzes and sending them an additional report. The matter was urgent. The reliefs had been reserved by Hans Weihrauch, then Director of the Bavarian National Museum and a well-known authority on Italian bronzes, and our chance of getting the reliefs depended on our acting faster. Weihrauch was having some difficulty in raising the money, and the owner of the reliefs was getting impatient.

I flew to Munich and inspected the reliefs in the gallery of Julius Boehler. They were (and are) two superb late sixteenth-century casts, with a wealth of chased details that seemed to me much livelier and sharper in execution than those in Padua. There was no doubt in my mind that we should by all means try to secure them for the Museum. As to their relationship to the Paduan reliefs, I simply could not find a satisfactory answer. One could hardly doubt either the authenticity or the date of the reliefs in Padua, which were still attached to the altar for which Aspetti made them in 1592. I wondered whether the bronzes in Munich could not be second versions, executed by the sculptor with special care and more accurate finish for a specific patron. Given their high quality, it was unlikely that they were later versions, executed in the seventeenth century after Aspetti's models. But I felt that I could not write a conclusive report without examining the originals in Padua and comparing the measurements of both sets. I explained this to Boehler and convinced him that he should reserve the reliefs for us for eight days in spite of the option held by the Bavarian National Museum.

I had a day to wait when I reached Padua, since it was Sunday and Masses were being celebrated at the main altar of the cathedral, directly above my research area. As an interim project I visited the Santo, where there were four bronze figures of the Virtues by Aspetti. The vast sanctuary was in near darkness and buzzing with hundreds of pilgrims who had parked their buses outside, in front of Donatello's *Gattamelata,* and were crawling around, chanting and carrying candles to the tomb of Saint Anthony. Aspetti's *Virtues* were standing on the balustrade of the main altar. Examining them with my flashlight made me feel slightly sacrilegious, surrounded as I was by the praying faithful. Still, I maneuvered myself from one to the other, carefully scanning their surfaces. To my surprise, they had an impressive similarity in terms of workmanship,

FIGURES 36, 37. Tiziano Aspetti (1565–1607, Italian). *Saint Daniel Being Dragged by a Horse* and *Saint Daniel Being Nailed between Two Boards*. 1592/1593. Bronze relief made for the altar of Saint Daniel in the Cathedral of Padua. Purchase, Fletcher and Edith Perry Chapman Funds, 1970.264.1,2

FIGURES 38, 39. Bronze replicas of the Aspetti reliefs. From the Cathedral of Padua.
Photographs: Böhm

patina, ornamental borders, modeling, and yellowish color of metal to the reliefs in Munich. All that surface animation and goldsmithlike detail that had delighted but puzzled me were here again, in the draperies, the gestures, the faces. These *Virtues* are known to have been executed by Aspetti in 1594, only two years after the reliefs in the cathedral. I wondered anew why the appearance of the reliefs in the photographs seemed to be so different.

On Monday I went to the cathedral. The only person in sight was a janitor, cleaning the floor. I approached him, tip in hand, to ask him to take me to the crypt. He indicated that the door was open and told me I could go down by myself. There was no light in the crypt. With my flashlight, I found my way to the altar. It was an Early Christian free-standing marble sarcophagus. On the back side was one of the Aspetti reliefs enclosed in a Renaissance marble facing: the scene of Daniel nailed under a slab. The other relief, showing Daniel being dragged by a horse, had been removed from the front of the altar. Since I was alone, I settled down behind the altar to examine the bronze at ease. But what a disappointing sight! A reddish metal was clearly visible underneath a thin opaque patina. The figures were identical with those in the Munich version, but the surface had a bland look. The ring of the metal, when tapped, was thin and hollow. The faces were anodyne rather than expressive. The hair fell in heavy, rather than crisp, locks. The clothes, the background, the feet of the table underneath the saint were without any engraved details, flaccid and uninteresting in form and texture. When I took careful measurements of some of the figures and compared them with those I had taken in Munich, they were smaller by an average of 3/4 of an inch to an inch. The only possible explanation of these differences was that the relief in front of me was a fairly modern reproduction. The consistent shrinkage in size indicated that it had been cast from a plaster mold taken from the original relief. As to the dull surface, it was typical of nineteenth-century routine reproductions. The conclusion was inescapable: the reliefs in Munich were the reliefs that Aspetti had made for this altar in 1592. The relief before me was a miserable replacement, made sometime before 1921 when its photograph was first published by Leo Planiscig, an Austrian scholar who may never have bothered to come down to the crypt or who simply used available photographs.

All this was so startling that I felt slightly dizzy from excitement. I decided that I must see the second relief as well. As every connoisseur of bronzes knows, the reverse of a bronze cast will tell one much concerning its age and technique. The second relief was stored in the treasury of the cathedral. I saw it there, later in the day. The front of it was a perfect match in disappointing quality to the first one. The back showed me a pinkish copper-colored bronze, without any trace of oxidation. Again I took measurements. Again they turned out to be consistently smaller than those of the corresponding Munich relief.

That very night I telephoned the Museum the result of my investigation, and two days later the Boehler reliefs were on a plane to New York. In acquiring them we not only added a famous work to our collections but also recognized and recovered a key example of Italian Renaissance art that had long ago vanished from its original location. Once more, discovery and acquisition had become inseparably linked.

The Long Wait and the Quick Draw

HELMUT NICKEL

Curator of Arms and Armor

In the middle of nowhere, at a sharp bend in the road from Mérida to Chichen Itzá, there stands a huge dead tree. The road runs straight for miles on either side of this bend. Now and then an automobile comes speeding along, and here and there a cow or mule ambles across. Half a dozen vultures perch in that tree, patiently keeping their beady eyes open, waiting for something to happen . . . .

An important part of a museum curator's life is also spent in the long wait, and every so often I feel a strange sympathy for those patient watchers in that tree at the bend in the road to Chichen Itzá. One of the legends of the Arms and Armor Department has it that its founder and first curator, Bashford Dean, waited nearly twenty years for a certain Turkish provincial governor to fall into disfavor in order to obtain for the Museum a coveted hoard of armor found on an Aegean island. For the celebrated Riggs collection, which forms a substantial part of our holdings, negotiations dragged on from 1872 to 1913. In the case of our prize recent accession—the fowling piece of Louis XIII of France, acquired in 1972—the long wait started in the 1920s and spanned the terms of office of all three of my predecessors: Bashford Dean, Stephen V. Grancsay, and Randolph Bullock.

This fowling piece is not only thought of as the most elegant seventeenth-century long gun in existence, it is also of the greatest possible historical importance, for it is one of the three flintlock guns known that can be proved—by signatures or documentation—to have been made in the workshop of the inventors of this ignition system, the three brothers Le Bourgeoys in Lisieux, and it is documented as part of the celebrated Cabinet d'Armes of Louis XIII, whose interest in firearms earned him the nickname Louis l'Arcquebusier. (He is better known today, though, as the king in Alexandre Dumas's *Three Musketeers*.)

It is difficult to decide which one of the Le Bourgeoys brothers—Jean, Marin, or Pierre—was the mechanical genius who "invented" the beautifully simple action of the flintlock (or better, streamlined it from earlier systems). Jean (died 1615) is recorded in Lisieux as a gunsmith and also a clockmaker; he was in charge of the town clock. A mark with his initials, IB, flanking a tiny crossbow is said to be stamped on the barrels of three wheellock pistols in London, Berlin, and Paris. Marin (died 1634), whose name appears engraved on mountings of the highly decorated stocks of two early flintlock guns, one in the Musée de l'Armée in Paris (M 435) and one in the State Hermitage Museum, Leningrad (F 281), was appointed "peintre ordinaire" to the governor of Normandy, François de

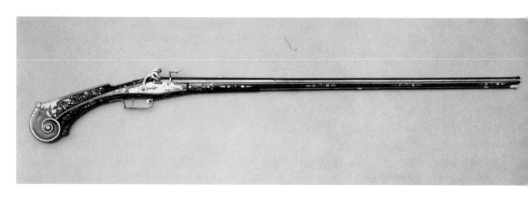

FIGURE 40. Flintlock fowling piece. French (Lisieux). About 1615. By Pierre and Marin Le Bourgeoys. Rogers and Harris Brisbane Dick Funds, 1972.223

Bourbon, Duke of Montpensier, in 1589 and was painter to the king from 1598 through 1633. From this and his signature—on the stocks and not on the locks—it can be assumed that he was the decorator and designer, but in 1608, when he received a *brevet de logement* for the recently completed Louvre Gallery, he is mentioned as "peintre et vallet de chambre et ouvrier en globes mouvans, sculpteur, et aultres inventions mécaniques." The third brother, Pierre (died 1627), seems to have been a barrelmaker, as a mark with his initials, PB, flanking a tiny crossbow appears on several firearms in the Le Bourgeoys style.

Our gun bears this mark. On the stock it has the crowned cipher of Louis XIII as part of its rich decoration, and on the underside of the stock there is stamped the number 134. The inventory of Louis XIII's Cabinet d'Armes identifies number 134 as

> Un beau fusil de 4 pieds 4 pouces, fait à Lizieux, le canon rond, couleau d'eau, ayant une arreste sur le devant et à pams sur le derrière, doré de rinceaux en trois endroits, la platine unie ornée de quelques petittes dorées sur un beau bois de poirier noircy, enrichy de plusieurs petits ornemens d'argent et de nacre de perle, la crosse terminée en consolle par le dessous, sur laquelle il y a une longue fueuille de cuivre doré de rapport, et sur le poulcier un mascaron d'argent et une L couronnée vis à vis la lumière.

Before the flintlock, the standard ignition system until well into the nineteenth century, there were—if we discount the matchlock, which

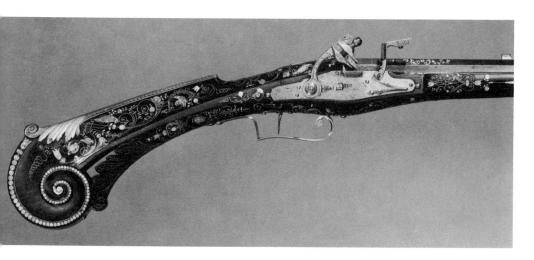

FIGURE 41. Detail of Figure 40, showing lock side

required a separately lit slow-burning fuse—the wheellock (sometimes called the "German" lock) and the snaphaunces (the "Netherlandish," with steel and pancover separated, and the "Italian" and "Spanish," with steel and pancover joined into a battery). The new "French" flintlock had fewer moving parts with the main action sheltered on the inside, and it used the battery, which made it sturdier and its ignition a fraction of a second faster than the other systems, whose more complicated inner mechanisms engaged the outer wheel or hammer through slots in the lockplate. This faster action was designed for shooting birds on the wing, and therefore, not surprisingly, the early flintlock guns from the Le Bourgeoys workshop are fine hunting weapons. Admittedly, the forward motion of the hammer gave it a tiny jerk, in contrast to the smooth release of the wheellock, but this would be more than compensated for by its greater weather resistance and easy maintenance.

Of the 455 objects listed in the inventory of the Cabinet d'Armes, nearly one hundred still exist and can be identified; forty-eight are in the Musée de l'Armée in Paris. The Metropolitan Museum owns eight objects that were once owned by Louis XIII, among them a wheellock carbine with the Cabinet d'Armes number 52, a pair of wheellock pistols with the *PB* mark attributable to Pierre Le Bourgeoys, and another pair signed by the Bourgeoys's competitor, François Duclos. Private collections that could boast of more than two objects from the Cabinet d'Armes were those of Georges Pauilhac, in Paris, of William Goodwin Renwick, in Arizona, and of W. Keith Neal, in Warminster, Wilts. Of these only the Keith Neal collection still exists; the Pauilhac collection is now incorporated into the Musée de l'Armée, and it is about the dispersal of the Renwick collection that this article is concerned.

The provenance of both the Paris and Leningrad flintlock guns signed by Marin Le Bourgeoys lacks any mystery. The Paris gun practically never left Paris, simply moving from the Cabinet d'Armes into the Musée de l'Armée; the Leningrad gun entered the Hermitage from the armory of Prince Condé at Chantilly. However, the third gun appeared as suddenly and mysteriously in the Renwick collection, in the 1920s, as did the Bury St. Edmunds cross, a generation later, in the collection of Topic-Mimara.

William G. Renwick had brought together one of the largest and most important collections of firearms in America. In his later life he was considered a recluse; he kept his collection locked up in his home in

Tucson, Arizona. The Louis XIII gun was seen by the public only once, in a great loan exhibition from private collections here at the Metropolitan, in 1931. It was published a couple of times, though less often than such an important object deserved, and even then in a way—as in Torsten Lenk's *The Flintlock* (1939)—that indicated the author was working from photographs only. With time, rumors grew among collectors and connoisseurs about the fabulous treasures hidden in Tuscon. Some of the great pieces, it was darkly hinted, with fitting expressions of frustration, were rusting away in condensation puddles in the supposedly overcooled air-conditioned cases. Other rumors, uttered in similar frustration, had it that whatever was left after these envisioned ravages would "go to the Smithsonian." Personally, I could never quite understand why this should be thought a fate worse than death. After all, at the Smithsonian the objects would be properly cared for and accessible to the public. It would be too wonderful for words, though, if there was any chance at all for us to acquire the fabulous Louis XIII gun . . . .

William Renwick died in 1972. Waves of excitement spread through the world of arms collecting when it was revealed that only a couple of hundred pieces had been bequeathed to the Smithsonian Institution, and that the bulk of the collection would be auctioned at Sotheby's of London in at least four large sales. The most dizzying detail was that the Louis XIII gun was not among the pieces willed to the Smithsonian, but would be the pièce de résistance of the second sale, scheduled for November 21, 1972.

In his will Renwick bequeathed to the Metropolitan a fine seventeenth-century Netherlandish snaphaunce-revolver gun. Curator Emeritus Stephen V. Grancsay, who arranged the 1931 exhibition with the thinly disguised goal of persuading as many lenders as possible to eventually donate or bequeath objects to the Museum, had repeatedly pointed out to me that the acquisition of the Louis XIII gun would be a crowning achievement for the department. Apparently there had once been the possibility that this gun would be bequeathed to the Museum, perhaps with more significant objects than the snaphaunce-revolver, but this plan had long before been changed.

As soon as the sales catalogue appeared, featuring the Louis XIII gun on a color page, friends of the department called from all sides to make sure that we would "of course" try to win this prize. Sotheby's estimate for the gun was £45,000, or about $100,000, a formidable sum in the field of arms and armor, even in the light of a previous attempt by a group of American dealers to buy the entire Renwick collection for half a million dollars, a patriotic enterprise to keep the money within the American economy.

Wheels were set rolling in the Arms and Armor Department. Dossiers were accumulated, forms were filled out, educated guesses were made about the amount to be sought from the Acquisitions Committee. There is a rule of thumb that the auction price of a desirable object may climb to twice that of its estimate. Keeping in mind that the previous year we had paid an auction price of $100,000 for the presumably last Boutet garniture de luxe—a hunting rifle and two pistols richly mounted in silver—I was convinced that $250,000 would be the least the Louis XIII gun would bring. The memoranda grew more and more eloquent, stressing the esthetic importance of the fowling piece as the finest available firearm of its period and pointing out its cultural significance for an American museum; after all, the flintlock gun was a key factor in the settlement of America.

There were barely two weeks between the issuance of the estimate from Sotheby's and the sale. A meeting of the Acquisitions Committee was scheduled for Monday, November 20. Since the sale was to be the next afternoon, there would be just enough time to cable our bid—provided, of course, that the Acquisitions Committee approved of our making a bid.

Things happened very fast. A week before the sale the Director called me for a brief interview; he was enthusiastic about the project: "This is just great, and we must do everything to get it—but you never have seen the object? All right, get to London as fast as you can, take a long good look at the piece—there will be only Friday, I doubt you will have a chance on Saturday—and be back on Monday in time for the Acquisitions Committee meeting."

I quickly obtained travel funds and reservations, called my wife about Situation Red Alert, and flew to London. On my way to Sotheby's I stopped at the Wallace Collection to inspect its Le Bourgeoys pistol and carbine—both wheellocks—and other pieces from the Cabinet d'Armes. (The Wallace Collection, as a closed national collection, could afford to stay aloof from the upcoming scramble for the new acquisition.) I particularly wanted to check the mark on the barrel of the Collection's pistol. The mark had been read and published both as *IB* and *PB*. The first reading, interpretable as the initials of Jean Le Bourgeoys, would date the pistol to between 1610, the year of Louis's accession, and 1615, the year of Jean's death. The second reading would make the mark that of Pierre Le Bourgeoys, who lived until 1627. A similar uncertainty had existed about the mark on the Renwick gun, though John Hayward, the Sotheby cataloguer, identified it as *PB*. Vesey Norman, Assistant Director of the Wallace Collection, showed me the Le Bourgeoys pieces, and the mark of the pistol—even though it was a tiny bit blurred—was indeed *IB*. The mark on the carbine, however, was definitely *PB*.

With this useful bit of information and the stylistic image of the Wallace Collection's pieces firmly in mind, I went on to Sotheby's and there, in the delightfully Dickensian atmosphere of rambling offices and storerooms, was most cordially received by Mr. Hayward and his assistant, Diane Keith Neal, daughter of W. Keith Neal, the collector. I soon had the fowling piece in my cotton-gloved hands. Here I will have to admit that, though I consider arms and armor one of the most fascinating fields in all cultural history, my enthusiasm for firearms is limited, no doubt having to do with an overexposure to them in World War II. But the legendary Renwick gun was something else. It looked much more impressive in hand than it did in its photographs. Its elegant outline, with its boldly curved butt spiral, and its perfect balance that made it appear almost weightless, were breathtaking. The gun was in excellent condition. Evidently it had been given a first-class overhaul. No traces of the darkly rumored irreparable damages were to be seen. I looked at the mark. Sure enough, *PB*—exactly as on the Wallace Collection's carbine. So it was Pierre after all, and the date, consequently, before 1627. However, by reason of the king's crowned cipher, in its form as used before 1620, it could be dated as early as 1610, and, because its construction was practically identical to that of the Leningrad gun, which bears the arms of France and Navarre and is therefore attributed to Louis's father, Henry IV, the traditional dating 1610–1615 was probably right.

But I would worry later about the exact chronology. After all, that's what research is for. Relaxing, I went over the gun inch by inch with my magnifying glass, delighting in the delicate scrolled inlays of silver wire in the dark pearwood stock, and the charming little birds and rabbits—inlaid with silver, gilt-bronze, and mother-of-pearl—gamboling in the silver vines, apparently without a thought about the sinister purpose of the object they adorned.

When I reported back to the Director on Monday, it was agreed that

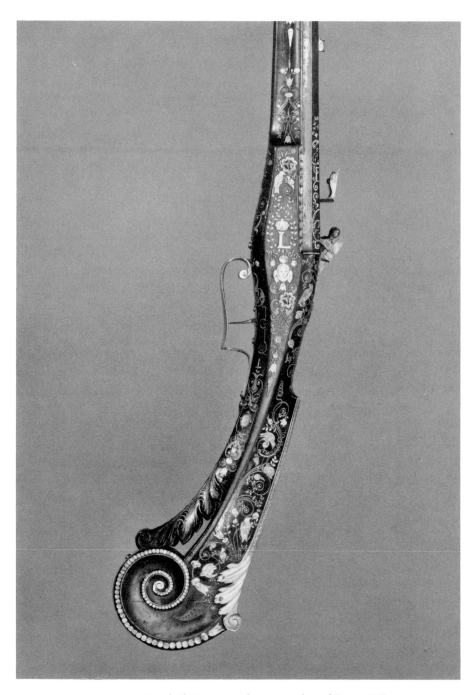

FIGURE 42. Detail of Figure 40, showing cipher of Louis XIII

a London dealer should do the bidding for us. We telephoned Frank Partridge, who had acted as agent for the department on two earlier purchases. He suggested that we should be prepared to pay much more than the $100,000 estimated, and even more than the $250,000 I had proposed as a realistic figure in my purchase application form.

By the time of the Acquisitions Committee meeting jet-lag had caught up with me, and everything in sight had rather fuzzy edges. I remember little of my oral case for buying the gun except that I stressed the importance of the invention of the flintlock, pointing out that our civilization would have had difficulties spreading beyond Plymouth Rock without it. I must have been sufficiently eloquent, because the Trustees, on the advice of the Director, who quoted Mr. Partridge's suggestion, allocated a staggering sum for the purchase.

The morning after the auction came the eagerly awaited call from the Director: "Congratulations, you are the proud owner of the most beautiful gun in the world!" The newspapers, calling it "the world's most expensive gun," made much of the purchase price of $300,000. When I proudly announced the acquisition to Stephen Grancsay, he remarked thoughtfully, "I'm glad that we finally got it, but if we could have bought it right after the exhibition in 1931, we could have had it for a lot less."

The Stuff That Wasn't in the Metropolitan: Notes on Collecting Primitive Art

DOUGLAS NEWTON, *Chairman*

JULIE JONES, *Curator*

SUSAN VOGEL, *Associate Curator*
Primitive Art

Why anyone who is not a squirrel, packrat, or bowerbird collects anything, heaven knows. At least one hopes that heaven knows, for nobody else has a clear opinion about the process, not even that inveterate accumulator Sigmund Freud. Religion frowns upon it, and convenience is not served by it, for collecting and collections entail, in more senses of the word than one, care. The bowerbird's motives are clear enough, though: he disposes pretty oddments around his bower in a display intended to tempt his prospective mate. It is pleasing and slightly flattering to note that this art collector among birds is, on just these grounds, said by ornithologists to be further up the evolutionary rungs than his more glamorous relatives, the effervescently plumed birds of paradise.

But why *primitive* art? and, at that, what is primitive art?

The orthodox answer is, of course, "The visual arts of Africa, the Pacific Basin, and Precolumbian and Native America." This is startlingly comprehensive: it covers the art of almost three continents (including Australia) and a vast number of islands, over a time span of at least three thousand years. Primitive art is not, be it noted, *"art sauvage,"* or even the "art of primitive peoples," since it includes the high civilizations of Middle and South America. "Primitive," for the time being, remains a useful catchall sort of adjective, about as accurate as "Gothic"; its days of further use may well be numbered.

There are other definitions, however.

There used to be a sort of riddle going the rounds among people interested in the subject; Robert Goldwater told it to me, and it is possible he made it up. It goes like this:

Q: "What's primitive art?"

A: "The stuff that isn't in the Metropolitan."

The reasons for the expansion of taste that took place through the first part of the twentieth century and allowed the acceptance of primitive art by people born to Western traditions are a study in themselves—far too complicated to describe here. Why it was not in the Metropolitan before and why it now is, involves historical changes in the public view of what art is, in trends in collecting, and in the Museum's policy. Most of these changes have accelerated over the last few decades.

The Metropolitan Museum did in fact acquire its first objects in the field as early as 1882—with a group of Peruvian antiquities—only a dozen years after it opened its doors, but this promising beginning failed to flourish. In succeeding decades, the collections that it owned were regarded with indifference by the Metropolitan's administrators, and indeed they were bundled off to the American Museum of Natural History, where it was felt they more properly belonged. It is no secret that one director, himself an eminent archaeologist, displayed what amounted to hostility

FIGURE 43. Relief slab: eagle devouring heart. Northern Veracruz, near Tampico, Mexico (?). Early Postclassic period, 1000–1200. Limestone with traces of stucco and paint. Gift of Frederic E. Church, 93.27.1

toward concrete proposals for the reanimation and expansion of the Precolumbian collections.

This did nothing to deter the formation of private collections of primitive art. The most important of these was made by Nelson A. Rockefeller in a manner which combined his own connoisseurship with the expertise of René d'Harnoncourt, the Director of the Museum of Modern Art. Apart from his long involvement with Precolumbian art, d'Harnoncourt had organized and installed at the Museum of Modern Art the exhibitions of *Indian Art of the United States* (1941) and *Arts of the South Seas* (1946), a series which continued with *Ancient Art of the Andes* (1954), each a monument to the works displayed. D'Harnoncourt hit upon a device to give Rockefeller's growing collection a goal and system. A fine draughtsman, he compiled a series of notebooks with drawings of exemplary objects from the cultures to be covered. As equivalent objects were acquired, he added a photograph and extracted the drawing, so that gradually the ideal became transmuted into the real under the collector's eyes. Eventually the collection reached a level of quantity and quality which justified its being made a public institution. The Museum of Primitive Art was founded in 1954 and opened its doors to the public in 1957, with Nelson Rockefeller the Founder and President, René d'Harnoncourt the Vice-President, and Robert Goldwater the Director.

The collecting process became rather more formalized. The curatorial staff scouted for suitable works and presented them to an Acquisitions Committee, which made recommendations to the President. The aim was to continue assembling works of high quality that augmented existing holdings. Everything was done on the basis of single objects: by set policy, no other collections might be bought *en bloc,* and no collecting in the field was ever sponsored. In practice, this meant purchasing from dealers and runners in New York and Europe. It so happened that at the time remarkable discoveries were being made in various parts of the world, the objects were circulating freely, and the Museum was able to make the most of opportunities that will not recur. The accession records are, in fact, something of a document of the state of the market in those days. As a result, the Museum's collection, as it grew, retained a quality that was saved from subjectivity by rather strict standards. This is not to say that nobody made mistakes. The purchases reflected the attitudes of gather-ye-roses-while-ye-may and wait-and-see, and both, we know now, sometimes led to injudicious acquisitions and to serious omissions. More often, however, both attitudes paid off.

FIGURE 44. Ancestor poles. Asmat tribe, New Guinea. Wood, paint, fiber. Collected by Michael C. Rockefeller. Installation photograph from *Art of Oceania, Africa, and the Americas from the Museum of Primitive Art,* 1969

In the years 1957–1973 the collection vastly increased, over 70 exhibitions were organized, and a stream of books, catalogues, and studies, mostly written by the staff, were published. Many of the exhibitions broke new ground, and a number of the books remain standard works. The public effect was striking: thousands of visitors to the Museum became aware of an enormous range of art styles to which they had never before been exposed. Since the physical dimensions of the Museum were small—a converted brownstone on 54th Street—the extent of the collection could never be properly understood. It was partly revealed in *The World of Primitive Art,* a large show held in 1966 in the old premises of the Whitney Museum, and more extensively revealed in 1969 in the exhibition *Art of Oceania, Africa, and the Americas,* held at the Metropolitan Museum.

For, over the years, the Metropolitan had changed. Its original devotion to mainly western art had been affected by its great accessions of oriental, Islamic, and ancient Egyptian art. Now that it was increasingly clear that the Metropolitan would go on to become an encyclopaedic institution, it could be seen that primitive art was the one field still largely missing.

The Museum of Primitive Art had long outgrown its home, to the extent that its potential was stunted. Appropriate space would become available in the Metropolitan. So it was a happy occasion when Nelson Rockefeller announced, at the opening of the 1969 show, that he would give the Metropolitan his collection, upon completion of a building to be called the Michael C. Rockefeller Wing in memory of the son who had made such great contributions to his father's museum.

A Department of Primitive Art was set up, under the aegis of Dudley T. Easby, formerly the Metropolitan's Secretary. The knowledge and taste of Easby's lifetime enthusiasm was embodied in *Before Cortés,* the dazzling Precolumbian exhibition of 1970. The department was off to a brilliant start. Since then, work has gone ahead on the Wing, and the end of the period of preparation is in sight. With its completion, primitive art will take its place in the only museum that shows it as part of the spectrum of the world's art.   DN

The earliest collectors of Precolumbian art were, it might be said, the sixteenth-century explorers and conquerers of the New World who sent back to Europe things of astonishing imagery and flamboyant workmanship meant to amaze kings and bedazzle popes. "All sorts of wonderful things for various uses . . . much more beautiful to behold than things

FIGURE 45. Standing warrior with club [right]. Candelaria River drainage (?), Campeche, Mexico. A.D. 800–1000. Maya-Toltec. Marble. Harris Brisbane Dick Fund, 66.181. Installation photograph from *Before Cortés, Sculpture of Middle America,* 1970–1971

of which miracles are made," wrote Albrecht Dürer in admiration of Fernando Cortés's 1520 offering to Charles V. The sense of wonder and astonishment at the American treasures did not carry through, unfortunately, and few of the many sixteenth-century treasures from the great Indian kingdoms of the Western Hemisphere can be found in European collections today; these few are among the "aristocracy" of Precolumbian objects, and as with many an "aristocrat," they have often wandered and been unloved. Today, these aristocrats of Precolumbian art are part of a much bigger family, one that has grown large only in the past century.

The growth began when the vast, reclusive Spanish viceroyalties allowed foreigners into their American domains in the early nineteenth century. Scientific travelers, of which Alexander von Humboldt was the initial notable example, were granted permission to travel on the American continents, and they returned to Europe with all manner of data, with collections of flora and fauna, with theories and opinions, and with strange and exotic objects. The best-known traveler from the United States was John Lloyd Stevens, who, in the late 1830s journeyed through Central America and Yucatan and collected a number of "vases, figures, idols and other relics." In 1842 these were exhibited in New York, the first exhibition of Precolumbian antiquities to take place in the United States.

By the end of the nineteenth century archaeological traveling had become archaeological collecting. Scientists of antiquarian bent began to preserve and investigate objects and collections of objects. On both sides of the Atlantic, natural history museums, many of them newly formed, were eager to fill their exhibition halls with indigenous products of the New World. In 1892 the Exposición-Historico-Americana, organized to commemorate the four-hundredth anniversary of the discovery of America, took place in Madrid and had an enormous impact not only on Europe, where great new interest in Indian America was generated, but on the participating Latin American republics as well. In amassing the material to send to Madrid, many of the American countries focused for the first time on the tangible realities of their ancient Indian heritage. One of the chief attractions of the Madrid exposition was the display from Colombia, consisting primarily of Precolumbian gold objects: "The numerous magnificent specimens of native gold work . . . excited the admiration of those of antiquarian taste, from their novelty as well as for the perfection of their designs."

In the United States an early interest in our own Indians had led to the founding of such societies as the American Antiquarian Society, which was organized in 1812 to study, collect, and preserve the antiquities of this country. It was at the meetings of these societies that ancient objects were shown and discussed among the members. Later, the forum for Indian subjects was enlarged when professional staffs were employed by the new natural history museums. In 1869 the American Museum of Natural History was founded in New York; four years later the Department of Anthropology was formed and acquired its first collection of Indian materials.

The collecting of American antiquities was to remain in the hands of the natural history museums until the 1930s, when attitudes and interests began to change. The natural history museums in Europe and the United States had filled not only their exhibition halls but their storerooms as well, and professional anthropological interest turned more and more to excavation and away from what was called, with increasing condescension as the years passed, material culture. At the same time as the "scientific" interest began to wane, an "artistic" interest began to grow. This latter interest was intimately tied in with, as the oft-told tale would have it, modern art. While the salient "primitive" role in that well-known drama is unequivocally allotted to African art, Precolumbian art is not without a part in the events. In the largest sense it was a part primarily of bystander, for, as the 1933 exhibition *American Sources of Modern Art* stated: "There is no intention here to insist that ancient American art is a major source of modern art. . . . It is intended, simply . . . to indicate that its influence is present."

American Sources of Modern Art was the first major exhibition of Precolumbian art, as such, in this country, and it is fitting that it should have taken place at the Museum of Modern Art. If Precolumbian art had no great influence on modern art, early twentieth-century modernism, on the other hand and albeit indirectly, had enormous influence on our response to Precolumbian art. As the art of the West was so radically redirected at that time, the eyes that could perceive the redirection could also see works from other times and places, works of vastly different formal means, works made outside of Christian iconographic systems, works made in media previously considered insignificant, and even works that were simply functional or useful in nature. The exotic and the pagan could once again be wondered at and admired, and perhaps this time be truly incorporated into the world of art.

JJ

The history of collecting African art can be seen as a history of the delicate interplay among museums, galleries, and collectors. The currents of interest in African art began moving in Europe, especially in Paris, in the first decade of this century. Artists, excited by the visual freshness of the primitive art they discovered at world fairs and in ethnographic museums, excited a small group of collectors and, later, dealers with their new discovery.

When it came to exhibiting African art as *art*, New York started out where one might expect—in the vanguard. Masks hung on the walls, figures stood on pedestals and platforms, the look was clean and modern, the date was 1914, and the place was Fifth Avenue—Alfred Steiglitz's 291 Gallery. *Camera Work* proclaimed: "This was the first time in the history of exhibitions either in this country or elsewhere, that Negro statuary was shown solely from the point of view of art." In those early days, an esthetic approach to African art (as opposed to the prevailing anthropological vision) was just beginning to gain ground; the opposing camps were sharply distinguished.

An exhibition that would be noteworthy even today marked the arrival of African art on the New York museum scene. In 1923 the Brooklyn Museum's Department of Ethnology mounted *Primitive Negro Art,* a show of almost 1,500 Congolese objects of all kinds, ranging from superb figures and masks to baskets, arms, costumes, and pipes. "The entire collection," wrote Stewart Culin in the catalogue, "whatever may have been its original uses, is shown under the classification of art; as representing a creative impulse, and not for the purpose of illustrating the customs of the African peoples." He describes the short history of European interest in primitive art, and the ethnography museums where the objects could be seen, lamenting that "in the majority of these collections their artistic significance is obscured by the wealth of material, and lost, not infrequently, in the efforts made for its elucidation." Information enlisted by the anthropological approach had already become anathema to esthetic presentation.

Four years later African art had reached Fifty-seventh Street in Manhattan (a locale that quickly became one of its natural habitats), where a collection belonging to *Theatre Arts Monthly* went on view. Alain Locke, a Black writer and collector, wrote in the catalogue that the purpose of the show was not only to "bring to America a fine representation of this increasingly prized primitive art, but also to promote the contribution which it can make to contemporary art and life." It was 1927, and African

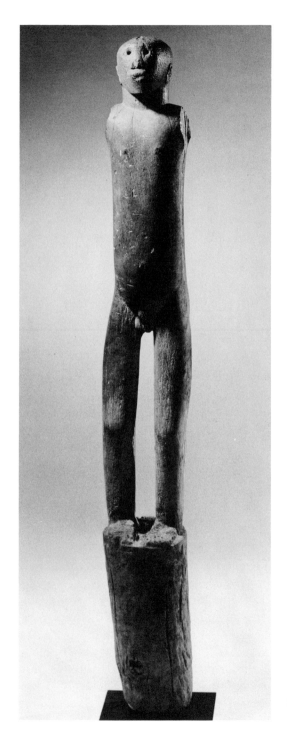

FIGURE 46. Tomb figure. Bongo, Republic of Sudan. Wood. Louis V. Bell and Harris Brisbane Dick Funds, Joseph Pulitzer Bequest, 1973.264. Photograph: Justin Kerr

influences were being felt in graphic, furniture, and textile design, in jazz, and even more in painting and sculpture. Like the Brooklyn Museum, Locke exhibited a great number of utilitarian objects as works of art, stating that "often the finesse of the decorative quality (according to our distinction between the fine and the useful arts) is sufficient to reclassify the object as an object of fine art."

Three years later, when a show called *Rare African Sculptures* opened on the same street, it was apparently felt that this kind of art no longer needed an introduction. The catalogue presented an extreme of the esthetic approach: all 74 pieces appeared in large illustrations without a scrap of text. In 1930, it seems, African art could stand on its own merits in some New York circles.

A landmark exhibition, *African Negro Art,* held at the Museum of Modern Art in 1935, was enormously influential, and for many years exhibitions of African art followed the pattern it had established: sculpture, no decorative arts, presented for its esthetic appeal with little or no information to distract the visitor. James Johnson Sweeney, who directed the exhibition, wrote a catalogue essay that was in fact a manifesto. He particularly warned of the dangers of information:

> In the end, however, it is not the tribal characteristics of Negro art nor its strangeness that are interesting. It is its plastic qualities. Picturesque or exotic features as well as historical and ethnographic considerations have a tendency to blind us to its true worth. This was realized at once by its earliest amateurs. Today with the advances we have made during the last thirty years in our knowledge of Africa it has become an even graver danger. . . . The art of Negro Africa is a sculptor's art. As a sculptural tradition in the last century it has had no rival. It is as sculpture we should approach it.

Back on Fifty-seventh Street,'in the fall of that same year, the stirrings of a third approach to African art were felt in Knoedler's show called *Bronzes and Ivories from the old Kingdom of Benin.* This exhibition had overtones of a new, "justifying" approach in its presentation of objects not because they were great sculpture, but because they were royal, ancient, and finely crafted of prestigious materials. "Old Kingdom" conjures up Egypt; bronze and ivory command respect. Unlike most African art, these works were relatively naturalistic and thus acceptable to more conservative tastes. The catalogue described the difference between this court art and the rest of African art in terms of quality: "The art of Benin is far removed from the geometric stylization which, under the name of 'art negre,' became the fashion of Paris of a few years ago. It has been

FIGURE 47. Saltcellar. Bini-Portuguese. Early 16th century. Ivory. Louis V. Bell and Rogers Funds, 1972.63

supposed that the essence of African art was a geometric sculpture, more or less of indigenous nature. However, it is the art of Benin that represents the true face of African art at its best."

Six months later the "justifying" approach to African art dominated *Sculptures of Old African Civilizations* at the Jacques Seligman gallery. The catalogue entries pointed to similarities between the African works and art from more established traditions. Greek and Roman art, the "geometric style," medieval art, the commedia dell' arte, even cubism, Modigliani, and Picasso were named to lend respectability and familiarity to African art. A comment in the catalogue by the art critic Roger Fry (once Curator of Paintings at the Metropolitan), pointed to one source of the uneasiness about this art:

> We have the habit of thinking that the power to create expressive plastic form is one of the greatest of human achievements, and the names of great sculptors are handed down from generation to generation, so that it seems unfair to be forced to admit that certain nameless savages have possessed this power, not only in a higher degree than we at this moment, but than we as a nation have *ever* possessed it.

While the anthropological and esthetic approaches were confident of the material they presented, the justifiers were not. Bothered because it had been made by "nameless savages," by its apparent newness, and the fact that most of the works were small and wooden, the justifiers would exhibit, collect, and sell African art for the associative virtues they could find in it.

By this time, the justifying approach was necessary because African art no longer astonished a public that had been exposed to modern art for a couple of decades. It had also moved beyond the small avant-garde circles that had been its first audience and now faced a wider, less sophisticated public. This public lacked the confidence in their own eyes that the early collectors, mainly artists and critics, had depended on.

All three approaches, in full flower by the mid-thirties, survive in altered form today. The esthetic and the anthropological schools of thought have tended to converge and now rather resemble each other. Available information, no longer considered the danger it once was, has enormously expanded and sharpened our ideas about African art. The "justifiers" have thought of new associations to validate their choices, but collectors and museums continue to say, as Alain Locke did in the twenties, "the significance of African art is incontestable; at this stage it needs no apologia."   sv

The Price
Was Not
Too High

MARGARETTA SALINGER

Curator Emeritus, European Paintings

When I joined the Department of European Paintings in the spring of 1930 the entire institution was still vibrating with the new life poured into the collections through the nearly two thousand items that constituted the magnificent gift of the Havemeyer collection. The grim events of the preceding autumn had paralyzed the luxury trades, and the sale of pictures in the Fifty-seventh Street galleries had slowed to a halt. But the splendor of the Havemeyer objects and their impressive number were revitalizing for the Museum and its visitors. Six galleries were swept clean of their usual displays and dedicated from March to November to our new treasures. Sixteen years had elapsed since the bequest of Benjamin Altman had brought the Museum a roughly comparable gift. But within two years, in 1931, the institution was once more enriched with a remarkable collection, that of Colonel Michael Friedsam, remarkable in its variety of objects and for the extraordinarily high quality of the individual items. With this bequest there came to the galleries of paintings some of the finest of our Flemish primitives, including the famous, much-debated *Annunciation* from the circle of the Van Eycks and Rogier van der Weyden's portrait of Francesco d'Este, one of the most beautiful likenesses ever painted in the Low Countries. I still remember vividly my first study trip to the storeroom where the pictures lay exposed and the excitement of discovery as a brilliant ray of sun touched Francesco's portrait, revealing the raised outline of a finger ring, painted out with dark pigment, but since made visible, explaining the curious, puzzling, and otherwise meaningless position of the bony Gothic fingers.

Here was a treasure of material mutely awaiting examination, study, comparisons, and interpretation. And best of all, the provisions of my employment in the department meant, as I often said, that I was being paid for doing what I most wanted to do anyway!

As I think back over those early years in the Museum, however, I realize that the greatest pleasures and the greatest satisfactions did not come from looking all those gift horses thoroughly and conscientiously in the mouth, as young research assistants are expected to do. The highest points came with the preparations for a major purchase: the inquiries about former ownership, about scholarly opinions, the search for significant, perhaps previously overlooked publications, the discovery of another version, and its assessment as a copy or a rival replica claiming to be also from the hand of the master to whom the work was attributed, and all this carried on with admonishments about discretion and secrecy and usually, especially in the case of an upcoming auction, under great pressure of time. The curator weighs and marshals all this research and information in preparation for his presentation to the Trustees. The availability of funds preoccupies him, of course, but only in a limited way; the spectacular acquisitions of the last two decades have shown that miracles of generosity follow the conviction of incomparable worth.

Almost routinely in the course of considering a purchase there arises the question whether opportunity will ever knock again, with a comparable, perhaps even greater, work by the same artist. This involves a knowledge of the whereabouts of this artist's major work (how often I have been reminded of the opening question on my first quiz in the history of art: "List the authentic works of Leonardo da Vinci"). The paintings of greatest distinction and value that are still in private hands may by innumerable turns of fortune be shaken loose; death, bankruptcy, and international conflict have played their grim roles in the exchange of works of art, and so has the indifference of an heir to his inheritance.

There was no question of waiting for a second chance with the three uniquely important purchases that were made in 1933, 1934, and 1935. In those three successive years the Museum bought the *Crucifixion and*

FIGURES 48, 49. Jan van Eyck (active by 1422–1441, Flemish). *The Crucifixion; The Last Judgment*. Tempera and oil on canvas, transferred from wood. Fletcher Fund, 33.92a,b

Last Judgment by the Brothers Van Eyck, Watteau's *Mezzetin,* both from the Hermitage Museum in Leningrad, and the *Birth of the Virgin* by the Master of the Barberini Panels.

No more than two or three paintings then in America laid any decent claim to being by the Van Eycks. The two slender little panels we bought, crowded with lively, highly individualized figures, rich as enamels in color, were still in their original carved frames. They had been acquired in Spain in the first half of the nineteenth century by Prince Tatistcheff, the Russian ambassador, along with an *Adoration of the Magi,* with which they had formed a triptych. This central panel, according to the earliest publication of these gems of painting, had "unfortunately" been "taken away from" the ambassador, but the word that the German writer employed, *entwendet,* leaves a shade of doubt as to whether he lost it by direct theft or by some subtle shady dealing that had deprived him of the center of his prize. In any case the finding of this precious lost panel has for decades been a major fantasy for many of us.

The negotiations, long and tedious, were finally concluded through the offices of Charles R. Henschel, the courtly president of Knoedler's. The complicated monetary arrangements were carried on in Zurich. The panels themselves were examined and approved in Berlin by William M. Ivins, at that time the Museum's distinguished curator of prints, who was supposed to accompany them to America on the *Europa,* sailing from Bremen. Codes and secrecy seem to have rendered the transport nerve-wracking, as evidenced by a series of frantic cables. The pictures were expected on the French Line's *Champlain,* but on that ship no trace of them was found. Two weeks later the Museum's Registrar reported to the Director that they had not come by the *Europa* either, and there is a memo stating that perhaps they were coming by the *Albert Ballin.* Finally they arrived. On June 22, 1933, a letter of gratitude from Herbert Winlock, then Director, to Charles Henschel in London, informed him that the pictures made "a far more immediate and successful impression on our Board than we had dared to hope." The purchase had received "unbounded approval." "The longer all of us looked at it," Winlock wrote, of the pair of panels, "the more it grew until eventually we had the feeling that it was as large as 'The Last Judgement' in the Sistine Chapel."

Watteau's rare and exquisite painting of *Mezzetin* presents with wit and wistfulness one of the sad and slightly reprehensible stock figures of the troupe of Italian comedians who had come back from exile in Watteau's lifetime to delight Paris with their songs and jokes. The painting had been in this country for two years when we bought it from the Wildenstein

FIGURE 50. Jean Antoine Watteau (1684–1721, French). *Mezzetin*. Oil on canvas. Munsey Fund, 34.138

Galleries. Its pedigree was brief but remarkably unassailable. It had belonged to Watteau's friend and patron Jean de Jullienne, and at his sale went directly to Empress Catherine the Great. Harry B. Wehle's persuasive curatorial letter called it the most important Watteau he had seen on the market in his fifteen years at the Museum, and quoted Paul Jamot, then Curator at the Louvre, as having said, "I don't know where another Watteau so fine could ever come from again. The best ones are all in museums." And thus another of the best ones found a home in a museum!

If the preparations for publishing the *Mezzetin* included the most delightful rummaging through works on the *commedia dell'arte*, searchings through prints and drawings, and weeks savoring the perfumed ambience of the early eighteenth century, the research into which we plunged the following year in an effort to unravel the mystery of the Barberini panels was pure joy. For six weeks a colleague and I, the youngest members of the department, combed the libraries and print rooms of New York City. We were provided with the scent and then released like hunting dogs, challenged to find in other works of art a recurrence of the innumerable motifs that combine to give the Museum's *Birth of the Virgin* as well as the *Presentation* in the Museum of Fine Arts, Boston, their unique character.

The two pictures had been in the Barberini collection, then had passed into possession of the Corsini branch of the family. They were on sale directly from the Barberini palace in Rome. The negotiations were halting and prolonged, from the moment when the word went out that the two panels might be for sale until the final pact. The Museum's archival records contain, among offers made and offers refused and the usual effort to lower what seemed in 1934 to be a highly unrealistic price, the outlines of a very humorous situation. Like the warriors who sprang up from the dragon's teeth in the story of the Argonauts, a crop of agents, all claiming to represent the vendors, began trying to arrange the sale. None of them were authorized and neither their stories nor their prices agreed. The Frick Collection, the Boston Museum, and our own Trustee, Maitland Griggs, who had the most discriminating adoration of vintage Italian primitives, were all said to be feeling an active interest in the panels. Eventually, the Boston Museum bought its companion, and the *Birth of the Virgin* was sold to us by Knoedler's.

It would be pointless to mention all the great buys of the next quarter-century, but two paintings bought at auction in recent years deserve a place in my consideration of memorable purchases. The acquisition of

FIGURE 51. The Master of the Barberini Panels (active third quarter of 15th century, Italian). *Birth of the Virgin.* Oil and tempera on wood. Rogers and Gwynne M. Andrews Funds, 35.121

Rembrandt's *Aristotle with a Bust of Homer* in 1961 and of Monet's *Terrace at Sainte Adresse* in 1967 had something in common, besides the fact that both were spectacularly expensive. In both cases the supreme effort and determination to secure the pictures for the Museum was not one bit weakened by the consideration that Rembrandt and Monet were already well represented in the collection. The Museum began wondering about the terms of Alfred Erickson's will and the ultimate destiny of the Rembrandt in 1953, while Mrs. Erickson was still alive. The curators and other scholars invited to drink tea in her library with Aristotle and Homer came away spellbound, convinced as long as eight years before the auction that the picture was one that must ultimately come to the Museum. At this time our holdings in the Dutch school were already distinguished by no less than twenty-eight pictures by Rembrandt, all gifts or bequests, most of them accepted by authorities of the time as authentic works. There were three others cautiously catalogued with a question mark after the artist's name.

Why then, one might ask (and many undoubtedly did ask), should the Museum make the Herculean effort to outbid all its competitors at the auction and secure the prize at an expenditure of two million three hundred thousand dollars? It would not be too simple to reply that it was because the picture is unique among Rembrandt's works and unique among the greatest pictures in the world.

Rembrandt painted *Aristotle with a Bust of Homer* for a Sicilian nobleman, Don Antonio Ruffo, in 1652–53 and ten years later obliged the same connoisseur with two other pictures. These were the only commissions he ever carried out for a foreign patron. The external facts about the shipping and delivery of the picture to Messina are well known. The shipping charges, the cost of the crate, and Rembrandt's own fee of 500 florins are all recorded, but we do not know which pictures by Rembrandt had inspired Don Antonio to covet one for himself, nor who supplied Rembrandt with his classical theme. Such themes are rare among Rembrandt's works, numbering only about twenty-five out of his very large oeuvre.

At the beginning of June 1961, the *New York Times* announced the sale that was to take place in November and ran an illustrated story about the picture. During the months that followed there was never a moment of hesitation or doubt in the minds of the Director, James Rorimer, the curator of the department, Theodore Rousseau, or of any members of the staff of the department, that this was a painting that the Museum had to get. To clarify our thinking about the high position the *Aristotle* occu-

FIGURE 52. Rembrandt van Rijn (1606–1669, Dutch). *Aristotle with a Bust of Homer.* Oil on canvas. Purchased with special funds and gifts of friends of the Museum, 61.198

pied among all the works by Rembrandt we invented a game, each of us submitting on ten separate slips of paper the names of the pictures we regarded as his ten greatest. *Aristotle* inevitably appeared in every group. Nearly all of the Trustees shared our enthusiasm, to such an extent that at a special meeting of the Purchasing Committee, held two days before the auction, they authorized a sum even larger than the very high price that ultimately brought down the auctioneer's hammer.

The indisputable beauty of the picture as a triumph of handling paint has never been gainsaid. When Rembrandt painted it he had arrived at a point of artistic and technical development at which he could do, and do superbly, anything he chose. The very impasto of the richly glittering golden chain and of the much-gathered stuff that forms the huge sleeves of the fantastic costume, is evidence of a virtuosity that only a genius could keep in subordination to the tender and poignant mood that is so basic an element of the picture's beauty.

Only two or three other paintings by Rembrandt show the same depth of feeling. The *Prodigal Son* of the Hermitage and the *Jewish Bride* of the Rijksmuseum portray the force of love between two human beings. The *Bathsheba* of the Louvre is an incomparable expression of a state of the soul. In *Aristotle* the tender contact of the infinitely gentle hand with the inanimate bust adds to the philosopher's pose and expression a shade of symbolism that imparts to the philosopher's emotion an element of thought. Here is the ultimate human activity of heart and mind. In spiritual depth this painting has for peers Piero della Francesca's *Resurrection*, the *Pietà of Avignon*, and Titian's *Portrait of Charles V in an Armchair*. Its price was not too high!

If the sheer weight of numbers of paintings already in the Museum was ever a cogent reason for not buying another by the same artist, we would never have acquired the *Terrace at Sainte Adresse*. When the Reverend Theodore Pitcairn announced in the fall of 1967 that he was going to sell it at Christie's in London, the Museum's remarkably large and representative collection of French Impressionist paintings included some thirty-odd paintings by Monet. Among these were early works as well as late, and even *The Beach at Sainte Adresse,* a view of the sands and shore of the same little suburb of Le Havre, painted within a year of the *Terrace*. But how different these two pictures are, how different indeed is the *Terrace at Sainte Adresse* from every picture Monet had painted before it and from all of those that followed!

Thomas Hoving had seen the *Terrace* several years earlier at Bryn Athyn, where it shone among the soberer paintings of the Pitcairn collection with an astonishing brightness. The Reverend Pitcairn, son of the founder of the Pittsburgh Plate Glass Company, had begun his career as a missionary in Basutoland. Soon after his return to America he had broken away from the main branch of the Swedenborgian faith and in 1927 founded The Lord's New Church in Bryn Athyn, of which he became the pastor. The year before, walking with his wife on Fifty-seventh Street in New York, he had seen the *Terrace* in the window of the American branch of Durand-Ruel, and walked in and bought it, one presumes with the same appetite and forthright speedy decision that were to motivate

FIGURE 53. Claude Monet (1840-1926, French). *Terrace at Sainte Adresse*. Oil on canvas. Purchased with special contributions and purchase funds given or bequeathed by friends of the Museum, 67.241

Thomas Hoving, Theodore Rousseau, and the President of the Museum's Board, Arthur Houghton, forty-one years later.

Between Christie's announcement of the sale and the day of the auction, December 1, 1967, there was little time to set in motion the machinery of appropriation of funds. No one had any doubt, considering the prices that Impressionist paintings had begun to bring, that the successful bid was going to be a very high one. The picture had already gone to London and the presentation to the Trustees had to be done with a colored slide, projected on the wall of the Director's office, carefully scaled by Philippe de Montebello to the actual size of the absent painting. The hurried trip that the Director and the Curator made to London and Paris, to see the *Terrace* and to look at Monet's other great works in the Jeu de Paume, is a vivid illustration of the way air travel has made possible a whole new mode of studying works of art. The fresh visual image is surely more dependable than the old reliance on a black-and-white photograph.

The *Terrace at Sainte Adresse* made a new auction record for an Impressionist painting. Degas, as an old man, felt a certain resigned exasperation when he learned of the huge price that his *Dancers at the Bar* fetched at the Rouart sale, comparing himself to a horse who has won the Grand Prix but gets nothing for it but his oats. In this connection one cannot help reflecting that when Monet painted the *Terrace,* and for some time after, he was still in the clutches of humiliating poverty.

If a painting may be said to strike one single note, however, the *Terrace's* dazzling color and its brisk invigorating air strike the single note of unalloyed joy. All his life, work made Monet happy, and in this painting his skills and techniques are so patently in the process of becoming that we can see him intoxicated with each telling passage in which he has managed to get the effect he craved. Areas of traditional local color are juxtaposed to areas of brilliant, short, clear-colored brushstrokes, so that in this paean to sun and wind the whole pageant of Impressionism is unrolled. None of us, I think, would question the essential rightness of adding to a great collection this one more very great example.

Since 1967 we have bought many other notable pictures, including, of course, the Velázquez portrait of Pareja. Wonderful things come on the market less frequently now, but there are still many artists not yet represented in the Metropolitan. No one dares hope for a Leonardo, and probably not for a Piero della Francesca. But we might some day get a chance to buy a Stefan Lochner, or a Saenredam, or a Seghers, and the staff that works to bring about the purchase will taste the keenest pleasure of curatorial work.

Collecting Period Rooms: Frank Lloyd Wright's Francis W. Little House

MORRISON H. HECKSCHER

Curator, American Wing

In 1972 the Museum purchased a large living room designed by Frank Lloyd Wright for a house built in Wayzata, Minnesota, between 1912 and 1915. It is the most important of the several American rooms, staircases, and other parts of buildings acquired in recent years for installation in the new American Bicentennial Wing.

The use by museums of period rooms—whole rooms taken from historic buildings and reinstalled with appropriate, contemporary furnishings—has always provoked debate among museum curators, architectural historians, and preservationists. The causes of concern are not far to seek.

Period rooms require a permanent and inflexible commitment of space within a museum, they are costly to install, and they do not provide as good visibility for the objects shown in them as do regular museum galleries. On the other hand, the period room does what nothing else in a museum can: it provides a visually and spatially appropriate setting for the chosen works of art. Objects that may seem nearly meaningless by themselves can be understood in their original context. Furthermore, the period room can be the means of preserving at least a portion of an important building that is being demolished.

Our decision to acquire the Wright room, however, was not based upon these criteria so much as upon the special character of the existing collections of the American Wing. To explain the nature of these collections a little history is in order.

For the first forty years of its existence, from 1870 to 1910, the Metropolitan was deeply involved with modern American art. Decorative arts, including glass by Tiffany and furniture by the best New York firms, was displayed in line with the Museum's stated intention to improve the quality of our domestic manufactures.

All this changed with the city-wide Hudson-Fulton Celebration of 1909. The contemporary arts fell from favor, and the colonial period came to the fore. At the instigation of Henry Watson Kent, the Museum's Assistant Secretary, and Robert W. deForest, Vice-President of the Board of Trustees, the Museum mounted a major loan show of colonial portraits, antique furniture, and silver. It was an instant success. Even though the Director, Edward Robinson, did not think these American things were worthy of the Museum (a sentiment still occasionally voiced, by the way), key members of the Board thought otherwise. Only the crowding of the objects onto platforms in our large galleries bothered them. Accordingly, it was decided that the domestic arts required suitable domestic settings for their proper permanent display. The answer was to use rooms taken, either in whole or in part, from seventeenth- and eighteenth-century American houses. Thus, the idea of our American period rooms was born, and our approach to American decorative arts was fundamentally altered.

The search for rooms, as well as for the collections that they were to house, began in 1910. The quest intensified after deForest became President of the Board in 1913 and encouraged it. By the early 1920s portions of more than twenty rooms, some of great architectural importance, had been collected. In 1922 Mr. and Mrs. deForest themselves gave funds to build a new wing that had been designed to house the collection. In 1924 the American Wing was opened, and, ever since, it has been one of the most popular parts of the Museum.

Opening off a central gallery on each of three floors were eighteen old rooms, suitably furnished, dating from the seventeenth to the early nineteenth century. The idea behind these rooms changed during the decade of collecting the woodwork and its final installation in the American Wing. Elements that had originally been acquired as sympathetic backgrounds were now considered works of art themselves.

During the next forty years more rooms were acquired, but they served to improve and refine the existing collection rather than to enlarge its scope. The only architecture and decorative arts thought to be collectible were those made prior to about 1815, before the advent of industrial mechanization. The problem was not just a matter of taste. With all those eighteenth-century rooms, it was impossible to make space in the existing wing for objects, much less rooms, of the later nineteenth century. With no reasonable expectation of ever being able to house works from the nineteenth century, the Museum simply did not collect them.

In the mid-1960s the picture changed. James Biddle, Curator of the Wing, began a drive to enlarge its space. By 1967 the conception of a vastly bigger American Wing was on paper at least as Museum policy. The old Wing was to stay as the core of the new building. After fifty years, beloved by a wide public, it had become, itself, a historical monument.

The existence of the rooms representing American architecture up to 1815 left the staff little choice except to continue the collection through the nineteenth and into the twentieth century. Otherwise it would appear that we regarded the architecture of the Victorian period as unworthy of representation.

With real prospects for the new building, the department began to collect the arts of the nineteenth century with conviction. The Museum's centennial exhibition, *19th Century America*, gave us the chance to preview some of our new rooms. Berry B. Tracy, the Wing's new curator, using woodwork acquired for permanent installation in the future Wing, created five temporary period rooms representing significant architectural styles up to 1870.

But this exhibition, splendid full dress rehearsal though it was, demon-

FIGURE 54. Northome about 1915

strated some weaknesses in the American Wing's collections. The first
American architects to have international significance, H. H. Richardson,
Louis Sullivan, and Frank Lloyd Wright, were not represented. We were
too late for Richardson; with one exception his greatest domestic interiors
had been destroyed. Sullivan, a designer of commercial buildings, had
never been considered. Wright's prairie houses still dotted the midwestern
landscape, but they were not considered museum pieces. This was the
situation when I joined the staff in 1968 as an assistant curator.

Against this background, you can imagine my interest when, in 1971,
I learned that Northome, the large summer house designed by Wright in
Minnesota for Francis W. Little, was probably going to be demolished.

Located far from most of Wright's other work, Northome was relatively unknown, even to architectural historians. I knew it only from photographs, which now interested me anew. My eyes were drawn to the great living room in its own almost free-standing pavilion. It was big. Henry-Russell Hitchcock called it "the most spacious domestic interior Wright had ever designed." And it was beautiful. Light poured in from long banks of patterned glass windows, and the flat-coved ceiling appeared to float above the room. But there was something more. Unlike many of Wright's domestic living rooms, this one was entirely self-contained; it did not blend spatially into adjoining rooms. It could be treated on its own. In brief, it was both spectacular and eminently suitable for installation in a museum. I tried to put that thought out of my mind. How could anyone even think of tearing down such a house?

My informant about the house and the present owners' plans for it was Edgar Tafel, a New York architect who had first been referred to me by Arthur Rosenblatt, the Museum's Vice-Director for Architecture and Planning. Tafel had been one of Wright's students at Taliesen and remained an ardent admirer of his work. He had recently restored a Wright house in Buffalo and was concerned with what might happen to Northome. Friends of his in Minnesota, including Don Loveness, another Wright buff, were keeping him apprised of developments.

I alternated between greedy admiration for that living room and absolute horror at the thought that Wright's house was going to disappear. As a curator, I saw something splendid for the Metropolitan Museum; as an architectural historian concerned with preservation, I saw defeat in demolition. It was the classic dilemma. The safest course would have been to write a couple of letters of indignant protest about the situation and wash my hands of another American tragedy. But that I didn't do. The collecting instinct won out.

The situation was this: Northome was owned by Mr. and Mrs. Raymond V. Stevenson, the daughter and son-in-law of the man for whom Wright had built it. After living in it year-round for more than twenty years, the Stevensons now found the house much too big for themselves or for any of their children. Efforts to sell it to a sympathetic private buyer had not succeeded, and local ordinances would not permit its use for anything other than a single-family dwelling. Proposals to turn it into a restaurant or a museum had been rejected as unsuited to the suburban neighborhood. The local authorities had permitted the Stevensons to begin building a new, smaller house just below the big one, with the understanding that, in accordance with the local zoning regulations, those parts of Wright's house closest to the new building would be taken down. The closest parts were the great living room and its entrance vestibule. Obviously, if the Museum was to save anything, it would have to act fast.

In November 1971, Berry Tracy, Edgar Tafel, and I flew out to Wayzata to see what could be done. The Stevensons were most hospitable. They were also, I think, eager to meet us. Don Loveness had already discussed with them the Metropolitan's possible interest in the room. Our proposal obviously had some appeal. First, the Museum would be paying for the privilege of taking away those parts of the house that would have to be removed anyway. Second, the negative aspects of the destruction would be lessened if significant parts of the house could be saved.

The Stevensons ushered us into the room. I won't readily forget that first overwhelming impression. It was much more wonderful than photographs could portray: a sublime space, exquisitely detailed with natural materials and soft earth colors. The room had hardly been touched since its completion in 1915. The wood trim still had its original wax finish, the plaster its original earth-tone washes; even the original furniture was still in place. And all was flooded with autumnal light. Berry and I agreed that if the house must come down, we must have the room and all its furnishings. We would install it in the new Wing with a view, through the banks of patterned glass, into Central Park.

From experience I knew that our Director's enthusiastic support would be essential for any such major acquisition. The permanent commitment of space in the new building, as well as the costs of disassembly, transportation, and installation were matters that would not be treated lightly. We were fortunate, however, that, through the munificent bequest of Emily Crane Chadbourne in 1965, funds were available for projects relating to the new American Wing building. As it turned out, Tom Hoving himself had seen Northome years before. It took only a few of Edgar Tafel's seductive color slides to refresh his memory of the room. I spoke of the Museum's long-term involvement with American period rooms and their increasing importance in the proposed new building and noted that we had nothing to represent the major architects of the end of the nineteenth century. The Northome living room, I concluded, would give our collection of American rooms something of international stature. And with it we would obtain the original furniture and even some of the architec-

FIGURE 55. The living room at Northome in 1972. White oak, electroglazed glass. The Emily C. Chadbourne Bequest, 1972.60.1

tural drawings and correspondence dealing with the design and construction of the house. Hoving agreed that we should buy the room.

Now, a new question arose. If the Museum bought the great room, what would happen to the rest of the house? It contained a library and three bedrooms, each eminently adaptable for museum use, as well as some 200 casement units of ornamental "leaded" glass. The glass had good market value and would probably be saved, come what might. The rooms were something else; they would most likely be destroyed. In the end it was decided that the Museum should offer to buy the whole house and salvage all the glass and finish trim. The extra rooms and glass would be offered to other museums, and the proceeds would help to cover the costs of salvage. Though temporarily burdensome, this course of action would best assure the proper disposition of all the elements. It might also reduce some of the criticism the Museum would inevitably get for being associated with the demolition of a Wright house.

The Stevensons, going ahead with the building of their new house, wanted a quick decision. In December, Tom Hoving, Arthur Rosenblatt, and I flew to Minneapolis. We arrived at Northome, met the Stevensons, and went to the room. I didn't have to say a word.

Later, we met with the Stevensons and their lawyer. In an hour all was settled. The Museum would purchase the entire house but not the land on which it stood. The house would be dismantled in the spring or summer, as soon as the Stevensons had moved into their new one. It was decided that the transaction should not be immediately publicized. While the Stevensons had always tried to make the house available to visitors with a genuine interest in Wright's work, the quantity of rubberneckers was growing all the time. The house was becoming unlivable.

I flew back to New York with a paper shopping bag stuffed with drawings and correspondence related to the building of the house. Some of these documents I had seen before; others Mrs. Stevenson had found recently, after learning of my interest in every scrap of documentation. These papers were rich with suggestions of the tension between the strong-willed client and the strong-willed architect who together had created Northome. Such records would be priceless in our efforts to make the room come alive in the Museum.

In New York the Trustee Acquisitions Committee was chitted for approval of the transaction, and it was granted. With the chase completed, excitement ebbed, and we realized that the work had just begun.

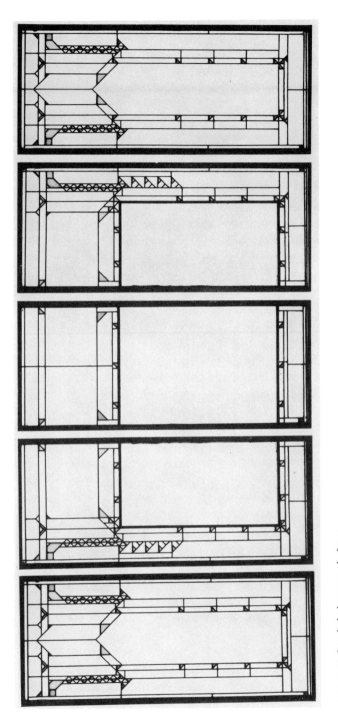

FIGURE 56. Leaded glass panels from the living room, Northome

FIGURE 57. Gate-leg table designed by Wright about 1902 for the Littles' Peoria, Illinois, house. White oak. The Emily C. Chadbourne Bequest, 1972.60.8a,b

The first priority was that the house be properly recorded before its demolition. In January 1972 I accompanied an appraiser to Wayzata. He listed and described all the important interior architectural elements and all of the original furnishings, as well as some additional Wright-related books and drawings I had found. The temperature outside, as we did our recording, was −15°, and in the great room it must have been near zero. Ball-point pens froze. At the end of two days, job done, I left Wayzata with a cold that wanted to qualify as pneumonia.

The next task was to make measured drawings and a full set of record photographs of the house. We waited for warmer weather. In March, Kevin Roche and John Dinkeloo Associates, the Museum's architects and the firm that would ultimately incorporate parts of the house into the American Bicentennial Wing, sent a three-man team to do that job.

On my several visits to Wayzata I had gotten to know the Stevensons quite well. They had grown very interested in our plans for installing the room in New York. Now they wanted to have a last great party in the house and to invite, rather as guests of honor, Tom Hoving and other members of the Museum's staff. On Friday, the 12th of May, Northome was at its most beautiful. Two hundred people moved effortlessly in and around what was now our great room. It worked wonderfully well with a large crowd. Except for our Museum contingent, the Stevensons' guests were family, friends, and neighbors. At least three of them, during the evening, expressed their pleasure to me about the transaction that had solved the Stevensons' problem and then asked *sotto voce*, "But what is it about this old house that is of interest to your Museum?" Looking at the room around me, I realized that we still had a lot of eyes to open.

The final bittersweet day came in June. On the day that demolition began Ada Louise Huxtable, in the *New York Times*, reviewed our purchase as "one of the most important acquisitions in the field of American art by any museum."

Creating a New Department

HENRY GELDZAHLER
Curator, Twentieth Century Art

U ntil 1967 the responsibility for twentieth-century art in the Metropolitan Museum was divided somewhat chaotically among several departments. This was the result not so much of indifference toward our own time as a disinclination to regard it systemically. Modern painting, sculpture, and drawing were cared for by three departments, each of whose responsibilities went so far back in time that the art of the twentieth century seemed incidental. Only twentieth-century American paintings and sculpture were husbanded together under one curator, and that only since 1949, when American artists demonstrated and wrote letters to the *New York Times* insisting that the Metropolitan fulfill its role in support of contemporary art through a judicious use of the George and Arthur Hearn Funds, established for just such a purpose in 1906 and 1911.

Among the incorporators of the Museum in 1870 were several well-known artists: the painters John F. Kensett, Frederic E. Church, and Eastman Johnson, the sculptor John Q. A. Ward, the architect Richard

Morris Hunt, the landscape architect Frederick Law Olmsted, and a poet, William Cullen Bryant. The wording of the charter made it clear that the Museum was incorporated "for the purpose of . . . encouraging and developing the study of the fine arts, and the application of arts to manufacture and practical life, of advancing the general knowledge of kindred subjects, and to that end, of furnishing popular instruction." Thus the art of our time was one of the founders' primary concerns.

Several urgencies led to the creation of the Department of American Paintings and Sculpture in 1949. Francis Henry Taylor, the Director, was under pressure from a New York art world beginning to sense that its contribution was no longer tentative and provincial: artists were conscious of the availability of the Hearn Funds for the purchase of paintings by living Americans, and the Museum had no adequate way of caring for the magnificent Alfred Stieglitz bequest, which included numerous works by such American artists as O'Keeffe, Dove, Marin, Hartley, and Demuth.

When Robert Beverly Hale was named first curator of the new department, the Metropolitan recognized its responsibility to living art and to its public. An artist himself and the most successful instructor in artistic anatomy in our time, Hale acquired magnificent paintings for the collection—Jackson Pollock's *Autumn Rhythm,* Willem de Kooning's *Easter Monday,* and Arshile Gorky's *Water of the Flowery Mill,* to name only three. His success is the more admirable in light of the hostility he encountered from a Board of Trustees singularly uninterested in contemporary art and outrightly offended by abstraction. Bob Hale literally shed tears of emotion and frustration at the meeting of the Acquisitions Committee at which he presented *Autumn Rhythm.* This taciturn man's emotion convinced the Trustees, but in order to acquire the painting he had to turn back a smaller Pollock, purchased five years earlier. This Pollock is now in the collection of S. I. Newhouse, Jr.

American painting was well on its way to a handsome and persuasive representation at the Museum in the nineteen-fifties and early sixties. But what of American sculpture, for which there were no restricted funds? What of modern European paintings and sculpture? What of twentieth-century decorative arts, American and European? Thanks to the munificence of donors and the canniness of curators, none of these areas had been totally neglected. Gertrude Stein had willed her historic portrait by Picasso to the Metropolitan, and Joseph Breck had bought handsomely from the key 1925 Paris Exposition of Decorative Arts; the Stieglitz bequest included drawings by Picasso and Matisse and a Brancusi sculpture; and Robert Hale had induced the Trustees to purchase, with unrestricted funds, Isamu Noguchi's handsome marble *Kouros*.

After Hale's retirement in 1966 and the advent of a new Director, Thomas Hoving, in 1967, it became apparent that a new department was needed to collect the art of the twentieth century more systemically. By this time it was an inescapable fact that the modernist movement was in the process of becoming a discrete entity and, as such, a necessary part of any encyclopaedic museum.

Since New York during the war had surpassed Paris as a center of artistic ferment, and American and European modernists were influencing each other and competing as members of an international movement, it was no longer appropriate to divide responsibility for recent painting and sculpture among four departments. The inclusion of the decorative arts in the new department also made sense from the standpoint of the new postwar internationalism but had more to do with the need to act quickly if New York was ever to have an impressive collection of art deco furniture and objects. Interest in art deco and other neglected realms of collecting was still in the pioneer stage, but it was clear that once a market developed it would skyrocket.

The new department's first name, Contemporary Arts, was unsatisfactory; contemporary sounded temporary and *arts* is one of those words, like monies, that is diminished in the plural. Modern Art sounded too much like a historical period, and anyway had been pre-empted by another great museum. Twentieth Century Art was the name finally chosen; it encompassed the necessary disciplines and could be effective for several decades as the Museum's collection was brought into the continuing present. Twentieth Century Art is, of course, a temporary designation. While there will always be a certain amount of interest in how this Museum dealt with the art of its own time in the first full century of its existence, it seems clear that eventually the painting, sculpture, and decorative arts of our time will be set in a larger perspective with the past, with the best that has been done. And that is as it should be.

There is necessarily something of this kind of historical perspective always at work in an art-historical museum that shows contemporary art. A Francis Bacon exhibition at the Guggenheim Museum is judged and felt differently than a Francis Bacon exhibition at the Metropolitan, because of the proximity of Velázquez, Rembrandt, Goya, and Manet at the Met. A painting by Willem de Kooning hanging fifty yards from a roomful of Rembrandts is judged according to the artist's highest ambition; the stakes are higher and the game more passionate. This is not to argue against the museum that specializes in recent and current art; it is to explicate the role of recent art within the context of the encyclopaedic museum.

The spirit of monopoly, borrowed from American business and sometimes encouraged by the art press, has no place in the community effort of New York museums; surely it is an advantage that more than one institution is busy collecting the best art that is being produced. In this way the definition of the best is not in limited hands; three or four teams are out there. Also, if the flight of impressionist and twentieth-century paintings from France is any example, the more American museums that accumulate our heritage, the better we will be served in the future. That there are Hofmanns, Averys, and David Smiths in five New York museums is not a failure of the system; it is its glory.

There are eighteen curatorial departments at the Met. When the history of art is divided into eighteen chapters the results are understandably both logical and arbitrary. Which department is responsible for Scythian gold, for Fayum portraits, for art nouveau furniture? But, then, the vitality of an institution is not as dependent on rational organization as it is on the enthusiasms of individuals; the collections of a century-old museum are the result of the cumulative wisdom, eccentricity, passions, and lapses of hundreds of artists, trustees, collectors, dealers, art historians, critics, and curators.

An argument frequently heard at Acquisitions Committee meetings is that an object proposed for purchase will fill a gap in the collection, as if we were aiming for a seamless web. The process of acquisition often involves the awareness of a serious gap, granted, but is inspired far more by the availability of a particular work of art—such as the appearance on the market of a David Smith sculpture that haunts the memory and that may never be available again. The need for excellence, not merely chronology, must be satisfied.

The purchase by exchange of David Smith's *Becca* in 1972 was the subject of a great deal of journalistic concern. The practice of museums' selling and exchanging works of art, though much discussed, was not the central issue. After all, every major museum, in and out of New York, had quietly exchanged and improved its collections for many years without provoking scandal. To cite just one example, if the Museum of Modern

Art had not disposed of a Cézanne watercolor to make the purchase possible, New York and America would not now have Picasso's *Demoiselles d'Avignon.*

It was not so much the Metropolitan's purchase by exchange that was questionable; rather, it was the Museum's failure to inform the public and the heirs of the donor whose gifts were being exchanged. Following a long-established tradition among museums of keeping such transactions

FIGURE 58. David Smith (1906–1965, American). *Becca.* Stainless steel. Bequest of Miss Adelaide Milton de Groot (1876–1967), by exchange, 1972.127

quiet, the Metropolitan's first responses to inquiries were guarded. The critics of this secretiveness were correct. A change of policy was indeed overdue. One result of the press coverage of this and other exchanges and sales at the time is that the Attorney General's office has given the state's museums welcome guidelines to help protect the public interest.

Had the Museum announced that it was planning to exchange six specific paintings from the bequest of Adelaide Milton de Groot for *Becca* by David Smith and *Ocean Park #30* by Richard Diebenkorn, it is doubtful that there would have been much controversy. As it was, journalistic critics without adequate knowledge of the paintings being deaccessioned suggested that since the Museum had traded works by such historical masters as Renoir, Bonnard, Picasso, Gris, and Modigliani for a Smith and a Diebenkorn, future generations were losing the benefit of priceless treasures.

In fact, the six paintings exchanged were minor works of Renoir, Bonnard, Modigliani, and Picasso, each of whom is represented in the collection by far better examples, and neither of the two small paintings by Gris was significant enough to represent him adequately. The paintings had been at the Museum since 1952. Several curators had tried to hang them in the public galleries only to find again and again that they were simply not of prime quality.

I had to bring *Becca* before the Trustees more than once before we acquired it. In the interval of two years, pursuant to Smith's testamentary instructions, and to the aggressive style of the Marlborough Gallery, then agents for the Smith estate, the sculpture went up in price by fifty thousand dollars and then by an additional one hundred thousand dollars, reflecting the artist's increasing international stature, the importance of *Becca* as a late great work, and the acquisition of other major Smiths by public collections. Almost every member of the Acquisitions Committee was enthusiastic about *Becca* when it was presented the second time, displayed at an evening meeting in the Hall of Arms and Armor, steel against steel, a marvelously apt temporary setting.

There was genuine admiration for *Becca,* but there was simply no money available to purchase it. We have never had money specifically marked for modern sculpture, no fund for sculpture equivalent to the Hearn Funds for American paintings. As a result, while the Metropolitan was building a persuasive collection of first-rate postwar American paintings, the sculpture of the period was collected only sporadically.

When it became apparent that six paintings on a previously compiled list of works to be deaccessioned could be exchanged for *Becca,* I recommended this procedure and the Acquisitions Committee agreed.

Along with Isamu Noguchi and Alexander Calder, David Smith produced American sculpture of international quality. We have several Calders and a great Noguchi. We also have Smith's *Tank Totem II,* acquired in 1953, a pleasant example of an aspect of his work of that decade but one that does not adequately represent his achievement. There were 408 works in our exhibition *New York Painting and Sculpture 1940–1970;* 22 of them were by Smith. My conviction about the supreme quality of his *Becca* (named after one of this daughters, Rebecca) was such that it stood at the head of the grand staircase at the entrance to the exhibition. Executed in 1965, the last year of his life, *Becca* sums up both David Smith's lifelong debt to cubism and the correspondence in his work to that of his contemporaries the abstract expressionists and their immediate heirs, the color-field painters. It is a superb three-dimensional mate to Jackson Pollock's *Autumn Rhythm* and Morris Louis's *Alpha Pi.* Even though she never saw *Becca,* I believe that Adelaide Milton de Groot's memory is enhanced by the permanent linking of her name with the purchase by exchange of this masterpiece.

In 1964 Barnett Newman's painting *Concord* was hanging in the back room at Betty Parsons's gallery. It had been part of her own collection since 1950 when she exhibited it in the artist's first one-man show. In 1950 the audience for Newman's work was restricted; we can almost count them—Tony Smith, Clement Greenberg, Jackson Pollock, Betty Parsons, and Annalee Newman. Though Newman had a reputation among artists, it was not until the late fifties and early sixties that he was seen more generally as a major contributor to the glory of postwar American art.

I asked Mrs. Parsons if she would consider selling *Concord* to us. She answered that it was not for sale, but that if it were to go to the Museum she would let us have it for $30,000. The price was reasonable, the picture excellent, and the provenance impeccable. Newman himself agreed with the choice. There being sufficient income in the Hearn Funds, I presented *Concord* to the Acquisitions Committee in 1964 and pleaded the case for abstract expressionism as a movement, Barnett Newman as an artist, and *Concord* as a prime example of his work. There was some discussion about the durability of the painting: the two vertical elements that divided the canvas in the middle were made of masking tape with some paint

FIGURE 59. Barnett Newman (1905–1970, American). *Concord*. Oil and masking tape on canvas. George A. Hearn Fund, 68.178

overlaid. The Curator of Prints, Hyatt Mayor, asked for his opinion, said that masking tape might conceivably not last forever. After curators have made their cases to the Acquisitions Committee they leave the room and the Trustees deliberate. It's a bit like school. The next day it was announced that the painting had been turned down.

Several years later, under a new administration, I went back to Betty Parsons and said, "Can we try again with your Newman?"

She said, "Yes, for the Museum."

I asked, "How much is it now?"

She said, a bit surprised, "thirty thousand dollars."

I was grateful to her. She could legitimately have asked more, but she was not out to make a killing; she was interested in the Met's acquiring an excellent painting.

The Trustees were presented with the same painting at the same price. Nobody mentioned the earlier effort, nobody questioned the longevity of masking tape. Indeed, the question of the masking tape never even came up. We bought the painting I consider to be one of the most beautiful in our collection.

But the masking tape continues to nag at my memory and conscience. We collect not only for the present but for the future. Hyatt Mayor was perfectly correct. Masking tape, unaided by scientific conservation, will not last forever. We keep a weather eye on *Concord*'s condition, and twice have had to glue down tiny edges of tape. Our responsibility is clear. We will keep an accurate photographic record of the tape in its present state and be ready to reproduce it, when necessary, in a more stable material.

Artists have always experimented with new materials. Leonardo and Delacroix spring to mind. Leonardo's *The Battle of Anghiari* blistered off the wall almost before it was finished and, in the nineteenth century, bitumin turned out to be a fugitive material. Imaginative scientific conservation can go a long way toward arresting the effects of self-destructing innovation. If by its esthetic quality a work insists on being preserved, a sympathetic scientific conservator can do wonders.

The parameters of the activity of the Department of Twentieth Century Art in decorative arts are indicated by the acquisition of a major set of windows by Frank Lloyd Wright, a collection of sixteen superb hand-turned bowls by the American craftsman James Prestini, a chair by the Spanish art nouveau architect Gaudí, four extraordinary pieces of furniture by his Italian contemporary Carlo Bugatti, and products of the Wiener Werkstatte.

Perhaps our most telling accomplishment has been in the collection of masterworks produced in Paris in the nineteen-twenties by artist-craftsmen such as the furniture designer Jacques-Emile Ruhlmann, the innovator in glass Maurice Marinot, and the silversmith Jean Puiforcat. At an auction in Paris in 1972 we made dramatic acquisitions in this field: an African-inspired stool by Pierre Legrain (already represented in the collection by several handsome leather-bound books) and a small table of ebony, ivory, and sharkskin by Clement Rousseau. Both had been commissioned by the French couturier, collector, and Maecenas, Jacques Doucet for his new apartment, which was barely completed at the time of his death in 1929. They represent the third phase of Doucet's collecting: he moved with grace from painting, sculpture, and furnishings of the eighteenth century to the work of Picasso and the Douanier Rousseau and then to the new design sense that was to triumph as art deco. Much of Doucet's furniture had been given to the Musée des Arts Decoratifs in Paris. The news that more pieces of comparable quality remained in private hands and through an inheritance dispute were to come up for auction at the Hôtel Drouot called for action. I requested twenty thousand dollars of the Trustees' funds to buy, I thought, a handsome sofa by Coard. We needed the unrestricted funds because we had spent the interest and capital of the Edward C. Moore Fund, the only long-standing money available for modern decorative arts, and we had plans for expending a handsome gift from Edgar Kaufmann on the purchase of a superb Ruhlmann desk.

It quickly became apparent, once I was in Paris, that my twenty thousand dollars were not going to buy the Coard couch. Everywhere I went I heard that Yves St. Laurent would be bidding, and Madame Helen Rochas, and a wealthy American from Richmond, Virginia, then unknown to me, as well as the clutch of Parisian art deco dealers. My sense of the competition was correct. The couch brought thirty thousand dollars and is now in the home of Sydney Lewis in Richmond.

When I saw the Clement Rousseau table, I felt simultaneously an extraordinary weakness and exaltation. In other words, I had to have it. This feeling does not come over the curator often, but when it does he becomes wild, canny, daring and, need I say, somewhat unreasonable. Tom Hoving describes these feelings in his pages on the Bury St. Edmunds cross. I was going to return to New York with the table and, if possible, with something else as well from among the Doucet masterpieces. I fixed on several stools by Pierre Legrain, who had been primarily a bookbinder until encouraged by Doucet to try his hand at furniture. The one I wanted most got away; it went to Madame Rochas and thus stayed in Paris. The Legrain stool I was able to acquire is a perfectly stylized French echo of its African progenitor.

This was my first auction in French. The bidding was in five-hundred-franc jumps. I was bidding against pros and collectors who could go much higher than I could. I had to figure in the auction house's commission,

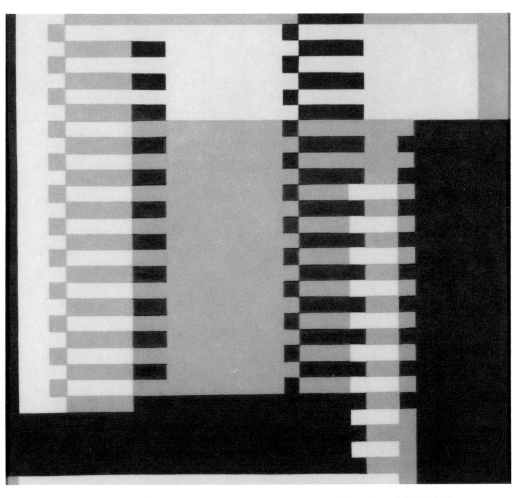

FIGURE 60. Josef Albers (1888– , American). *Pillars.* Sandblasted and flashed glass. George A. Hearn Fund, 1970.139

which varied as the price went up, and the shipping charges to New York. It was, of course, also a point of honor to return to general funds as little of the money voted for this auction as possible; my job was to buy the best, not to save pennies. On the other hand I had no authorization to exceed twenty thousand dollars. It was a close game. I had hired at a modest fee a French auction expert. He was to do the actual bidding. We sat in the first row. I didn't realize that all the collectors and dealers were buzzing that the infinitely wealthy Metropolitan Museum was there to walk away with what it wanted. I had discussed the pieces that interested me with my expert, and we had set the top bids on the few pieces I was after. When the Rousseau table came up, it quickly became clear that the price would exceed my limit. I whispered to the man to keep bidding. He refused. He believed in respecting the cool decision made previous to the heat and excitement of the auction. I poked him hard with my elbow. Nothing happened. My heart thumping with fear and excitement, I shot my hand up at several of the five-hundred-franc jumps that seemed as if they would wipe out my money and then some if the bidding continued for even one more round. At twelve thousand five hundred dollars the bidding stopped and the piece was ours. I had meant to stop at eight thousand. I had just enough money left to buy the Legrain stool. Months later I learned that the underbidder on the table was Sydney Lewis. Lewis had thought he was bidding against all the wealth of a powerful museum. Gentleman that he is, he is happy to see the table at the Metropolitan. We have since become fast friends.

When the table arrived in the Museum, it was sent to Conservation for cleaning and minor restoration. There, a young conservator, Rudolph Colban, found a plug of wood on the underside securing a medal implanted by Clement Rousseau. The medal's inscription reads "Je veux passer mon ciel à faire du bien sur la terre" (I want to spend my time in heaven secure in the knowledge that I have done well on earth). Could this hidden thought have drawn me to the table in the auction room? The table's delicacy, strength, exquisite proportions, and delectable combination of materials—not to mention the drama of its purchase—make this my favorite twentieth-century decorative arts acquisition.

My second meeting with Josef Albers was unexpected though not unannounced. He called to say that he was coming to the Museum the following day at eleven. He arrived early, with a package under his arm. In it was *Pillars,* a magnificent black, red, and white sand-blasted, flashed

FIGURE 61. Clement Rousseau (1872–   , French). *Table*, dated 1924. Ebony, ivory, sharkskin. Fletcher Fund, 1972.283.2

glass work from his Bauhaus days. "Is it a gift, a loan, or an offer for purchase?" I inquired, apprehensive of giving offense but eager to set things straight. "Nine thousand dollars," he replied. I thanked him and presented *Pillars* at the next meeting of the Acquisitions Committee. It was purchased. Bob Hale had acquired three of Albers's *Homage to the Square* paintings in the 1950s, and Albers had given us two more paintings in 1969, but we still had nothing from his early period.

I soon realized that we were being tested by this serious man—serious, but with a twinkle. Several subsequent visits to his home in Orange, Connecticut ("Orange! That's good for Albers!" said his wife, Anni, on my first visit), and the gentle yet forceful intervention of Albers's lawyer, adviser, and friend, Lee Eastman, led to a retrospective exhibition of one hundred paintings by the artist, ninety-eight of them from his own collection. The Museum benefited magnificently from this effort when Albers invited me to accept twelve paintings of my choice for the Department of Twentieth Century Art. Furthermore, he gave a full set of his prints to the Department of Prints and Photographs.

My first meeting with Albers occurred in 1969, when I was preparing the exhibition *New York Painting and Sculpture, 1940–1970.* It was a stormy one. Albers wanted assurances that his work would be treated seriously. As it turned out, he was pleased with his representation: thirteen works in a room devoted to him.

We passed our tests with Albers, and now we have the best representation of his work to be found in any public institution.

The outstanding promised gift made to the Department of Twentieth Century Art is that of Hans Hofmann's nine paintings of 1965, the *Renate Series.* In 1975 one of the nine, *Rhapsody,* was formally given to the Museum. In his last full working year Hofmann painted these pictures and dedicated them to his young wife, Renate, who in turn promised them to us. It was Hofmann's intention that the pictures be kept together and given to a museum, from which we can conclude that he regarded the series as an esthetic testament. During his lifetime, Hofmann gave forty-seven paintings, spanning his work from 1935 to the mid-sixties, to the University of California at Berkeley. He made this gift in thankful recognition of the university's invitation to him to come to America in 1930 to teach a summer session. He ascribed his subsequent decision to live in America to this generous gesture and responded in kind. The Berkeley gift was a conscious effort on his part to represent the three decades of his American career.

The presence of the *Renate Series* at the Metropolitan, along with *Window* (1950) and *Veluti in Speculum* (1962), both acquired soon after their execution, make us, after Berkeley, the leading collector of this still underappreciated master.

After the collecting of twentieth-century art, there comes the problem of how to exhibit it adequately. The New York institutions that specialize in the art of their time are: the Whitney Museum of American Art, which grew out of the old Whitney Club of the early twenties; the Museum of Modern Art, founded by energetic enthusiasts in 1929; and the Guggenheim Museum, which began its career in 1939 when Hilla Rebay interested Solomon Guggenheim in nonobjective art. Now, after fifty years of accomplishment in collecting and exhibiting, these institutions seem to be facing two alternatives: to continue to collect and exhibit, entailing costly expansion of both plant and staff to house and curate the art of the present and future in addition to all they have so far accumulated, or to limit themselves to some period, for instance 1870–1950, and assume less responsibility for the state of contemporary culture. The procedure of having special exhibitions practically prohibits the Whitney and the Guggenheim from showing the known collections. The Museum of Modern Art and the Metropolitan, while they have special exhibition galleries, still can hang only parts of their collections. At any given time there are numerous works of high quality in storage. This situation is not only wasteful of existing resources, it gives a false impression of an embarrassment of riches that discourages patronage at a time when New York should be energetically expanding its far from adequate public collections of postwar American and European art. Recognizing that, since the Whitney left its Eighth Street quarters in 1954, there has been no major museum in the neighborhood where artists live and work, the suggestion arises that the New York museums with public and private aid join forces to rent or buy a large building in Soho, which could be used to exhibit segments of their permanent collections.

An example of recent art that could be shown in the jointly operated exhibition space I propose is the *Renate Series*. I have been able to show these paintings as a group only twice since they came to the Museum. I always have as many of them hanging as possible, but the public would be better served if the series was on view more often while we wait for the Metropolitan's expansion program to be completed. Other examples of works not often enough on view are the Guggenheim's Kandinskys, the Modern's contemporary American paintings and sculpture, which must be rotated in the first floor gallery for reasons of space, and the Whitney's Gorky, *The Artist and His Mother.* The dialogue between the new museum and Soho's galleries could be resounding.